From Front Office to Front Line

Essential Issues for Health Care Leaders

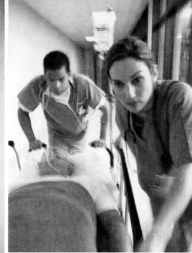

Second Edition

Joint Commission
Resources

Joint Commission
International

Foreword by
Ross Wilson, M.D.

FROM FRONT OFFICE TO FRONT LINE:
Essential Issues for Health Care Leaders | Second Edition

Executive Editor: Steven Berman
Senior Project Manager: Cheryl Firestone
Manager, Publications: Paul Reis
Associate Director, Production: Johanna Harris
Executive Director: Catherine Chopp Hinckley, Ph.D.
Joint Commission/JCR Reviewers: Pat Adamski, Lynne Bergero, Patty Craig, Linda Hanold, Catherine Chopp Hinckley, Karen Kolbusz, Richard Koss, Michael Kulczycki, Ana McKee, Paul Reis, Elvira Ryan, Stephen Schmaltz, Sharon Sprenger, Paul VanOstenberg, Ann Watt, Scott Williams

Joint Commission Resources Mission
The mission of Joint Commission Resources (JCR) is to continuously improve the safety and quality of care in the United States and in the international community through the provision of education and consultation services and international accreditation.

Joint Commission International
A division of Joint Commission Resources, Inc.
The mission of Joint Commission International (JCI) is to improve the safety and quality of care in the international community through the provision of education, publications, consultation, and evaluation services.

Joint Commission Resources educational programs and publications support, but are separate from, the accreditation activities of Joint Commission International. Attendees at Joint Commission Resources educational programs and purchasers of Joint Commission Resources publications receive no special consideration or treatment in, or confidential information about, the accreditation process.

The inclusion of an organization name, product, or service in a Joint Commission Resources publication should not be construed as an endorsement of such organization, product, or services nor is failure to include an organization name, product, or service to be construed as disapproval.

Printed in the U.S.A. 5 4 3 2 1

Requests for permission to make copies of any part of this work should be mailed to
Permissions Editor
Department of Publications
Joint Commission Resources
One Renaissance Boulevard
Oakbrook Terrace, Illinois 60181 U.S.A.
permissions@jcrinc.com

ISBN: 978-1-59940-617-6
Library of Congress Control Number: 2011928893

For more information about Joint Commission Resources, please visit http://www.jcrinc.com.
For more information about Joint Commission International, please visit http://www.jointcommissioninternational.org.

Contents

Contributors

Chapter 1. Balancing Systems and Individual Accountability in a Safety Culture
Gerald B. Hickson, M.D., is Assistant Vice Chancellor for Health Affairs; Associate Dean for Faculty Affairs; Joseph C. Ross Chair in Medical Education and Administration; and Director, Center for Patient and Professional Advocacy, Vanderbilt University School of Medicine, Nashville, Tennessee. **Ilene N. Moore, M.D., J.D.,** is Assistant Professor of Medical Education and Administration and Assistant Professor of Family Medicine, Vanderbilt University School of Medicine. **James W. Pichert, Ph.D.,** is Professor of Medical Education and Administration; and Codirector, Center for Patient and Professional Advocacy. **Manuel Benegas, Jr. J.D.,** is Program Administrator, Quality Systems Strategy, Vanderbilt University Medical Center.

Chapter 2. Identifying and Responding to Patient Safety Problems
Christine Goeschel, Sc.D., M.P.A., M.P.S., R.N., is Assistant Professor and Director, Strategic Development and Research Initiatives, Armstrong Institute for Patient Safety and Quality, Johns Hopkins University School of Medicine, Baltimore. **Michael A. Rosen, Ph.D.,** is Assistant Professor, Department of Anesthesiology and Critical Care Medicine; and Staff Member, Armstrong Institute. **Lisa Lubomski, Ph.D.,** is Assistant Professor, Armstrong Institute. **David A. Thompson, D.N.Sc., M.S., R.N.,** is Assistant Professor, Armstrong Institute and Johns Hopkins School of Nursing. **Julius Cuong Pham, M.D., Ph.D.,** is Assistant Professor, Department of Emergency Medicine and Department of Anesthesia and Critical Care Medicine, and

Armstrong Institute. **Peter J. Pronovost, M.D., Ph.D,** is Professor of Anesthesiology and Critical Care Medicine and Surgery; Senior Vice President for Patient Safety and Quality; Director, Armstrong Institute; and Professor of Health Policy and Management, The Johns Hopkins Bloomberg School of Public Health. **Sean Berenholtz, M.D., M.H.S.,** is Associate Professor, Department of Anesthesiology and Critical Care Medicine and Armstrong Institute.

Chapter 3. Training Physician and Nursing Leaders for Quality Improvement
Paul Convery, M.D., M.M.M., is Senior Vice President and Chief Medical Officer, Baylor Health Care System, Dallas. **Carl E. Couch, M.D., M.M.M.,** is President, Baylor Quality Health Care Alliance, Baylor Health Care System. **Rosemary Luquire, R.N., Ph.D, F.A.A.N., N.E.A.-B.C.,** is Senior Vice President and Chief Nursing Officer, Baylor Health System.

Chapter 4. The Role of Health Information Technology in Quality and Safety
David W. Bates, M.D., M.Sc., is Chief, Division of General Internal Medicine and Primary Care, Brigham and Women's Hospital; and Professor, Harvard Medical School and Harvard School of Public Health, Boston. **Gilad J. Kuperman, M.D., Ph.D.,** is Director of Interoperability Informatics, Department of Information Systems, New York–Presbyterian Hospital, New York City; and Associate Professor, Department of Biomedical Informatics, Columbia University, New York City.

Chapter 5. Engaging Patients in Patient Safety
Saul N. Weingart, M.D., Ph.D., is Vice Pres-

ident for Quality Improvement and Patient Safety, and Director, Center for Patient Safety, Dana-Farber Cancer Institute, Boston.

Chapter 6. Improving Management of Chronic Disease
William G. Weppner, M.D., M.P.H., F.A.C.P., is Assistant Director, Center for Excellence in Rural and Regional Patient Centered Education, Veterans Affairs Medical Center, Boise, Idaho; and Acting Assistant Professor of Medicine, University of Washington, Seattle. **Katie Coleman, M.S.P.H.,** is Research Associate II, MacColl Institute for Healthcare Innovation, Group Health Research Institute, Seattle. **Robert J. Reid, M.D. Ph.D.,** is Associate Medical Director of Health Services

Research and Knowledge Translation, Group Health Research Institute; and Adjunct Professor, Department of Health Care and Epidemiology, University of British Columbia, Vancouver, British Columbia, Canada. **Eric B. Larson, M.D., M.P.H., M.A.C.P.,** is Executive Director, Group Health Research Institute; and Professor of Medicine, University of Washington.

Chapter 7. Implementing, Sustaining and Spreading Quality Improvement
John Øvretveit, Ph.D., C.Psychol, C.Sci., is Director of Research, Professor of Health Innovation Implementation and Evaluation, Medical Management Centre, Karolinska Institutet, Stockholm.

Foreword

Ross Wilson, M.D., Senior Vice President, Quality; and Corporate Chief Medical Officer, New York City Health and Hospital Corporation, New York City

There is an evolving appreciation throughout the world that the performance of health care organizations needs dramatic improvement. In the past 15 years or so, seminal reports in many countries have called attention to the size and nature of shortcomings in the quality, safety, and value of health care, which has then led to broad expressions of commitment to change. Improvements have generally fallen short, despite the dedication of an ever-increasing percentage of gross domestic product as annual increases in health care costs outpace economic growth. This "burning platform" might appear differently to providers and patients and to employers, governments, and other payers, but there is no doubt of its looming shadow. This is the context for this second edition of *From Front Office to Front Line: Essential Issues for Health Care Leaders.*

The imperative to achieve sustained improvement of care at lower cost (or at least a lower rate of cost increases) is manifest in the United States, for example, in two Centers for Medicare & Medicaid Services (CMS) initiatives, each of which represents a further move to pay for performance. Under the Value-Based Purchasing Program, CMS will make value-based incentive payments to acute care hospitals on the basis of how well the hospitals perform on certain quality measures or on the extent of improvement from baseline levels.[1] Through the Shared Savings Program, incentives will be provided to physicians, hospitals, long term care organizations, and other health care providers to work together with accountable care organizations to treat an individual patient across care settings while decreasing the growth in health care costs and meeting performance standards on quality of care.[2] In September 2010, Donald Berwick, CMS Administrator, described CMS's direction in terms of a "triple aim" plan—improved care (as represented by the six domains in the Institute of Medicine report *Crossing the Quality Chasm*[3]), improved health of the population being served, and reduction of per capita costs.[4] This triple aim is an enormous but appropriate challenge for the future of all health systems—not just in the United States but throughout the world. It should underpin the thinking of all leaders in health care. It moves the conversation from independent consideration of quality and cost to an intertwined dual accountability for both, while adding the responsibility to ensure that the care provided has effectively improved the health of those we serve.

So the challenge and its urgency are clear. However, it can be argued that this is not really new; problematic performance on both quality and cost has long been known. In the past decade, there has been increasingly transparent evidence of poor quality combined with health care costs that grew faster than economies could afford, particularly after the global economic downturn that started in 2008. One possible conclusion to account for the inadequacy of the progress made is that the task is very complex and difficult. Even when we know what needs to be done, actually implementing at scale with sustainability is difficult to achieve. We have now reached the point that continued underappreciation of the complexity of implementing improvement is incompatible with success for health leaders or their organizations. The understanding that relatively simple performance improvement initiatives, however well intentioned, are unlikely to lead to success is starting to take hold. Thankfully, the idea that if an health care organization demonstrates a gap in performance, then its clinicians and managers will be able to close that gap on a sustained basis by simply "trying harder," without the support of the necessary organizational culture, infrastructure, and training, is disappearing as more and more organizations move to higher levels of performance. This book is an excellent resource for how we should implement improvement of quality and safety. Given the complexity of health care it would certainly not be practical to attempt to cover all improvement-related issues, but this book succeeds in addressing the pressing issues facing health care organizations and their leaders, and does so by providing clear guidance and proven solutions.

In varying ways, this book show us how to operationalize key factors in driving improvement at the level of the whole organization: Development of leadership; accurate, timely, and transparent performance measurement; proven improvement methodologies; and an organizational safety-minded culture with accountability at all levels. Each chapter provides a judicious guide to the literature and practical strategies that are immediately applicable across the variety of health care organizations.

Chapter 1 provides a thoughtful exposition of issues that influence organizational safety cultures. The authors also highlight how explicit, agreed-on values and practical tools contribute to balancing system and individual accountability in the quest for improving performance.

In Chapter 2, the authors, in surveying the challenges of identifying and responding to patient safety problems, make the vital observation that "every patient care area is a world of inherited risks, hidden in the protocols, procedures, and common practices of the people who work there" (page 50). The chapter elucidates how health care organizations can learn from rather than simply recover from mistakes, as they practice "proactive patient safety."

Chapter 3, which addresses training of clinical leaders for performance improvement, conveys two important messages: First, we cannot improve performance without clinical leadership, and, second, to optimize clinical leadership, health care organizations should provide or make available specific training that is not routinely part of clinical education.

Chapter 4 explores the complex topic of health information technology and its role as a "thoughtful component" of a comprehensive approach to the improvement of quality, safety, and efficiency" (page 103). The authors provide an exceptionally useful up-to-date summary of the evolving capabilities and expectations for health information technology, including and beyond the electronic health record, to extend to its use in partnering with patients and in decreasing costs and improving quality and safety.

Chapter 5 provides an excellent review of and practical guidance on the important topic of engaging patients and their families in all levels of the delivery of care. The report showing a proven reduction in harm to patients who are better engaged in their care than patients who are not so engaged provides a concrete platform for each organization's efforts in this area.

Chapter 6 discusses improvement in the care of patients with one or more chronic diseases, an issue now being recognized with increasing urgency in many countries, given the growing social and financial costs. The authors make the pointed observation that patients with spend 99% of their time outside hospitals or clinics. The implications are obvious for the efforts that we need to make to ensure the central role of patients as partners in the continuity of care. The authors also highlight the primacy of primary care practice settings, where most care of patients with chronic diseases occurs, in the care delivery system. Models based on the Chronic Care Model and, more recently, the Patient Centered Medical Home, are essential to improving performance.

Chapter 7 provides a clear understanding of the increasing evidence base for improving health care performance and reinforces the need for more research. The author effectively conveys the concept of improvement as a science, with evidence-based knowledge and skill sets that needs to be learned if implementation is to be effective.

If we are able to implement all the wisdom in this book, the care of our patients and the financial health of our organizations will be dramatically improved. Although the need for more knowledge through research and evaluation is clear, given what we do know, we can do better right now . . . and we all need to! I commend to you this book as an excellent addition to your learning resources.

References

1. U.S. Centers for Medicare & Medicaid Services: *Quality Initiatives.* https://www.cms.gov/hospitalqualityinits/ (accessed Oct. 6, 2011).

2. U.S. Centers for Medicare & Medicaid Services: Overview: *The Website for Information on the Medicare Shared Savings Program (Shared Savings Program).* https://www.cms.gov/sharedsavingsprogram/ (accessed Oct. 6, 2011).

3. Institute of Medicine: *Crossing the Quality Chasm: A New Health System for the 21st Century.* Washington, DC: National Academy Press, 2001.

4. Silva C.: New CMS chief to focus on quality, organization and costs. *American Medical News Reports,* Sep. 27, 2010. http://www.ama-assn.org/amednews/2010/09/27/gvsa0927.htm (accessed Oct. 6, 2011).

Introduction

THIS BOOK'S PURPOSE AND AUDIENCE

This book, *From Front Office to Front Line: Essential Issues for Health Care Leaders*, Second Edition, is an all-new edition of a 2005 book. Each of the seven chapters in this new edition describes an essential issue in terms of its importance and implications for the quality, patient safety, and value of care; chief findings from the literature; practical guidance and suggestions; lessons learned; and ongoing challenges. Although ongoing policy efforts regarding these essential issues vary throughout the world, the need for health care organizations to develop their own strategies to address these issues is universal.

From *Front Office to Front Line: Essential Issues for Health Care Leaders*, Second Edition, was developed for a global audience of CEOs, chief medical officers, chief operations officers, and other health care executives; quality and safety officers; and other clinical and administrative leaders and their staff in hospitals, health systems, ambulatory care organizations, behavioral health care organizations, critical access hospitals, hospitals, and long term care organizations.

ACKNOWLEDGMENTS

This publication has greatly benefited from the invaluable guidance of the following reviewers, who commented on earlier versions of chapters: Jack Cox, Allan Frankel, Karen Grimley, Stephen R. Mayfield, Wilson Pace, Nancy L. Szaflarski, Mark VanKooy, and Ian Watt.

Joint Commission Resources (JCR) also thanks the internal Joint Commission and JCR staff members, as listed on page ii, who provided expert review of the book's content. Finally, JCR thanks Joint Commission International Editorial Advisory Board members LEE Chien Earn, Virginia Maripolsky, and Jorge César Martinez for their instructive comments.

Their advice is much appreciated. Finally, we extend heartfelt thanks to the contributors for generously giving of their time to share their knowledge and experience.

CHAPTER 1

Balancing Systems and Individual Accountability in a Safety Culture

Gerald B. Hickson, M.D.; Ilene N. Moore, M.D., J.D.; James W. Pichert, Ph.D.; Manuel Benegas Jr., J.D.

Countless patients worldwide suffer avoidable events, disabilities, and death from health care errors.[1-3] In spite of calls for improvement, little evidence suggests that delivery of health care is more reliable now than it was 20 years ago. Although we know much about the causes of medical error,[4-7] and although strides have been made in some areas of practice, medical mishaps persist. Failures to identify and to address unsafe systems and to hold individuals accountable for their performance may explain at least a portion of our limited progress.

Hospitals and medical groups are highly complex. So, too, are the humans who work in them. Outcome failures can result from human-to-human interaction and/or the interface between humans and complex medical systems. Individuals vary in their backgrounds, training, and experiences as well as their abilities to handle fatigue or stress. Some individuals have "challenging" personalities and may not be aware of how they interact with others or how their behavior affects team performance. Behavior can either promote trust and effective communication among team members or disrupt work flow and create risk.

Balancing systems and individual accountability is therefore central to the operation of a safety culture. Disproportionate focus on systems ignores problems posed by untrained, distracted, irresponsible, or impaired humans. Disproportionate focus on individual humans ignores problems posed by outdated or flawed systems. Health care leaders face three challenges in balancing systems and individual accountability. In the face of an adverse event, they must first determine whether care delivery systems failed and, if so, whether and how human behavior contributed to or caused the event. Second, they must determine actions that will improve systems and human performance. At a minimum, systems need to provide safety nets for human error and, more expectantly, support the ability of humans to achieve extraordinary outcomes.[8] Finally, leaders create opportunities for excellent performance by holding people accountable as individuals, as members of a team, and as observers and reporters of systems issues.

In this chapter, we first discuss health care's reliability problem and outline underpinnings for a safety culture, variously termed "just culture,"[9] "fair and just culture,"[10] or "safety culture."[11] In this chapter, we use the term *safety culture* because not only must patient safety be one of an organization's primary goals, but the path to achieving safety lies in team members feeling safe to lead the organization there. Within a safety culture, leaders recognize that adverse (or "bad") outcomes occur because of systems and/or individuals' contributions. Having a balanced approach to analyzing and acting to address either contribution promotes and sustains a safety culture. We then describe tools and practices that help leaders improve quality and safety by balancing the roles of systems and individual accountability.

We now present the first two parts (*see* below and on page 4) of a case example that represents a composite of actual events involving a blood transfusion error. Later in the chapter, we return to part 3 of the case example to follow its progression.

CASE EXAMPLE, PART 1. A CASE OF THE WRONG BLOOD: SYSTEMS PROBLEMS, HUMAN ERRORS, OR BOTH?

You are a medical center leader (chief medical officer, chief nursing officer, chief executive officer, administrator-on-call, unit manager, chief of staff) and receive a 0500 call. A 25-year-old man was transported to your emergency department (ED) following a collision resulting from icy roads. A tractor-trailer struck six cars. Cardiopulmonary resuscitation was administered, and the victim was transported to your hospital. Your ED team identified multiple orthopedic injuries and intra-abdominal bleeding, requiring multiple transfusions in the ED.

It appears that the patient received two incompatible units of packed red blood cells, developed multisystem failure, and died. Whether this fatality was related to the transfusion error is uncertain. While cleaning up, a team member identified the incompatible units and reported the error.

The ED nurse who was believed to have administered the incompatible units is experienced. Because transfusion of an incompatible unit is a "never" event, regulators will pursue further reporting and investigation.

You drive to the hospital. On the way, you see a billboard declaring that the wait time in what you advertise as a "quick" ED is 56 minutes. The ED is busy. The trauma service is treating other victims of the motor vehicle collision. Apparently, 10 patients are also waiting for admission to the hospital; the current census is greater than 95%.

In spite of such stressors, you expect professionals to perform the basics. A policy directs personnel to confirm two identifiers before administering blood products. After a "close call" (also termed *near miss*) a year earlier, all ED and operating room (OR) personnel were required to retrain.

Your institution's quality and risk teams will review records and schedule interviews. Policy directs a root cause analysis to be attended by involved personnel. Other thoughts come to mind, such as, "I wonder what has been shared with the family." You can only imagine what they must be going through. You also think about your team—nurses, physicians, or others—who are involved. You want to make sure that the wellness program director is alerted.

As you turn into the hospital parking lot, you remember that the board liaison needs to be notified, as does the news and public affairs office in case this event finds its way to the press.

HEALTH CARE'S RELIABILITY PROBLEM

The Institute of Medicine's 2000 report, *To Err Is Human,* estimated that 98,000 persons die in hospitals in the United States each year because of preventable medical errors.[12] Many health care organizations and professionals were already aware of the safety problem on the basis of the 1991 study by Brennan and colleagues, in which they measured the magnitude of errors for hospitalized patients in New York State.[13] Patients suffered adverse outcomes in 3.7% of hospitalizations (6% for the elderly), with medical negligence contributing to 28% of the cases.

Little seems to have changed.[11,14–17] A recent study examining care in 10 North Carolina hospitals is a case in point.[18] The study identified 25.1 harms per 100 admissions, almost two thirds of which were preventable. Despite various initiatives, the overall harms rate did not change between 2002 and 2007. Although not powered to confirm differences, findings appeared to vary by hospital site, suggesting that some may have infrastructures and/or cultures better equipped to effect change.

Variation in results is not surprising because some institutions have reduced certain risks for patients.[19–23] For example, consider the following:

- Baptist Memorial Hospital–Desoto (Mississippi) joined the Institute for Healthcare Improvement (IHI) IMPACT ICU collaborative. ICU nosocomial infection rates fell during the implementation year. Significant declines were seen in ventilator-associated pneumonia rates (7.5 to 3.2 per 1,000 ventilator days) and bloodstream infection rates (5.9 to 3.1 per 1,000 line days).[19]
- The Michigan Health & Hospital Association (MHA) Keystone ICU project resulted in a greater than 60% reduction in central line-associated bloodstream infections (CLABSIs) from baseline sustained at 36 months post-implementation of interventions.[20] A second study compared mortality rates of MHA ICU patients and ICU patients in control hospitals. All hospitals had similar pre-implementation mortality rates. Post-implementation, MHA ICU patients experienced a significant reduction in mortality compared with controls

through the 22-month study, suggesting further benefit from the project.[21]

- At Cincinnati Children's Hospital, baseline airway clearance therapy (ACT) for hospitalized adolescent patients with cystic fibrosis met 21% qualitative and 41% quantitative best-practice standards.[22] Using the Plan-Do-Study-Act model[24] to increase compliance, a multidisciplinary team that included clinicians, patients, and parents identified barriers to achieving best practice. Educating patients and staff about the importance of ACT and reinforcing cooperative behaviors increased ACT quality and quantity to 73% and 64%, respectively.[22]
- At Southmead Hospital in Bristol, United Kingdom, mean alcohol gel compliance was 24% for all persons entering the surgical ward. After a line of bright red tape was placed along the entryway corridor, terminating in an arrowhead pointing to two wall-mounted alcohol gel dispensers, mean compliance for the subsequent six months was 62%, with significant improvement in rates among physicians, nurses, transporters, visitors, and patients. Two methicillin-resistant *Staphylococcus aureus* (MRSA) cases occurred during the pre-intervention six-month period, but no cases developed during the subsequent six months.[23]

These studies reported five elements, as follows, that appeared to influence the success of the projects:

1. Clear leadership commitment
2. Articulated goals
3. Changes in work patterns to create teams that facilitate communication and participation in decision making
4. Elimination of unnecessary variation[25–30] by using "bundles" of best practices
5. Measures for tracking progress with feedback to the project team

None of the studies mentioned whether any team member's actions threatened team functioning or project outcomes. We therefore propose an additional element for success:

6. Stepwise, graduated interventions for personnel exhibiting non-teamwork-promoting disruptive behavior[31,32]

Disruptive or unprofessional behavior takes several forms. "Yelling, spitting, and cussing" are readily recognizable aggressive behaviors. Most disruptive behavior, however, is not as obvious. An individual who fails to speak up when a team member harasses another demonstrates passive unprofessional behavior. Those who remain silent during meetings but later mock the group's consensus illustrate passive-aggressive disruptive behavior. All these behaviors can affect team dynamics and, consequently, care delivery. We therefore define disruptive behavior as any conduct by a team member that interferes, or has the potential to interfere, with the team's ability to achieve intended outcomes.[12,33]

Disruptive behavior is inconsistent with a commitment to professionalism. Professionals are committed to clear and effective communication, in which they model respect and maintain awareness of how they affect others within the team. Professionalism also requires a commitment to self- and group regulation in a fair but progressive manner as required. Behavior that can impair team performance must be recognized and fairly addressed.

The Michigan, Mississippi, Cincinnati, and Bristol projects suggest what reliable health care looks like, but successes may remain local and limited unless similar processes can be implemented on a larger scale. Health care organizations with committed leadership, well-functioning teams, high levels of compliance with best practices, and good monitoring tools are in position to help transform health care delivery. However, increasing pressure to contain costs may challenge any system's best intentions. In theory, anticipated savings from providing evidence-based care, eliminating waste, and ending medical injury will help defray the costs of increasing safety. On the other hand, it is not unreasonable to hypothesize that forces to control costs may sometimes result in health care that is less safe. One reason for concern is that a negative effect of change may be so small early on that its impact may be undetected for years. Therefore, we add a cautionary note that unintended consequences of new models to control cost may not be quickly apparent; deleterious health care outcomes may be missed without large system, multisite, or national collaboratives.

Consider the study by Needleman et al., which examined the relationship between nurse staffing patterns and inpatient mortality.[34] Analyzing data from almost 200,000 admissions, the authors identified a significant association between mortality and increased exposure to units with gaps in registered nurse (R.N.) staffing. It is not too difficult to envision scenarios in which hospital leaders reduce staffing in response to pressures to curb costs without recognizing the impact of the decision on the patients served.

CASE EXAMPLE, PART 2

As the medical center leader (as in Part 1), you know that thousands of patients are injured each year, making a compelling case for building a more reliable system, but your commitment to act often loses to the incessant demands of running your unit. Now, as you enter to debrief with your ED and trauma teams and contemplate meeting with the grieving family, you want to understand what happened and how your team can make sure that this "never event" never happens again.

IN SUPPORT OF A SAFETY CULTURE

Organizations committed to quality strive for reliability—that is, consistent performance of high levels of safety for an extended period of time. High-reliability organizations (HROs), such as commercial air travel and performance on aircraft carrier flight decks, handle extreme risk by maintaining aware and observant work-forces, fostering cultures in which team members feel comfortable speaking up when they see risk, and using disciplined approaches to solve safety threats.[5,35,36]

Team members in HROs, individually and collectively, maintain awareness that failures in processes set the stage for disaster. With this "collective mindfulness," team members are taught to be on guard for the smallest indication that a standard process has changed. In health care, as pointed out by Chassin and Loeb, "we are too often in the position of investigating severe adverse events *after* [our emphasis] they have injured patients, which means we have missed opportunities to pinpoint and correct quality problems before they cause harm."[11(p. 563)] Vigilance in HROs leads to observations that, when reported, allow early identification of threat. An HRO is able to sustain focus on awareness because its culture supports reporting without fear. Team members know they are accountable for their actions but also that they will not be blamed for system faults.

After deficiencies are identified, HROs drive improvement by using such disciplines as Six Sigma, Lean Management, and Change Management[37–42] to tease apart complex safety problems and deploy solutions. Although similar processes have been introduced into several health systems—Sentara Healthcare (Norfolk, Virginia), Virginia Mason (Seattle), and Scotland's National Health Service (NHS Scotland) are examples[43–45]—they are not yet commonplace.

Achieving patient safety requires vigilant systems to mitigate unintended harm to patients. Such a highly reliable system must be supported by the reinforcement of a safety culture. Leadership, tools, and processes make it possible.

In our view, four foundational elements—shared values and goals, effective leadership, teamwork,[46] and safety culture—affirm and mutually reinforce one another to make health care safer. After briefly discussing each, we set out a framework and discuss the practical tools that can help leaders balance systems and individual performances to achieve safe outcomes.

Shared Values and Goals: Mission Statement, Credo, and Professionalism

Organizations can successfully align goals, incentives, and actions if all team members understand and share core values. Organizational values, often captured in mission statements and/or credos to which team members are held accountable, may include statements about commitment to patient safety. Such statements affirm the organization's intentions toward and commitment to those it serves. Patient safety–specific commitment statements can be seen as mission statements with a special focus.[10] A statement about commitment to patient safety declares the institution's intent to deliver safe, effective care and to promote accountability. At Dana-Farber Cancer Institute and Partners HealthCare (both in Boston), teams developed their respective commitment statements, which were then endorsed by their boards of trustees.[10] Commitment statements may articulate the importance of teamwork, open communication, learning from adverse events, and reporting to patients and families, team members, leadership, and boards of directors.[10]

Some institutions have adopted credos that declare "who we are." At Vanderbilt University

Medical Center (VUMC), the credo defines standards of professionalism to which team members should ascribe. The credo was developed in 1995[47] by 900 team members working in focus groups and using art exercises to define "who we are." Thousands of hand-drawn illustrations of "what professionalism looks like" were distilled into the following six core principles, and specific credo behaviors were added in 2005:*
1. I make those I serve my highest priority.
2. I respect privacy and confidentiality.
3. I communicate effectively.
4. I conduct myself professionally.
5. I have a sense of ownership.
6. I am committed to my colleagues.

Team members publically sign the credo and attach it to their identification badges. Leadership takes opportunities to review the credo in staff and faculty meetings and to announce credo awards and testimonials about colleagues with distinguished performances. Credo principles are folded into performance evaluations.

The credo also supports professionalism and just culture. By framing core values as reference points, the credo can be used to help resolve conflicts and to address episodes of disruptive behavior in which one member's actions hinder work flow and team performance.

Effective Leadership

Leadership. Progress toward organizational goals cannot be made without leadership. Effective leaders are the spark; if charismatic, their enthusiasm can be contagious. They capture attention and articulate a vision for the way the organization will look to patients and to professionals in the future. They identify unifying themes by listening carefully to diverse messages from constituencies and bring people together toward shared goals.[48]

Leaders' authority derives from their organizational roles, policy directives, and hospital and medical staff bylaws, as reflected in accreditation standards.[49,50]†

However, written authority is only a starting point. Leaders must do the following:
- From the chief executive to the unit managers, understand the mission statement and credo, integrate their principles into all aspects of work, and help others appreciate their significance
- Work to establish and to respect processes that are transparent, data driven, and regularly reviewed
- Invest in and deploy resources commensurate with goals and staff needs
- Understand their own accountability to all stakeholders, from the board of directors to frontline staff, patients and families, accredi-

---

* The six principles are broken down, in turn, into more than 30 behaviors. The complete list can be found at http://www.mc.vanderbilt.edu/root/pdfs/elevate/8_5 credo.pdf.

† For example, see the "Leadership" (LD) standards chapter in The Joint Commission: *Comprehensive Accreditation Manual for Hospitals: The Official Handbook*. Oak Brook, IL: Joint Commission Resources, 2010. Standard LD.03.01.01 states, "Leaders create and maintain a culture of safety and quality throughout the hospital." The JCI standards (Joint Commission International: *Joint Commission International Accreditation Standards for Hospitals*, 4th ed. Oak Brook, IL: Joint Commission Resources, 2010) do not specifically use the term *culture of safety*, but they do require that staff and leaders work together in the interest of optimal patient (and staff) safety. For example, Management of Communication and Information (MCI) Standard MCI.5 specifies, "The leaders ensure that there is effective communication and coordination among those individuals and departments responsible for providing clinical services" (Intent: "To coordinate and to integrate patient care, the leaders develop a culture that emphasizes cooperation and communication.").

tation agencies, and public regulators

- Not "blink"—that is, seek or accept excuses or rationalize away concerns about performance of team members with special value—but rather hold all accountable to the mission and credo
- Be thoughtful as they assess systems issues versus individual accountability. Fact finding is critical and must be thorough. Leaders should not jump to conclusions on what seems to be a compelling story but should actively seek other viewpoints.
- Be willing to seek and to respond to feedback and be able to draw upon a wide repertoire of experience and tools to broaden communication, make good decisions, promote teamwork, and encourage professional growth of others
- Recognize and celebrate success. Appreciating positive behavior and performance reinforces organizational values, builds team members' morale and self-esteem, and encourages outstanding care quality.

Board Leadership. Many leaders understand how health care can be made safer yet find it difficult to recruit collaborators because others in the organization, or even on the board, send mixed messages. The board of directors (trustees) must assume a role beyond their customary focus on financial statements. As the ultimate authority, the board must establish the vision and hold leadership accountable for moving toward it.[51]

The board must aim to create high reliability, identify and prioritize goals, and assess progress. Directors should insist on reviewing data, learning about serious events, talking with patients and families affected by errors, and asking hard questions of leadership.[52] The board must envision high reliability; support the operational leaders, even when decisions prove unpopular

with those who are influential on the basis of specialty, seniority, or revenue production; and maintain the fortitude to shepherd fundamental change.

Safety Culture

Effective leaders understand the need to promote and to sustain growing "maturity" in safety culture. As Chassin and Loeb recommend, leaders self-assess the extent to which they and their organizations display characteristics associated with high reliability.[11] For example, a "mature" safety culture feels physically and psychologically safe to those working in it, promotes best practices, and improves outcomes because of a commitment to continuous learning. Physical and psychological hazards in the environment are minimized to the extent possible. Psychological safety is sufficient that people do not fear scorn or retribution if they speak up to identify a suspected variation in practice, to raise a question, or to ask for help. Safety culture requires commitment to and enforcement of best practices, and any member of the team can "stop the line"[53–56] or take a "time-out" to conduct an assessment.[57]

A safety culture develops and matures as team members respect, value, and support one another.[11] Moreover, health care professionals trust, report, and improve,[11] reflecting what Reason and Hobbs refer to as three mutually reinforcing imperatives.[58] A safety culture can help foster joy and meaning in work.[59] Because a safety culture includes the expectation of professional conduct, team members have confidence that unprofessional behavior will be noted and dealt with fairly, appropriately, and consistently. Perpetuation of unequal treatment within teams impairs their ability to function properly,[60] places patients at higher risk for errors, and leads to professional burnout and decisions to look for jobs elsewhere.[61] In a safety culture, leaders establish and enforce a code of conduct (consistent with the credo) and protect from retaliation those who speak up or report in good faith.

A safety culture will not happen without visibly active leadership. Team members know safety and quality are overarching priorities, because they see their leaders embrace the organization's mission and credo. Statements regarding the commitment to patient safety are posted on the walls, and that commitment is embodied in day-to-day operations and interactions. Team members know experientially whether such statements or professionalism credos represent the implicit or the explicit culture.[62] They know whether it is really "who we are" versus "who we *say* we are." Real leadership diffuses from the board to the CEO to the unit level. Because every lapse in performance or conduct threatens safety at that moment and undermines future culture sustainability, leaders provide ongoing feedback in a way that preserves team members' well-being and confidence.

If reliability and safety depend on organizational values, effective leadership, and a supportive culture, the challenge for any leader is how best to implement these concepts day-to-day. The critical elements are the following:

- A state of organizational readiness to address unsafe systems and/or unreliable individuals
- Multipronged "learning systems"
- Key persons in the organization who are well trained to achieve goals, address systems issues, and show their commitment to holding individuals accountable for past actions and for progress
- Methods and procedures to analyze events, identify actionable single events or patterns, and execute plans for improvement when an adverse outcome or close call occurs

Within this framework reside tools and techniques that provide leaders the means to become aware of variations in performance or process, to assess threats to safety (to identify causes or potential causes of harm), and to respond in ways that reduce the probability of recurrent risk.

First, we highlight tools and techniques associated with the first three elements. We then discuss methods that leaders may find helpful for analyzing events and improving quality through actions targeted at unsafe systems and providing feedback to individuals who demonstrate non-teamwork-promoting behavior.

TOOLS AND PRACTICES FOR SAFETY AND RELIABILITY
A State of Organizational Readiness

How does an organization know when it is ready to address faulty systems and human performance failures? Addressing quality and safety requires significant groundwork. An organization is poised to make improvements if leaders want to learn, embrace the opportunity to change what is broken, and commit to holding all team members accountable. Organizational readiness, then, is signaled when leadership consensus emerges around the following:

- Needed improvements are aligned with the organization's mission statement and goals.
- The organization has defined processes and models to assess performance, to provide feedback, and to guide improvement programs with detailed and specific implementation plans.
- Resources are allocated and available to key personnel who will manage existing problems and design needed improvement projects.

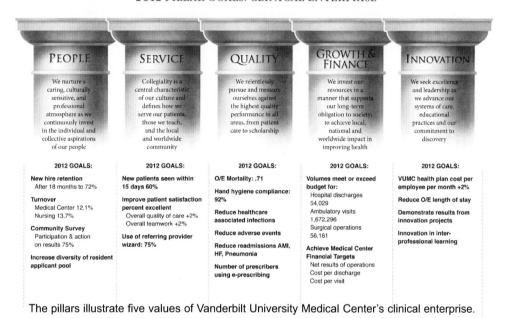

Figure 1-1. The Five Pillars at Vanderbilt University Medical Center

VANDERBILT UNIVERSITY MEDICAL CENTER
2012 PILLAR GOALS: CLINICAL ENTERPRISE

PEOPLE	SERVICE	QUALITY	GROWTH & FINANCE	INNOVATION
We nurture a caring, culturally sensitive, and professional atmosphere as we continuously invest in the individual and collective aspirations of our people	Collegiality is a central characteristic of our culture and defines how we serve our patients, those we teach, and the local and worldwide community	We relentlessly pursue and measure ourselves against the highest quality performance in all areas, from patient care to scholarship	We invest our resources in a manner that supports our long-term obligation to society, to achieve local, national and worldwide impact in improving health	We seek excellence and leadership as we advance our systems of care, educational practices and our commitment to discovery

2012 GOALS:	2012 GOALS:	2012 GOALS:	2012 GOALS:	2012 GOALS:
New hire retention After 18 months to 72% **Turnover** Medical Center 12.1% Nursing 13.7% **Community Survey** Participation & action on results 75% **Increase diversity of resident applicant pool**	**New patients seen within 15 days 60%** **Improve patient satisfaction percent excellent** Overall quality of care +2% Overall teamwork +2% **Use of referring provider wizard: 75%**	**O/E Mortality: .71** **Hand hygiene compliance: 92%** **Reduce healthcare associated infections** **Reduce adverse events** **Reduce readmissions AMI, HF, Pneumonia** **Number of prescribers using e-prescribing**	**Volumes meet or exceed budget for:** Hospital discharges 54,029 Ambulatory visits 1,672,296 Surgical operations 56,161 **Achieve Medical Center Financial Targets** Net results of operations Cost per discharge Cost per visit	**VUMC health plan cost per employee per month +2%** **Reduce O/E length of stay** **Demonstrate results from innovation projects** **Innovation in inter-professional learning**

The pillars illustrate five values of Vanderbilt University Medical Center's clinical enterprise.

Source: Vanderbilt University Medical Center, Nashville, TN. Used with permission.

1. Alignment. Figure 1-1 (above) illustrates five areas ("pillars" or values) of one medical center's clinical enterprise. Under the pillars are the goals of the enterprise. Note how the goals under the central pillar are consistent with the organization's stated value of clinical quality and the commitment, expressed and implied, to best-in-class performance. In setting goals, all constituencies provide input, weigh pros and cons of inclusion, and affirm alignment with values. In this medical center, incentives and evaluations at every level of leadership, from those in the "corporate suite" (including the chief medical and nursing officers) to the unit manager, are consistent with achievement of these goals.

2. Defined Processes and Models to Assess Performance. A defined and regularly practiced or simulated process is essential for learning the extent to which systems and/or individuals contributed to adverse events, close calls, or program/project failures. Everyone in the organization then knows which assessments and follow-up actions are expected from whom, when, and how. As a result, fidelity to processes promotes a sense of justice and fairness (the same rules apply to all), which in turn supports a safety culture. Furthermore, when individuals are subject to feedback or discipline stemming from acts that threaten safety, regular application of defined due process may improve acceptance and reduce the likelihood that the individual would prevail in a legal challenge.[63,64]

Reason's Unsafe Acts Algorithm[65] and an Accountability Pyramid to Promote Professional Performance[31,32] (see Figure 1-2, page 11) are two tools that illustrate how process regularity for evaluating individual accountability in face of an adverse event and responding to the result supports fairness. The Unsafe Algorithm has been adopted and adapted by many organizations for a quick assessment of human accountability for an adverse event.[10,66] The formulations screen for evidence of intent of harm, impairment, violation of policies, and/or unreasonable behavior. If none of those factors was involved in the event, it is reasonable to conclude that harm was caused entirely by a systems failure. If any individual performance (behavior) problem exists, there needs to be human accountability whether or not a concomitant systems failure occurred. A fifth question asks whether a currently accountable individual has a history of unsafe acts. If he or she does, this history will factor in when a leader addresses the current act, as we show later in this chapter.

The Accountability Pyramid provides a framework to help leaders decide how to best address an individual with accountability for an event. All steps of the pyramid have criteria for action. So, for example, suspected or observed "most egregious"[32] (intentional, dangerous, immoral and/or illegal) acts are promptly elevated to the top of the pyramid (Level 3) for evaluation and consideration of corrective/disciplinary action,[31,67] and, when appropriate, law-enforcement involvement. In contrast, other first-time unprofessional behavior or performance concerns are handled at lower tiers on the pyramid. Isolated incidents of unprofessional conduct generally respond to "cup-of-coffee" conversations—that is, quick, respectful, nonjudgmental feedback.[31] The person providing feedback shares what was observed and suggests that the behavior does not seem consistent with the credo.

The next tier, Level 1, applies to a serious (but not "most egregious") first-time act or data that suggest a pattern of unprofessional performance and/or behavior. The purpose of the leader's meeting with the individual is to bring "awareness."

Should the pattern persist, a leader would take a more active role (Level 2) and guide the individual (for example, to receive coaching, to undergo a medical or psychiatric evaluation, or to enroll in a course for distressed professionals). If the professional does not improve, he or she would be referred for consideration of Level 3 corrective/disciplinary action in accordance with the institution's bylaws and/or policies from human resources or other departments.

How do we know such a model works? Our experience comes from more than a decade of addressing the human side—that is, accountability for performance—in the arena of patient complaints. Two of the authors [G.B.H., J.W.P.] and others codeveloped the Vanderbilt Patient Advocacy Reporting System® (PARS®),[68] which is currently used to help mitigate risk in more than 40 hospitals and medical groups across the United States. Originally designed to address the problem of recurring malpractice claims among a relatively small subset of physicians, the PARS program identifies physicians and other health care providers associated with high numbers of patient and family unsolicited complaints, a marker for malpractice-claims risk.[69–71] Patient dissatisfaction with a provider's practice may also lead to noncompliance[72–75] and undermine outcomes of care.[76,77]

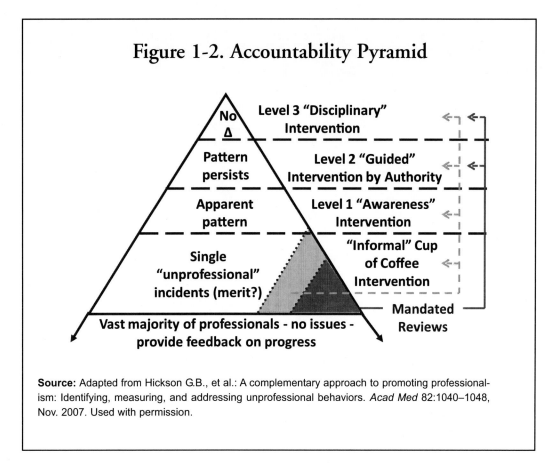

Figure 1-2. Accountability Pyramid

No Δ — Level 3 "Disciplinary" Intervention

Pattern persists — Level 2 "Guided" Intervention by Authority

Apparent pattern — Level 1 "Awareness" Intervention

Single "unprofessional" incidents (merit?) — "Informal" Cup of Coffee Intervention

Mandated Reviews

Vast majority of professionals - no issues - provide feedback on progress

Source: Adapted from Hickson G.B., et al.: A complementary approach to promoting professionalism: Identifying, measuring, and addressing unprofessional behaviors. *Acad Med* 82:1040–1048, Nov. 2007. Used with permission.

Learning about patient complaints promotes individuals' professionalism and provides institutions with a quality-improvement and risk-prevention data source.[67,78]

Many health care systems establish offices of patient relations (ombudsman) to record patient complaints, to provide real-time "service recovery"[79] (attempts to "make right what went wrong"), and to comply with U.S. Centers for Medicare & Medicaid Services (CMS) guidelines for resolving grievances.[80] As close observers, patients and families report exemplary care as well as behaviors that undermine teamwork and create risk. Their stories reflect individual and team performance. Patients may report, for example, poor communication, rudeness, provider inattention or unavailability,

delays in diagnosis or treatment, and/or failed treatments.[67,68]

PARS aggregates all complaint reports, codes each embedded complaint, and transforms complaint data into comparative local and national reports.[81,82] Using peer-based "awareness" interventions to share the data (Level 1, as described), individuals are given opportunities to reflect on what patients and families say and to address the reasons for high levels of dissatisfaction associated with their practices.

Most professionals who receive feedback make necessary changes to decrease complaints and to reduce risk. More than 800 physicians in the 40-plus hospitals and medical groups throughout the United States using this system have received Level 1 interventions (Figure 1-2); more than 70% have demonstrated significant improvement in their complaint numbers.[67] However, process regularity means that those who do not respond are predictably elevated to Level 2 "guided" interventions and then, for the occasional individual who still shows no improvement, Level 3. No physician is exempt from the process, irrespective of claims that his or her practice, patients, specialty, support systems, and so on differ from others'. Results reinforce the use of the Accountability Pyramid.

The Unsafe Act Algorithm and the Accountability Pyramid are tools that can be incorporated into change models. However, to be most effective, the change process should be implemented the same way for each opportunity to which it may apply. For example, the model for conducting step-wise tiered interventions can be adapted to other clinical quality initiatives, such as increasing hand hygiene rates.[83] The tools should be used skillfully and routinely. The same algorithm questions should be asked, and the same pyramid-guided conversations should be held. The tools help the leader remain focused and consistent, which can be challenging when a patient receives incompatible blood. Yet this is exactly the time process regularity helps humans (leaders) stay focused on doing the right things, not resorting to quick systems fixes or arbitrary disciplinary measures, thereby threatening the safety culture.

To achieve successes and to build momentum that reinforces the importance of process, many health care organizations start by adopting or adapting best-practices models for specific clinical issues, such as those advanced by the IHI 100,000 Lives and 5 Million Lives Campaigns.[84] These campaigns provide bundled best practices in a variety of areas, including improving medication reconciliation, preventing CLABSIs, and delivering evidence-based care for congestive heart failure. The U.S. Agency for Healthcare Research and Quality's Health Care Innovations Exchange also provides evidence-based innovations and quality tools to speed the implementation of safer, reliable care. Innovations and best practices are grouped by subject and are searchable.[85] Among international quality improvement collaboratives are the United States Agency for International Development (USAID) Health Care Improvement portal,[86] which supports widespread international application of the IHI approach in developing and middle-income countries; the World Health Organization (WHO) Blood Transfusion Safety program,[87] which strives to improve global blood transfusion safety by focusing on quality management, blood system strengthening, and donation testing and processing; and European eHealth Area,[88] a collaboration among major European Union health systems to promote standardization and improve access, safety, and quality.

The Internet and national conferences make it easier today to identify locally relevant and beta-tested model programs that identify emerging best practices. With planning for local adoption, models developed elsewhere can be tested via local rapid-cycle improvement projects, and results of novel interventions can be shared for others to consider.[89–91]

3. Resources. Discussion of readiness to address threats to safety would be incomplete without detailing some of the resources that improvement-project teams may need to achieve their aims, such as the following:

- Coordination of resources among and within departments
- Funds to support dedicated personnel for the project period
- Costs of training leaders

- Costs of surveillance systems for monitoring performance and outcomes
- Costs of internal and external audits and reviews
- Space for team meetings and personnel work areas
- Informatics and/or biostatistics support
- Consultations with mechanical and human factors engineers[37–42]
- Methodology for assessing and monitoring financial implications related to return on investment[92] and value-based purchasing[93]

Learning Systems

How do health care leaders learn about threats to safety within their organization? Best practices suggest that learning systems are characterized by four critical contributors: (1) surveillance systems; (2) needs assessments with accompanying impact analysis; (3) metrics, measurement systems, and tools; and (4) multilevel professional education in the use of the first three.

1. Surveillance Systems. Common surveillance tools in health care organizations include executive walk-arounds, team members' reports, safety culture surveys, patient and family complaints, reports from referring physicians, and trigger tools. Each tool provides a view of the organization through a different lens and identifies different or overlapping issues[94]:

- *Executive walk-arounds*[95,96] allow leaders the chance to visit units to observe, to hear, and to experience whether those on the front lines assess the safety culture differently from management,[97] and if so, why? Walk-around best practices, as described by Frankel and colleagues (Leadership WalkRounds™),[98] suggest that leaders ask questions that elicit information about events or near misses, consistency of event reporting, whether team

members know what happens to their reports, patient concerns about safety, the impact of team communication on care, and what they need to make care safer.

Leaders review events with the team to identify contributing factors. Contributors are coded and rated for frequency and impact. Summaries of data aggregated by contributing causes and weightings are provided to designated committees, which determine issues for referral to appropriate unit leaders for review, prioritization, and action. Walk-around meetings and subsequent analysis of recorded comments and discussion should be conducted under the protection of and in conformance with state peer review or quality statutes.

- *Team member reports identifying risks to quality and safety.* Centralizing reports in a designated area of the organization promotes consistent evaluation and follow-up, tracking, and trending. Best-practice policies direct reporting mechanisms and specify who reports and who provides initial review and management. Policies also specify what to report, which includes the following:
  - –"Incidents," "events," and "near misses." Reports are routed via electronic, paper-based, or oral mechanisms to the office of risk management. Risk managers share them with quality officers and other leaders with a need to know.[99]
  - –Unprofessional behavior in violation of the organization's credo, code of conduct, or other related policies. Reports may be filed via the same routes as "events."[31,32]
  - –Observed or suspected violations of regulatory requirements, including privacy breaches, incomplete or inaccurate medical records, billing/revenue/reimbursement irregularities, and illegal, unethical, or

improper conduct. Reports are filed in the compliance office.

–Harassment or discrimination complaints. Reports are filed in the Equal Opportunity Office.[100]

–Unsafe equipment and medications and equipment/product recalls.[101,102] Reports are filed with the quality or risk management departments.

- *Safety culture surveys*[103] of physicians and staff in inpatient and ambulatory areas of the organization
- *Unsolicited patient/family complaints*[69,70] or comments from satisfaction surveys and call-back feedback[104] centralized within the organization's patient relations (ombudsman) office. Concerns that meet "grievance" criteria are managed in accordance with CMS guidelines.[80]
- *Reports from referring physicians* called into a "physician liaison office" or collected during visits to affiliate physicians' offices by designated institutional "physician liaison" representatives.
- *Trigger tools*[45,105–108] systematically review patient charts to find markers that can identify harm. Sample surgery module triggers include return to surgery, change in procedure, admission to intensive care post-operatively, intraoperative administration of epinephrine or norepinephrine, pathology report with tissue unrelated to surgical diagnosis, and intraoperative procedure time longer than six hours.[108]

Beyond use of these surveillance tools, organizations must support a safety culture consistent with accreditation standards and regulatory requirements by affirming to reporters that all reports are reviewed and that retribution for good-faith reporting is not tolerated.[32,109] Designated reviewers must evaluate reports in real time to determine priority, potential impact, and opportunities to mediate or to remediate. For example, after receiving a report of an unexpected outcome involving a transfusion error, the risk manager may meet with the patient's physician to discuss the organization's credo-based accountability and how information will be shared in a family conference.[110,111] Another example, consistent with shared governance practices, happens when a hospital unit manager and medical director review a report about a team member's performance, such as a physician who yelled at a nurse. They would investigate, determine whether allegations are substantial, and provide appropriate feedback.

A further requirement to make optimum use of surveillance data would be for well-trained teams to have access to one or more of the data sets to look for patterns.[94] Wherever available, data should be compared with local, national, and global data sets, such as the National Healthcare Safety Network CLABSI benchmark comparisons,[112] American College of Surgeons National Surgical Quality Improvement Program data,[113] the WHO European Health for All Database (HFA-DB),[114] Scotland Performs: NHSScotland,[115] the Netherlands National Institute for Public Health and the Environment (RIVM),[116] Rand Europe,[117] vendors' patient survey data,[118,119] and patients' unsolicited complaints,[69,70] to place performance in context. For example, the institution might ask whether some inpatient units have more falls, CLABSIs, incidents of ventilator-associated pneumonia, or unsolicited patient complaint reports than do others.

Analysis of surveillance data may reveal areas or themes of elevated risk. Organizations can deepen their assessments of these areas through the use of proactive risk analysis tools, such as failure mode and effects analysis (FMEA)[120,121] and sociotechnical probabilistic risk assessment

(ST-PRA).[122] FMEA is a proactive approach to assessing when and how a process or plan might fail and how the odds of failure can be reduced or eliminated. ST-PRA is an industrial engineering tool that models and predicts multiple risks and ways to recover through the use of "fault trees." These tools enable organizations to refine the detection and mitigation of vulnerabilities in existing or new processes and equipment.

2. Needs Assessments. Organizations also learn by proactively soliciting information from their components about current and future needs. Those that invest attention to systems problems and individual accountability conduct periodic needs assessments with accompanying impact analysis. *Impact* is based on self-identified filters and criteria, such as compliance with accreditation standards, financial outcomes, or even harms. Health care organizations can use systematically collected surveillance data to identify, review, track, and trend personnel, operational areas, units, and community outreach programs that require focused attention, feedback, and follow-up data.[123]

At the strategic level, most organizations have planning processes to identify annual goals. In preparation, leadership may request a needs/gap assessment of potential areas for focus. As an example, one area of concern might be pressure ulcers. A focused evaluation may indicate opportunity for improvement. The issue can be translated to reflect not only the impact of pressure ulcers on care and outcomes of patients but also the financial impact when insurers refuse to pay for treatment.[124] If the impact of pressure ulcers is judged to be more significant than other identified opportunities for improvement, it becomes a candidate for strategic priority. The next step for priority setting includes determining organizational readiness for addressing the identified issue (*see* page 8).

Concurrent with organizational needs assessments, organizations also encourage locally initiated (for example, unit level or individual) needs assessments for driving improvements. Education and training to "fix what you can" must therefore include attention to orchestrating synergy across departments.

Although leadership plays a large role in promoting needs assessments and impact analysis,[125] frontline individuals or teams are just as likely to identify salient issues via suggestions, survey responses, or reports of close calls or adverse outcomes. After an issue is turned into an institutional priority and goals are developed, project champions look for organizational data that shed light on the extent of the problem. With a needs/impact assessment, health care executives and their leadership teams view the same information as they discuss, consider, develop recommendations, and make decisions.

3. Metrics. Leaders not only review event reports and needs/impacts assessments to learn about the past but use existing metrics, measurement systems, and measurement tools to monitor progress toward goals. In addition, they work with colleagues to improve existing measures and/or develop and share newer ones.[126] Leaders also seek data that permit within- and between-organization comparisons, such as may be available to members of University HealthSystem Consortium,[127,128] VHA,[129] Premier,[130] the IHI,[131] the Department of Veterans Affairs Medical Center collaboratives,[132] the Organisation for Economic Cooperation and Development's Health Care Quality Indicators project (an international, multicondition project examining quality measurement and improvement issues),[133] and the Danish Healthcare Quality Programme.[134] Some organizations choose to form their own local or regional collaboratives.[135]

4. Education and Training. To disseminate learning throughout the institution, safety-conscious health care organizations provide ongoing multilevel professional education and training. An on-boarding process, which at VUMC usually occurs within the first six months of employment, ensures that all team members are introduced to the culture and learn about safety tools and safety science. Leaders and team members become familiar with and are trained on the skills required to employ the organization's surveillance systems, needs assessments, and metrics and measurements. The goal is for all to be able to use and to correctly apply them. Extra training is provided to leaders for promoting quality and holding colleagues accountable for performance. The leaders decide what knowledge and skills must be required learning for various team members (for example, protocols for universal time-outs, catheter insertion bundles, hand hygiene practices) and then support the training with professional development opportunities.[136,137]

Four Types of Key Persons

Key persons represent the third critical contributor for addressing unsafe systems and individual behaviors. We focus on four groups: chief officers or corporate-suite leadership, project champions, dedicated project team members, and frontline managers.

1. Corporate-Suite Leadership. Leadership qualities are discussed earlier in the chapter. In addition, persons in the corporate suite do the following:

- Hold themselves accountable to all stakeholders, including the board of directors (trustees), and hold others accountable for their performances
- Proactively search for problems in care systems and protect from retaliation others who report safety threats

- Direct and support "project champions" to form "dedicated project teams" empowered to undertake activities with achievable aims in support of the organization's safety culture
- Endorse programmatic goals and support those tasked to achieve those goals

2. Project Champions. Health care leaders routinely identify individuals with promise to be project champions capable of producing results. During executive walk-arounds, leaders observe directly and hear from others about prior successes and their personal qualities. In choosing project champions, leaders pay little attention to titles, practice areas, revenue production, and longevity, lest they inadvertently appoint "token" champions. Instead, they look for persons with the following:

- Ability to persevere and to inspire others to overcome barriers to achieving aims
- Desire to see others succeed
- Ability to maintain confidentiality
- Courage to respectfully challenge an attitude of "we've always done it this way" and to recruit others to the vision
- Objectivity to analyze data and to understand their implications
- Willingness to learn and to apply improvement methods and to test new ideas
- Skill to put the right people together in a dedicated project team to effectively implement the project
- An element of humility

3. Dedicated Project Teams. With the support of leaders and project champions, members of dedicated project teams offer relevant content knowledge and positive attitudes. They are also characterized as the following:

- Thoughtful, reasonable individuals with good judgment who maintain equanimity in the face of obstacles and conflict. They are neither weak-willed nor overbearing.

- Willing and able to see tasks through to completion despite sometimes significant obstacles involving politics, resistance to change, and incomplete knowledge of systems and personnel
- Able managers who understand the roles of systems and human accountability in implementing change
- Appropriately experienced and well-placed for the task (again, no "token" members appointed not for ability to contribute but solely for title, practice area, revenue, or longevity)
- Able to speak up in support of improvement projects during formal and informal meetings when the activity is challenged
- Committed to robust "load leveling." This term refers to reducing variations in workloads, work flow, and work mix to improve productivity, quality, and safety. Dedicated project teams that level loads measure productivity improvements by higher yield of high-quality capacity or reduced costs.[53]

4. Frontline Managers. Many other persons are required to address adverse outcomes and to implement successful change management. These individuals, including unit managers, medical directors, affiliated professional group leaders, and "natural leaders" among frontline staff, do the following:
- Receive appropriate training
- Support and provide feedback to all team members who are affected by change
- Encourage all to report unnecessary variations and unsafe systems or behaviors
- Track data about quality, safety, and efficiency
- Decide how best to share the results with colleagues, patients, and families to promote and to sustain high-quality services

Event Analysis Methodologies

The fourth and final critical contributor to balancing system and individual accountability is using reliable methods to analyze close calls and adverse outcomes, such as the transfusion error that may have contributed to the death described in the case example at the beginning of this chapter. These tools are widely described in the literature. Therefore, we focus on how they can help organizations better understand how adverse events occurred and may be prevented in the future, by balancing the roles played by systems and individuals' performances.

We discuss three common event analysis techniques that committed health care leaders use to complement data obtained from existing surveillance systems: (1) root cause analysis (RCA), also known as multicausal event analysis to reflect the likely finding of multiple root causes; (2) multidisciplinary morbidity, mortality, and improvement (MM&I) conferences; and (3) risk management claims files review.

Variations exist for each tool; all have strengths and weaknesses. Used well, they support a balanced focus on systems and individual accountability. Used poorly, results can mislead or do little to prevent future occurrences.[138] If used to unjustly punish,[139] these tools may exacerbate existing threats to safety and stifle forward momentum by making it psychologically unsafe for team members to speak up or to report when they observe unsafe practices.[140]

1. Root Causes Analysis. The first tool for determining exactly what went wrong is RCA. RCA systems were developed to identify "the factors that underlie variation in performance, including the occurrence or possible occurrence of a sentinel event."[49(p. SE-2)] The tool systematically explores the primary systemic causes of an adverse outcome and identifies actions to prevent recurrences.[141] A trained facilitator guides a multidisciplinary team of individuals who were directly involved in the event, including medical and other professional staff, policy makers, and managers from the relevant services, through the analysis.[140] Widely adopted in health care since 1996, when The Joint Commission first advocated their use,[142] RCAs were implemented by the U.S. Department of Veterans Affairs' National Center for Patient Safety (NCPS) in 2000,[142–144] and other organizations soon followed worldwide.[142] Joint Commission International (JCI), The Joint Commission's international accreditation "arm," also requires its accredited organizations to conduct RCAs and prepare action plans in response to sentinel events.[50]

RCAs take various forms and formats[142,145] but are fundamentally designed to answer three questions: "What happened, why did it happen, and what can be done to prevent it from happening again?"[141] Wu and colleagues suggest also asking whether follow-up assessments confirm that reoccurrence has been reduced.[138]

As a practical matter, features of the RCA process[49,146] should ideally encompass the following:

- Application to sentinel and other organization-defined events[144]
- A timely manner in which to conduct the RCA and to develop an action plan. The Joint Commission and JCI direct organizations to prepare thorough and credible RCAs and action plans within 45 calendar days "of the event or of becoming aware of the event."[49(p. SE-9)]
- Partnership between risk managers and quality officers, with both groups clear on their respective scopes of responsibility[147]
- Physical presence of all involved parties[143]
- Analysis of primary causative factors using

coding schemes[139,143]

- Creation of a database of completed RCAs for internal review and improvement actions[138,139]
- Development of actions for improvement designed to prevent recurrence. These actions are most likely to have desired impacts if they focus on specific clinical changes, are supported by evidence, are more straightforward than complex, and require few organizational changes.[148] Modifications of policies and (re)educating staff are not generally effective, particularly when the underlying cause is not lack of knowledge but inadequate staffing or faulty systems[34,138]
- Dissemination of findings to leadership, including the board[52,53]
- Use of completed RCAs to inform a standardized safety curriculum for the hospital

Best practices, however, have not been established for analyzing results or for follow-up assessments,[138] so system-level studies and cost-benefit analyses of RCAs are needed to establish their effectiveness.[138,142] Other concerns about RCAs are as follows:

- Institutions cannot directly correct problems in circumstances in which product or equipment design is faulty—that is, when others, such as manufacturers and regulators,[149–154] must be involved in creating and implementing solutions.
- Forming causal statements and developing/implementing corrective actions can be challenging, particularly when contributing causes appear to include many systems and individual performance failures.
- RCAs consume 20–90 hours of professional time.[138]
- Participants' contributions in RCA discussions may reflect individual and hindsight biases[139,142] and a tendency to blame others.

- Some institutions may conduct RCAs primarily to comply with Joint Commission or JCI standards or other performance measures but may not include an implementation phase to pilot efforts to prevent recurrence of identified quality and safety issues.[142]

Reviews of the impact of RCAs on subsequent outcomes are mixed.[138,142] Percarpio and colleagues, for example, found 11 articles that reported safety improvements following RCAs.[142] Although all the studies employed uncontrolled designs, the results were sufficiently encouraging to promote continued use of RCAs. We conclude that RCAs best serve as a tool when supplemented by two other learning mechanisms—the MM&I conference and risk management claims files review.

2. Multidisciplinary Morbidity, Mortality, and Improvement Conferences. MM&I conferences are a second tool for learning and for helping create transparency, encourage accountability, level hierarchical cultures, affirm reporting, and model psychological safety because they focus on systems and on human contributions to adverse outcomes.[155–157] Traditional M&M (morbidity and mortality) conferences began among surgeons in the early twentieth century as an education forum for examining and learning from medical errors and adverse outcomes. M&M conferences often focused on ways in which health care professionals contributed to adverse outcomes. Undoubtedly, this process reinforced professional accountability. However, attendees often perceived the purpose of the meetings to be assignment of blame rather than improvement of safety.[158–160]

MM&I conferences offer an alternative approach. A multidisciplinary team uses a disciplined approach to review the multiple domains in which failures or errors resulted in preventable adverse outcomes. The MM&I conference is an educational forum focused on improvement.

During the general MM&I process followed at VUMC, a review group composed of physicians, nurses, administrators, and risk managers nominates cases for presentation and then plans each conference.[155] A dedicated project team, consisting of a senior quality professional and physicians, prepares for and moderates the MM&I session. The team's intent is to create a learning experience in which all attendees feel comfortable with suggesting areas, behaviors, and circumstances that created risk not only for the patient whose care is discussed but potentially for other patients. Attendees are physicians, nurses, clinical support staff (regardless of training level), and hospital administrators; leaders participate as learners and quality promoters who affirm commitment to the organization's mission and credo.

The session begins with case details, as summarized across a time line diagram. A brief literature review related to the case-specific disease process or illness is presented, which is followed by a discussion about the events. Use of a cause-and-effect diagram (Ishikawa diagram[161]) encourages attendees to think about all factors contributing to the adverse outcome, such as policies, environment, equipment, communication, procedures, people, and "other." As each potential contributor is identified, the moderator asks why the event might have occurred. Respondents are expected to respect their colleagues and the complexity of the systems in which they work as they articulate concerns. Two goals of the process are to not blame and to remove fear of repercussions from sharing observations.[9] Before the conference, some respondents may be encouraged to speak up and are coached on how to do so. Each MM&I

conference concludes with a discussion of potential actions that might be needed. The dedicated project team meets after the MM&I conference to identify priorities for follow-up action. A work group is tasked to develop and implement the action plans for specified follow-up and designates team members who are accountable for their completion within target time frames. The project team tracks progress and, at each subsequent MM&I session, reports on status to promote accountability.

The MM&I process supports accountability and sustains a safety culture because it is consistent with the organization's mission and commitment to those it serves. Furthermore, the persons involved often publicly announce their roles in the patient's care (transparency and culture leveling), discuss the rationale for their actions, and declare the importance of analysis.[155,156]

The MM&I process models the principles of a safety culture by doing the following:
- Affirming event reporters
- Revealing that errors often occur because of the complex interplay between systems and humans
- Demonstrating leadership's determination to address problems
- Providing follow-up meetings to affirm that group input helps create real solutions.

For example, a young child was admitted to a children's hospital at 10 A.M. with fever and poor feeding. Following admission, the parents reported to the nurse (a relatively recent graduate) that their child seemed to be less active and alert than on arrival. The nurse communicated the parents' observations to the attending physician, who, for whatever reason, did not appreciate their significance. The parents reiterated their concerns about their child's worsen-

ing status several times throughout the day. Late in the afternoon, the child experienced respiratory arrest requiring resuscitation.

When this event was reviewed at an MM&I conference, the participants agreed that health care team members sometimes fail to recognize a patient's deterioration until a code is called. Two solutions that emerged in the course of the conference were deployment of rapid response teams and empowerment of families to call those teams directly. The MM&I review highlighted the need for a system that minimizes failures, and, because family members can detect deterioration in their loved one's appearance, they were felt to be perfectly positioned to initiate calls for a rapid response team. In addition, creation of rapid response teams was consistent with principles for balancing systems issues and individual accountability.[155,156,162]

3. Risk Management Claims Files Review. A risk manager's traditional role is to determine potential liability. Structured review helps the institution understand what harm the patient suffered, what happened, how it happened, whether the harm was related to medical error, and what effect this outcome will have on the individual's life. Risk managers obtain expert reviews to help answer these questions. After probable liability is determined, risk managers weigh the injured patient and family's demand for compensation against the organization's assessment of damages. Although risk managers should seek to protect organizational assets, ethical risk managers understand the realistic financial needs of injured patients and advocate on their behalf for fair settlement offers.

Until recently, another common risk manager role was to ensure that information learned from reviews did not leave the protection of the risk and legal departments, for fear it would be rendered discoverable.[163,164] The outcome was that valuable information was kept from others in the organization who could use that information to make health care safer.[147,165] Today, the risk manager's role is evolving. Risk managers are a critical part of the process for conducting RCAs and MM&Is. Having experience with other medicolegal cases and knowing the types of failures commonly identified, they help RCA and MM&I teams identify possible causes of the failures. In addition, as organizations commit to ensuring safe and reliable health care, risk managers are increasingly aware that the data that they manage are valuable to a learning organization. Aggregated case data may be used to identify recurring safety and quality themes. Patterns may be discovered for a hospital, department, clinic, practice, or person, crossing locales and departments or clustering within a small number of groups. For example, analysis of risk management claims files identified several cases where nighttime physicians incorrectly read x-rays, resulting in misdiagnoses. Overreads by experienced radiologists the next morning identified the errors. These data prompted leadership to rearrange senior radiologists' schedules to provide in-house expertise 24 hours/day, 7 days/week. Similarly, claims based in part on a series of alleged failures of communication in a busy trauma service resulted in the institution of trauma service "family rounds."[166]

The main goal of studying adverse events is to identify contributory factors so that interventions can be designed to address them. Policies with unintended consequences, modes of ineffective communication, inadequate supervision, a steep hierarchical structure that inhibits speaking up, inadequate staffing, lack of equipment, inadequate training in procedures or on new equipment, or ineffective use of the chain of command are but a few of the factors identi-

fied in claims files studies for women's health,[167] pediatrics,[168,169] emergency medicine,[170] and trauma care.[171] A clear theme across all these studies was the role of communication failures and disruptive behavior. Such studies are limited by the fact that the generalizability of the data is usually unknown. One remedy is to share risk management data across large consortia.[172–174]

Whatever the technique(s) employed to learn why an adverse outcome (or series of adverse outcomes) occurred, the results may reveal contributions related to systems failures, individual performance, systems *and* individual issues (as we will see in the transfusion error case), or neither, such as when reviews determine that a patient experienced the natural history or known complications of a particular condition or disease[175] (*see* Figure 1-3, page 22).

We return for the last time to the case example, for which we now describe the RCA's findings and leaders' interactions with the staff involved in the transfusion error.

CASE EXAMPLE, PART 3. ROOT CAUSE ANALYSIS

As a leader (same as in Part 1), you participate in the RCA regarding the transfusion error. Attendees include the patient's attending, Dr. Trauma; the ED nurses who cared for the patient; the bloodbank director; and the OR staff who transferred the blood units. The results reveal the following:

The incompatible units were intended for a *second* trauma victim. The blood requisition for Victim 2 originated in the ED. After typing and crossing the units, the blood bank correctly delivered them via a pneumatic tube system to the surgery suite where trauma Victim 2 had been transported. Because the admitting and laboratory computer systems do not communi-

Figure 1-3. Action Grid

		Did the Event Analysis Reveal Systems Problem(s)?	
		Yes	No
Did Event Analysis Reveal Performance or Behavior Problem(s)?	Yes	Address system barriers, medical "family" problems; reengineer system to promote reliability and reduce potential human factors *Plus* Individual intervention at appropriate level of graduated feedback	Individual intervention at appropriate level of graduated feedback
	No	Address system barriers, medical "family" problems; reengineer system to promote reliability and to reduce potential human factors	Verify data; provide feedback to patients, families, and/or staff; be prepared to "agree to disagree" with those whose opinions differ

The transfusion case demonstrates the evident need to balance systems-based solutions and individual accountability. The grid simply reminds leaders to take balanced actions consistent with the event analysis data. Consider how this might apply to team members involved in the transfusion error scenario and the systems in which they work.

Source: Vanderbilt University Medical Center, Nashville, TN. Used with permission.

cate directly, the location on the blood was still listed as "Emergency Department." Wanting to be helpful, but without noting the patient's name, OR personnel forwarded the units to the ED via the pneumatic tube system, contrary to policy. On arrival in the ED, the units were assumed to be "trauma blood" and placed with the other O negative blood. During the frenzy of activity surrounding the resuscitation of Victim 1, a nurse was dispatched for trauma blood. By chance, he pulled the two units intended for Victim 2. As the nurse approached Victim 1's bedside, Dr. Trauma unleashed at him a barrage of expletives about getting the blood in. The nurse asserted that he had tried to explain that he was following procedure but that he then felt pressured to do as he was

ordered. Another team member—an R.N.—recognized the high-risk situation but reflected, "I just didn't speak up."

The RCA identifies several needed systems improvements, including the following:
• Creation of an interface between the admitting and laboratory systems to allow immediate updates of patient location
• Creation of a more reliable process for receiving and storing trauma blood in the ED

The event analysis also raises questions about the performance of the nurse who administered the blood, the nurse who did not feel comfortable speaking up, and the surgeon whose behavior might have affected team performance.

Leaders in the departments of emergency medicine and trauma decide that this case has identified several important lessons. They conduct an MM&I conference, which is well attended by many physicians and nurses, OR and blood bank staff, administrators, residents, and risk managers. The case is sobering for all.

Human Accountability and Feedback

As a medical center leader, you are able to instruct the chief of trauma surgery to meet with Dr. Trauma and the ED unit manager to meet with the nurses. For each individual, the responsible leader is asked to make two determinations: (1) the individual's accountability under the Unsafe Acts Algorithm,*[1] and (2) the appropriate administrative response. All three—Dr. Trauma and the nurses—are valued team members, and you want to provide feedback in a way that supports a safety culture and promotes their professional accountability.

Meeting with Dr. Trauma

As Dr. Trauma's chief, you speak with him about his behavior toward Nurse 1. You have no reason to believe he had intent to harm, and you have no evidence of chemical impairment. On the other hand, you recognize that some individuals may be impaired in their abilities to interact with others. It seems to you that Dr. Trauma's behavior in the ED unreasonably increased risk; your experience is that the vast majority of physicians do not behave like this in high-pressure situations. You have no way of knowing whether Dr. Trauma even recognizes that his behavior may have contributed to an error.

Dr. Trauma has high productivity. Nonetheless, you cannot offer excuses for his performance. Others in the department conduct themselves professionally. In addition, this is not the first time that Dr. Trauma has behaved this way. During the past two years, other team members submitted event reports that describe similar behaviors. Some of the coworker and patient complaints suggest that Dr. Trauma gets angry in pressured circumstances, as in the following vignettes:

Coworker (in a safety culture could be anyone): "Dr. Trauma arrived in the OR 45 minutes after the case was scheduled to start. He immediately reprimanded the residents, OR staff, and the C.R.N.A. [certified registered nurse anesthetist] because the patient was still awake and the abdomen not yet opened."

Patient: "I asked the doctor why he was seeing me so much later than my appointment time, which was 9:00 A.M. It was now 11:30. He started yelling, 'People can't get in to see me. You're lucky you got an appointment. I don't need this.'"

You previously spoke with Dr. Trauma about several complaints from coworkers and patients. You find it concerning that Dr. Trauma failed to self-correct after this feedback. Given the accumulation of patient and staff complaints and the current event analysis, you decide that what is right for Dr. Trauma and the organization is for you, as his chief, to conduct a Level 2 "guided" intervention. As permitted by medical staff bylaws and in coordination with the Physician Wellness Program, you will require Dr. Trauma to undergo a comprehensive mental health evaluation and, if indicated, a defined treatment plan. Failure to comply would subject the physician to loss of privileges.

---

* Cited references are listed on page 25.

Leader of Nurse 1 and 2 (Emergency Department Unit Manager) Meeting with Nurse 1

As the ED director of nursing, you have been instructed to meet with the nurse who administered the incompatible units. You know this nurse has an outstanding record with excellent performance evaluations. Reviewing the Unsafe Acts Algorithm, you determine that no evidence suggests that the nurse intended to harm, was impaired at the time of the event, or had a history of unsafe acts. However, the nurse is accountable for knowingly violating a policy.

You need to determine what level of intervention is appropriate. Using the Accountability Pyramid (Figure 1-2), because this is not a "most egregious" act[2] and there has not been a persistent pattern of violations, Level 3 disciplinary action is not appropriate. You briefly consider having a cup-of-coffee conversation with the nurse because it was an isolated event but reject that alternative because of the error's seriousness. Level 2 is indicated for patterns that do not respond to awareness feedback; this is the nurse's first event, and you do not see the need for drawing up a directed plan that will require periodic meetings to assess progress.

Although this nurse has not had a pattern of events, you believe a Level 1 "awareness" feedback intervention would be appropriate to allow the nurse, as a professional, to reflect on what happened. From your experience with Nurse 1, you expect that he will respond professionally. You also are aware that should there be no evidence of insight, you retain the option to proceed to a Level 2 "guided" intervention. The ultimate goal is to provide feedback in a way that is designed to protect other patients from similar lapses but to also protect the well-being of your team member.

Because you recognize that errors can have emotional impact on health care professionals,[3-5] the first thing you do at the meeting is to make certain that Nurse 1 is doing okay. He says he is, but you provide him with information about the services offered by the Employee Assistance Program (EAP).[6] You see no need to defer the discussion to a later time.

You begin by affirming to Nurse 1 that he is an important member of the team. You review some of the results of the RCA of the event, as follows:

- Failed systems allowed blood units to return to the ED.
- A team member created a challenging environment via his verbal statements.
- A second team member noted the behavior but did not speak up.

You add the following:

- "You" (Nurse 1) failed to verify patient identifiers before starting transfusions and deferred to a team member, who encouraged you to violate an important safeguard.

You state that the institution is addressing each finding, including making necessary changes to the systems to prevent blood from ending up in the wrong location.

Nurse 1 immediately tells you that he has reflected on what happened. He is particularly concerned that he allowed himself to be intimidated by another member of the team and abandoned an important safety procedure to the detriment of his patient. He has reviewed last year's training for blood administration and expresses interest in receiving coaching in assertive communication skills.[7,8]

You affirm him for his thoughtfulness and his stated plan. You thank him for his valued contributions to the team and ask if he has any questions. Finally, you state that at this time, you see no need to meet again about the matter unless he wishes to.

Meeting with Nurse 2

Again, as the ED director of nursing, you are also asked to meet with Nurse 2. Nurse 2 acknowledges that she recognized a problem but did not speak up. No evidence suggests that she intended harm, was impaired, has a history of unsafe acts, or knowingly violated a policy. You believe that other team members might well have behaved similarly. However, not speaking up when a team member is unprofessional toward a colleague not only increased risk in this case but, if repeated, could put future patients at risk. You follow up this isolated incident with an informal cup-of-coffee conversation and provide feedback that her omission did not seem consistent with the credo value of commitment to colleagues. You decide that this informal session will likely suffice for Nurse 2 to self-correct. However, should there be future episodes, you will follow up and begin to document them.

Of note, this kind of conversation between a nurse leader and staff nurses is possible only when the leader can categorically assure his or her staff that abusive behavior by physicians or other employees in the organization will not be tolerated.

Health System CEO Report to the Board

As the health system's CEO, you present the case details to the board and share the results of the RCA and MM&I, including the systems issues and professionals' behaviors that set the stage for the incompatible transfusion. You advise the board that the interface between the admitting and laboratory computer systems is being programmed to allow immediate updates of patient location and that the process for receiving and storing trauma blood in the ED is now improved. You also communicate that leaders met with each of the involved professionals and provided appropriate interventions. You confirm that the error was shared with the family and that the risk managers continue to communicate with them.

Case Example References

1. Reason J.: *Managing the Risks of Organizational Accidents.* Aldershot, UK: Ashgate Publishing, 1997.
2. The Joint Commission: Behaviors that undermine a culture of safety. *Sentinel Event Alert* 40, Jul. 9, 2008. http://www.jointcommission.org/assets/1/18/SEA_40.pdf (accessed Sep. 23, 2011).
3. Roesler R., Ward D., Short M.: Supporting staff recovery and reintegration after a critical incident resulting in infant death. *Adv Neonatal Care* 9:163–171, Aug. 2009.
4. Waterman A.D., et al.: The emotional impact of medical errors on practicing physicians in the United States and Canada. *Jt Comm J Qual Patient Saf* 33:467–476, Aug. 2007.
5. Scott S.D., et al.: The natural history of recovery for the healthcare provider "second victim" after adverse patient events. *Qual Saf Health Care* 18:325–330, Oct. 2009.
6. U.S. Department of Health & Human Services, Federal Occupational Health: *Use of Employee Assistance Programs Clearly Improves Employee Health and Productivity.* http://www.foh.dhhs.gov/NYCU/EAPimproves.asp (accessed Sep. 23, 2011).
7. Griffin M.: Teaching cognitive rehearsal as a shield for lateral violence: An intervention for newly licensed nurses. *J Contin Educ Nurs* 35:257–263, Nov.–Dec. 2004.
8. Buback D.: Assertiveness training to prevent verbal abuse in the OR. *AORN J* 79:148–150, 153–158, 161–164, Jan. 2004.

THE NEW PROJECT BUNDLE: LAUNCHING NEW INITIATIVES

Up to this point in the chapter, we have focused on setting the foundations for responding to an event. But how can you set the stage to promote systems and individual accountability as you launch new quality and safety initiatives?

Reflect on some of your quality and safety projects. Some take off, and others flounder. Is the success or failure determined by your plan, your systems, your team members, or alignment of

Figure 1-4. A Project Bundle Rating Form

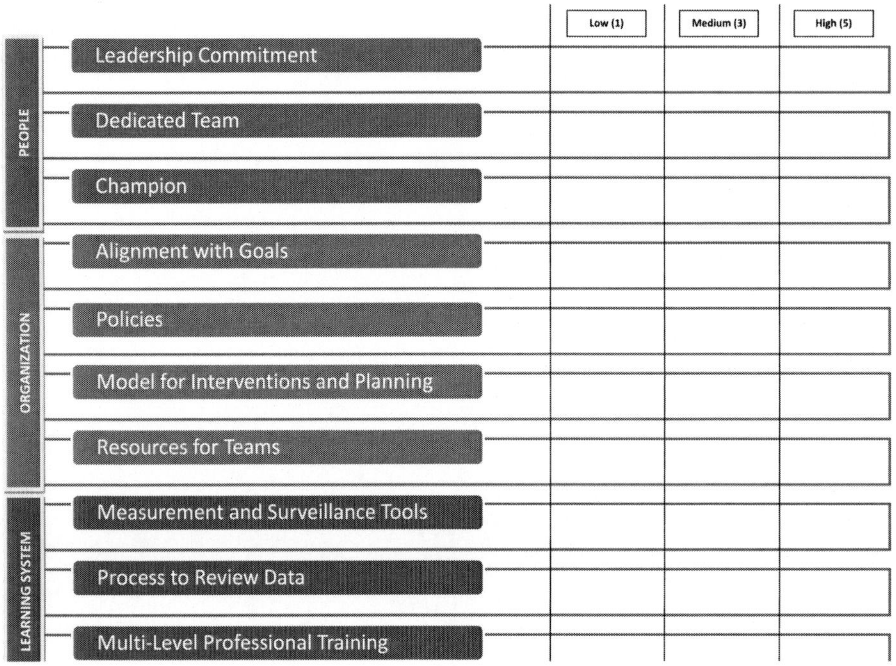

		Low (1)	Medium (3)	High (5)
PEOPLE	Leadership Commitment			
	Dedicated Team			
	Champion			
ORGANIZATION	Alignment with Goals			
	Policies			
	Model for Interventions and Planning			
	Resources for Teams			
LEARNING SYSTEM	Measurement and Surveillance Tools			
	Process to Review Data			
	Multi-Level Professional Training			

Source: Vanderbilt University Medical Center, Nashville, TN. Used with permission.

stars and planets? The next time you begin planning an initiative, consider using a "Project Bundle" (*see* Figure 1-4, above) to assess launch readiness. The tool may remind you of essential plan elements that may have been forgotten. Even leaders are subject to slips and lapses.

The "bundle" mirrors the previously described tools and processes for a safety culture and is divided into learning systems, people, and organizational readiness. Note that it includes a scoring system in which you, on the basis of your judgment, reflect on the strengths, commitment, and readiness of each element. Use the bundle to direct questions, as listed in

Sidebar 1-1 (pages 27–28) about your learning systems, people, and organizational readiness.

SUMMARY AND NEXT STEPS

Health care organizations have not achieved the goal of safe care at all times for all patients. A framework for pursuing quality and safety is supported by a culture in which (a) team members speak up when they see variation; (b) leaders and teams review event reports, adverse outcomes, and near misses to assess systems and individual performances; and (c) leaders address system vulnerabilities and conduct tiered interventions matched to individuals' levels of accountability.[176] We also describe a "project

Sidebar 1-1. Questions for the New Project Bundle

Learning Systems

- Is there really a need? Was this an isolated event? Or is there evidence of multiple events from one or multiple components of your surveillance system?

- What is the probability of reoccurrence, and how serious would the impact be?

- What is the impact analysis? Is it based on informal judgment or, for example, done in the context of changing reimbursement rules based on your higher-than-expected readmission rates? Your quality and finance teams should be positioned to assist. Whoever is on point, the key is capturing credible information in an attempt to create informed and structured opportunities for discussion. With a needs/impact assessment, a leader will know that his or her team has common ground for conversation, opinion, and recommendations for decision making.

- With respect to surveillance and measurement tools, does the proposed project have clearly defined metrics to assess performance? What pushback will you experience? Are you prepared to address the assertion that "my practice is unique"?

- With respect to education and training, do your team members have the time? Will their attempts bump up against other institutional priorities? Do you need to send individuals away to gain expertise or bring in outside resources?

People

- How do you really know that you have leadership commitment? If not, how will you get others on board? Will your informal leaders endorse and speak up at the right moments?

- In discussions to gain support, can you position a project in a way that is consistent with the organization's mission and vision, not "because of CMS [U.S. Centers for Medicare & Medicaid Services] and The Joint Commission (or Joint Commission International)" or other regulatory or accreditation requirement?

- With respect to a potential project champion leader, is this individual going to be a real champion and put in effort, or will he or she simply be a figurehead? Consider asking your project champions to commit to a list of tasks defining what is expected and the time frame. Of course, you should define the resources that are being committed, including your personal time for reviewing, coaching, and providing emotional support. Identify those with the "X factor," the ability to inspire and to bring others along.

- Do the project team members have a zeal for quality and safety? Warning: Persistence is critical, but being abrasive and judgmental may be destructive. Good team leaders find ways to promote insight and awareness of improvement opportunities without offending those who believe their work needs no improvement.

(continued on page 28)

Sidebar 1-1. Questions for the New Project Bundle (continued)

- Are all disciplines represented by individuals who will actually work? Will you overwhelm your team or the champion? If the organization is acting on multiple projects, can you do some "load leveling" and smooth out the distribution of effort? A portfolio of initiatives should contain work plans with sufficient details about required resources, areas of impact/change, and milestones so leaders are able to anticipate how to spread the work across areas or individuals.

Organizational Readiness
- Is your proposed project aligned with the organization's mission/vision statement? Will it be a "pillar" priority? Can you link leaders' performance evaluations to achievement of project goals?

- Are you adopting or adapting someone else's project or plan? A growing number of best practices allow organizations to take on various quality and safety challenges. Others' projects may be adopted in total because they have worked elsewhere and fit your culture. However, some team members may assert that your environment differs from that of the demonstration site, and they may be correct. Consequently, enthusiastic support for "our" plan may require you to invite key individuals and groups to recommend local adjustment(s) to the plan.

- Finally, in your leadership role, have you assigned sufficient resources to enable individuals to get the work done, or are you simply loading more requirements onto an already-stressed team? If the project is important, support it. Every successful launch builds confidence, trust, and support for your safety culture.

---

bundle" and component tools for supporting a safety culture. The bundle enables leaders to survey the organization's readiness to launch new plans, gain project momentum, evaluate systems and individual contributions to successes and failures, use feedback and tiered interventions to design midcourse corrections, and achieve successful outcomes.

VUMC has made substantial strides in encouraging reporting and intervening in ways that reinforce professionalism in patient and team interactions. Increasing rates of reporting about unprofessional performance/behavior and unsafe systems demonstrate increasing willing-

ness to speak up about concerns* and unit-level trust that the VUMC leadership holds individuals accountable to a credo, system goals, and one another.

Team members are trained to engage in cup-of-

---

* In a recent article, DuPree et al. (DuPree E., et al.: Professionalism: A necessary ingredient in a culture of safety. *Jt Comm J Qual Patient Saf* 37:447–455, Oct. 2011) described an obstetrics service's creation and roll-out of a Code of Professionalism, repeated encouragement to report errors and unacceptable behaviors as a means for fostering improvement, and implementation of a process for managing disruptive and inappropriate behaviors, which resulted in substantial increases in staff reporting.

coffee conversations with others, irrespective of position. Leaders routinely review various metrics to identify when more formal feedback is needed. As unit or individual data warrant and as guided by the Accountability Pyramid, leaders intervene with managers and team members to reengineer systems and to address individual accountability. Momentum is self-reinforcing. Units and individuals who once insisted "we're different" or "my patients are different" successfully improve systems and change behavior.

VUMC's leaders are using the project bundle to help decide which projects to initiate (those most likely to succeed because all elements are substantially in place) and which to defer (those projects that lack adequate leadership support, project champion commitment, or other essential threshold elements). Prior to implementation, project teams define criteria for Level 1, 2, and 3 interventions and determine which leaders will be involved at each stage. Using these processes, VUMC has reduced medical malpractice claims[67] and increased hand hygiene rates.[83] The next steps will include regular use of (1) the project bundle, to review proposed initiatives and to aid in their development and implementation and (2) the Accountability Pyramid, to ensure satisfactory performance in all units to which the initiative applies. The project bundle will also be used to reevaluate why a project is failing or stagnant.

The goal is to build VUMC's safety culture project by project, unit by unit, and department by department, using the tools and practices described in this chapter. We advocate patience but also active surveillance, innovation without abandoning what works, and a continuing commitment to sharing what we learn from successes and failures. By addressing deficiencies through a balanced approach to systems issues and individual accountability, we are promoting an increasingly reliable safety culture.

The authors thank Carol Farina for assistance with manuscript preparation; Margaret (Peggy) Westlake, M.L.S., for assistance with background research; and Allan Frankel, M.D., for prepublication review and comments.

References

1. Michel P., et al.: French national survey of inpatient adverse events prospectively assessed with ward staff. *Qual Saf Health Care* 16:369–377, Oct. 2007.

2. Aranaz-Andrés J.M., et al.: Impact and preventability of adverse events in Spanish public hospitals: Results of the Spanish National Study of Adverse Events (ENEAS). *Int J Qual Health Care* 21:408–414, Dec. 2009.

3. Wilson R.M., et al.: The Quality in Australian Health Care Study. *Med J Aust* 163:458–471, Nov. 6, 1995.

4. Reason J.: Human error: Models and management. *BMJ* 320(7237):768–770, Mar. 18, 2000.

5. Wachter R.M., Shojania K.G.: *Internal Bleeding: The Truth Behind America's Terrifying Epidemic of Medical Mistakes.* New York City: Rugged Land, LLC, 2004.

6. Sexton J.B., Thomas E.J., Helmreich R.L.: Error, stress, and teamwork in medicine and aviation: Cross sectional surveys. *BMJ*(7237) 320:745–749, Mar. 18, 2000.

7. Wilson R.M., et al.: An analysis of the causes of adverse events from the Quality in Australian Health Care Study. *Med J Aust* 170:411–415, May 3, 1999.

8. Reason J.T.: *The Human Contribution.* Burlington, VT: Ashgate Publishing Company, 2008.

9. Marx D.: *Patient Safety and the "Just Culture": A Primer for Health Care Executives.* New York City: Columbia University, 2001. http://psnet.ahrq.gov/resource.aspx?resourceID=1582 (accessed Sep. 23, 2011).

10. Frankel A.S., Leonard M.W., Denham C.R.: Fair and just culture, team behavior, and leadership engagement: The tools to achieve high reliability. *Health Serv Res* 41:1690–1709, Aug. 2006.

11. Chassin M.R, Loeb J.M.: The ongoing quality improvement journey: Next stop, high reliability. *Health Aff (Millwood)* 30:559–568, Apr. 2011.

12. Institute of Medicine: *To Err Is Human: Building a Safer Health System.* Washington, DC: National Academy Press, 2000.

13. Brennan T.A., et al.: Incidence of adverse events and negligence in hospitalized patients: Results of the Harvard Medical Practice Study I. *N Engl J Med* 324:370–376, Feb. 7, 1991.

14. Wachter R.M.: The end of the beginning: Patient safety five years after "To Err Is Human." *Health Aff (Millwood)* w4-534–w4-545, Jul.–Dec. 2004.

15. Leape L.L., Berwick D.M.: Five years after *To Err Is*

Human: What have we learned? *JAMA* 293:2384–2390, May 18, 2005.

16. Walsh K.E., et al.: Effect of computer order entry on prevention of serious medication errors in hospitalized children. *Pediatrics* 121:e421–e427, Mar. 2008.

17. Long A.L., et al.: The Leapfrog CPOE Evaluation Tool: One academic medical center's experience. *Patient Safety & Quality Healthcare,* Nov.–Dec. 2010.

18. Landrigan C.P., et al.: Temporal trends in rates of patient harm resulting from medical care. *N Engl J Med* 363:2124–2134, Nov. 25, 2010.

19. Jain M., et al.: Decline in ICU adverse events, nosocomial infections and cost through a quality improvement initiative focusing on teamwork and culture change. *Qual Saf Health Care* 15:235–239, Aug. 2006.

20. Pronovost P.J., et al.: Sustaining reductions in catheter related bloodstream infections in Michigan intensive care units: Observational study. *BMJ* 340:c309, Feb. 4, 2010.

21. Lipitz-Snyderman A., et al.: Impact of a statewide intensive care unit quality improvement initiative on hospital mortality and length of stay: Retrospective comparative analysis. *BMJ* 342:d219, Jan. 28, 2011.

22. Ernst M.M., et al.: Using quality improvement science to implement a multidisciplinary behavior intervention targeting pediatric inpatient airway clearance. *J Pediatr Psychol* 35:14–24, Jan.–Feb. 2010.

23. Davis C.R.: Infection-free surgery: How to improve hand-hygiene compliance and eradicate methicillin-resistant *Staphylococcus aureus* from surgical wards. *Ann R Coll Surg Engl* 92:316–319, May 2010.

24. Berwick D.M.: Developing and testing changes in delivery of care. *Ann Intern Med* 128:651–656, Apr. 15, 1998.

25. McPherson K., et al.: Small-area variations in the use of common surgical procedures: An international comparison of New England, England, and Norway. *N Engl J Med* 307:1310–1314, Nov. 18, 1982.

26. Raab S.S., et al.: Clinical impact and frequency of anatomic pathology errors in cancer diagnoses. *Cancer* 104:2205–2213, Nov. 15, 2005.

27. Rochon P.A., et al.: Variation in nursing home anti-psychotic prescribing rates. *Arch Intern Med* 167:676–683, Apr. 9, 2007.

28. Chassin M.R., Becher E.C.: The wrong patient. *Ann Intern Med* 136:826–833, Jun. 4, 2002.

29. National Health Service: *The NHS Atlas of Variation in Healthcare: Reducing Unwarranted Variation to Increase Value and Improve Quality.* Nov. 2010. http://www.rightcare.nhs.uk/atlas/qipp_nhs Atlas-LOW_261110c.pdf (accessed Sep. 23, 2011).

30. Nkoy F.L., et al.: Quality of care for children hospitalized with asthma. *Pediatrics* 122:1055–1063, Nov. 2008.

31. Hickson G.B., et al.: A complementary approach to promoting professionalism: Identifying, measuring, and addressing unprofessional behaviors. *Acad Med*

82:1040–1048, Nov. 2007.

32. The Joint Commission: Behaviors that undermine a culture of safety. *Sentinel Event Alert* 40, Jul. 9, 2008. http://www.jointcommission.org/assets/1/18/SEA_40.pdf (accessed Sep. 23, 2011).

33. Reason J.: *Human Error.* Cambridge, UK: Cambridge University Press, 1990.

34. Needleman J., et al.: Nurse staffing and inpatient hospital mortality. *N Engl J Med* 364:1037–1045, Mar. 17, 2011.

35. Speroff T., et al.: Organisational culture: Variation across hospitals and connection to patient safety climate. *Qual Saf Health Care* 19:592–596, Dec. 2010.

36. Keroack M.A., et al.: Organizational factors associated with high performance in quality and safety in academic medical centers. *Acad Med* 82:1178–1186, Dec. 2007.

37. DuPree E., et al.: Improving patient satisfaction with pain management using Six Sigma tools. *Jt Comm J Qual Patient Saf* 35:343–350, Jul. 2009.

38. DelliFraine J.L., Langabeer J.R. II, Nembhard I.M.: Assessing the evidence of Six Sigma and Lean in the health care industry. *Qual Manag Health Care* 19:211–215, Jul.–Sep. 2010.

39. Chassin M.R.: Is health care ready for Six Sigma quality? *Milbank Q* 76:565–591, Dec. 1998.

40. Poksinska B.: The current state of implementation of Lean in health care: Literature review. *Qual Manag Health Care* 19:319–329, Oct.–Dec. 2010.

41. Campbell R.J.: Change management in health care. *Health Care Manag (Frederick)* 27:23–39, Jan.–Mar. 2008.

42. Papadopoulos T., Radnor Z., Merali Y.: The role of actor associations in understanding the implementation of Lean thinking in healthcare. *International Journal of Operations & Production Management* 31:167–191, Feb. 2011.

43. McCarthy D., Klein S.: *Sentara Healthcare: Making Patient Safety an Enduring Organizational Value.* The Commonwealth Fund, Mar. 2011. http://www.commonwealthfund.org/~/media/Files/Publications/Case%20Study/2011/Mar/1476_McCarthy_Sentara_case_study_FINAL_March.pdf (accessed Sep. 23, 2011).

44. Nelson-Peterson D.L., Leppa C.J.: Creating an environment for caring using lean principles of the Virginia Mason Production System. *J Nurs Adm* 37:287–294, Jun. 2007.

45. Haraden C., Leitch J.: Scotland's successful national approach to improving patient safety in acute care. *Health Aff (Millwood)* 30:755–763, Apr. 2011.

46. Kozlowski S.W.J., Ilgen D.R.: Enhancing the effectiveness of work groups and teams. *Psychological Science in the Public Interest* 7:77–124, Dec. 2006.

47. Govern P.: Professional conduct standards take shape. *Reporter, Vanderbilt University Medical Center,* Jul. 8, 2005.

http://www.mc.vanderbilt.edu/reporter/index.html?
ID=4077 (accessed Sep. 23, 2011).

48. Frankel A., Gandhi T.K., Bates D.W.: Improving patient safety across a large integrated health care delivery system. *Int J Qual Health Care* 15:i31–i40, Dec. 2003.

49. The Joint Commission: *Comprehensive Accreditation Manual for Hospitals: The Official Handbook.* Oak Brook, IL: Joint Commission Resources, 2010.

50. Joint Commission International: *Joint Commission International Accreditation Standards for Hospitals,* 4th ed. Oak Brook, IL: Joint Commission Resources, 2010.

51. Joint Commission Resources: *Getting the Board on Board: What Your Board Needs to Know About Quality and Patient Safety,* 2nd ed. Oak Brook, IL: Joint Commission Resources, 2011.

52. Conway J.: Getting boards on board: Engaging governing boards in quality and safety. *Jt Comm J Qual Patient Saf* 34:214–220, Apr. 2008.

53. Liker J.K.: *The Toyota Way: 14 Management Principles from the World's Greatest Manufacturer.* New York City: McGraw Hill, 2004.

54. Kim C.S., et al.: Lean health care: What can hospitals learn from a world-class automaker? *J Hosp Med* 1:191–199, May 2006.

55. Spear S.J.: Fixing health care from the inside, today. *Harv Bus Rev* 83:78–91, Sep. 2005.

56. Jimmerson C., Weber D., Sobek D.K. II.: Reducing waste and errors: Piloting Lean principles at Intermountain Healthcare. *Jt Comm J Qual Patient Saf* 31:249–257, May 2005.

57. Reader T.W., et al.: Developing a team performance framework for the intensive care unit. *Crit Care Med* 37:1787–1793, May 2009.

58. Reason J., Hobbs A.: *Managing Maintenance Error: A Practical Guide.* Aldershot, UK: Ashgate Publishing, 2003.

59. Studer Q.: *Hardwiring Excellence: Purpose, Worthwhile Work, Making a Difference.* Gulf Breeze, FL: Fire Starter Publishing, 2003.

60. Felps W., Mitchell T.R., Byington E.: How, when, and why bad apples spoil the barrel: Negative group members and dysfunctional groups. In Staw B.M. (ed.): *Research in Organizational Behavior: An Annual Series of Analytical Essays and Critical Reviews,* vol. 27. Oxford, UK: Elsevier, 2006, pp. 175–222.

61. Rosenstein A.H., O'Daniel M.: Impact and implications of disruptive behavior in the perioperative arena. *J Am Coll Surg* 203:96–105, Jul. 2006.

62. Bendersky C.: Culture: The missing link in dispute systems design. *Negotiation Journal* 14:307–311, Oct. 1998.

63. Poliner v. Texas Health Systems 537 F.3d 368 (5th Cir. 2008).

64. Lubnau T.E. II, Bailey D.B.: Dealing with the disruptive physician. *Wyoming Law Review* 8(2):567–586, 2008.

65. Reason J.: *Managing the Risks of Organizational Accidents.* Aldershot, UK: Ashgate Publishing, 1997.

66. Roesler R., Ward D., Short M.: Supporting staff recovery and reintegration after a critical incident resulting in infant death. *Adv Neonatal Care* 9:163–171, Aug. 2009.

67. Hickson G.B., Pichert J.W.: Identifying and addressing physicians at high risk for medical malpractice claims. In Youngberg B.J. (ed.): *Patient Safety Handbook,* 2nd ed. Sudbury, MA: Jones & Bartlett Learning, forthcoming.

68. Hickson G.B., et al.: Development of an early identification and response model of malpractice prevention. *Law and Contemporary Problems* 60:7–29, Winter 1997.

69. Hickson G.B., et al.: Patient complaints and malpractice risk. *JAMA* 287:2951–2957, Jun. 12, 2002.

70. Hickson G.B., et al.: Patient complaints and malpractice risk in a regional healthcare center. *South Med J* 100:791–796, Aug. 2007.

71. Moore I.N., et al.: Rethinking peer review: Detecting and addressing medical malpractice claims risk. *Vanderbilt Law Review* 59:1175–1206, May 2006.

72. Düsing R., et al.: Changes in antihypertensive therapy: The role of adverse effects and compliance. *Blood Press* 7:313–315, Nov. 1998.

73. Ware J.E. Jr., Davies A.R.: Behavioral consequences of consumer dissatisfaction with medical care. *Eval Program Plann* 6(3–4): 291–297, 1983.

74. Kravitz R.L., et al.: Internal medicine patients' expectations for care during office visits. *J Gen Intern Med* 9:75–81, Feb. 1994.

75. Jackson J.L., Kroenke K.: The effect of unmet expectations among adults presenting with physical symptoms. *Ann Intern Med* 134:889–897, May 1, 2001.

76. Jayadevappa R., et al.: Satisfaction with care: A measure of quality of care in prostate cancer patients. *Med Decis Making* 30:234–245, Mar.–Apr. 2010.

77. Borras J.M., et al.: Compliance, satisfaction and quality of life of patients with colorectal cancer receiving home chemotherapy or outpatient treatment: A randomised controlled trial. *BMJ* (7290)322:1–5, Apr. 7, 2001.

78. Pichert J.W., Hickson G.B., Moore I.: Using patient complaints to promote patient safety. In Henriksen K., et al. (eds.): *Advances in Patient Safety: New Directions and Alternative Approaches,* vol. 2. U.S. Agency for Healthcare Research and Quality, 2008. http://www.ahrq.gov/downloads/pub/advances2/vol2/Advances-Pichert_51.pdf (accessed Sep. 23, 2011).

79. Hayden A.C., et al.: Best practices for basic and advanced skills in health care service recovery: A case study of a re-admitted patient. *Jt Comm J Qual Patient Saf* 36:310–318, Jul. 2010.

80. U.S. Centers for Medicare & Medicaid Services: *Revisions to Interpretive Guidelines for Centers for Medicare & Medicaid Services Hospital Conditions of*

Participation 42 CFR §§482.12, 482.13, 482.27 and 482.28. Aug. 18, 2005. http://www.cms.hhs.gov/SurveyCertificationGenInfo/downloads/SCLetter05-42.pdf (accessed Sep. 23, 2011).

81. Stimson C.J., et al.: Medical malpractice claims risk in urology: An empirical analysis of patient complaint data. *J Urol* 183:1971–1976, May 2010.

82. Mukherjee K., et al.: All trauma surgeons are not created equal: Asymmetric distribution of malpractice claims risk. *J Trauma* 69:549–554, Sep. 2010.

83. Johnson J.G., et al.: Using financial incentives to improve hand hygiene adherence. Poster presentation at the Society for Healthcare Epidemiology in America 21st Annual Scientific Meeting, Dallas, Apr. 2, 2011.

84. Institute for Healthcare Improvement: *What Was the 5 Million Lives Campaign?* http://www.ihi.org/offerings/Initiatives/PastStrategicInitiatives/5MillionLives Campaign/Pages/default.aspx (accessed Sep. 23, 2011).

85. U.S. Agency for Healthcare Research and Quality: *AHRQ Health Care Innovations Exchange.* http://www.innovations.ahrq.gov/index.aspx (accessed Sep. 23, 2011).

86. United States Agency for International Development Health Care Improvement Project: *A Global Knowledge Resource for Health Care Improvement.* http://www.hciproject.org/ (accessed Sep. 23, 2011).

87. World Health Organization: *Blood Transfusion Safety.* http://www.who.int/bloodsafety/en/ (accessed Sep. 23, 2011).

88. Health-EU: *eHealth.* http://ec.europa.eu/health-eu/care_for_me/e-health/index_en.htm (accessed Sep. 23, 2011).

89. Pelczarski K.M., Braun P.A., Young E.: Hospitals collaborate to prevent wrong-site surgery. *Patient Safety & Quality in Healthcare* 7:20–22, 25–26, Sep.–Oct. 2010.

90. Clarke J.R., Johnston J., Finley E.D.: Getting surgery right. *Ann Surg* 246:395–405, Sep. 2007.

91. Pennsylvania Patient Safety Authority: Insight into preventing wrong-site surgery. *Pennsylvania Patient Safety Reporting System Patient Safety Advisory* 4, Dec. 2007. http://patientsafetyauthority.org/ADVISORIES/AdvisoryLibrary/2007/dec4(4)/Pages/109b.aspx (accessed Sep. 23, 2011).

92. Brilli R.J., et al.: The business case for preventing ventilator-associated pneumonia in pediatric intensive care unit patients. *Jt Comm J Qual Pat Saf* 34:629–638, Nov. 2008.

93. U.S. Centers for Medicare & Medicaid Services: *Roadmap for Implementing Value Driven Healthcare in the Traditional Medicare Fee-for-Service Program.* https://www.cms.gov/QualityInitiativesGenInfo/downloads/VBPRoadmap_OEA_1-16_508.pdf (accessed Sep. 23, 2011).

94. Levtzion-Korach O., et al.: Integrating incident data from five reporting systems to assess patient safety: Making sense of the elephant. *Jt Comm J Qual Patient Saf* 36:402–410, Sep. 2010.

95. Frankel A., et al.: Patient Safety Leadership Walk-Rounds™ at Partners Healthcare: Learning from implementation. *Jt Comm J Qual Patient Saf* 31:423–437, Aug. 2005.

96. Pronovost P.J., et al.: Senior executive adopt-a-work unit: A model for safety improvement. *Jt Comm J Qual Saf* 30:59–68, Feb 2004.

97. Press Ganey: *Safety Culture and the Disconnect Between Front-line Staff and Administrators.* Oct. 2008. http://www.pressganey.com/researchResources/hospitals/whitePapers.aspx (accessed Sep. 23, 2011).

98. Frankel A., et al.: Patient Safety Leadership Walk-Rounds. *Jt Comm J Qual Saf* 29:16–26, Jan. 2003.

99. ECRI Institute: *Internal Event Reporting: An Essential Tool for Risk Management and Patient Safety.* May 19–20, 2010. http://bphc.hrsa.gov/ftca/riskmanagement/webinars/eventreporting.pdf (accessed Sep. 23, 2011).

100. U.S. Equal Employment Opportunity Commission: *Filing a Charge of Discrimination.* http://www.eeoc.gov/employees/charge.cfm (accessed Sep. 23, 2011).

101. Noblis: *Pharmacy Recalls Jump 33% in 2010.* Jan. 14, 2011. http://info.rasmas.noblis.org/ (accessed Sep. 23, 2011).

102. Roller S.T., Pippins R.R., Ngai J.W.: FDA's expanding postmarket authority to monitor and publicize food and consumer health product risks: The need for procedural safeguards to reduce "transparency" policy harms in the post-9/11 regulatory environment. *Food Drug Law J* 64(3):577–598, 2009.

103. Colla J.B., et al.: Measuring patient safety climate: A review of surveys. *Qual Saf Health Care* 14:364–366, Oct. 2005.

104. Dudas V., et al.: The impact of follow-up telephone calls to patients after hospitalization. *Dis Mon* 48:239–248, Apr. 2002.

105. Institute for Healthcare Improvement: *IHI Trigger Tool for Measuring Adverse Drug Events.* http://www.ihi.org/knowledge/Pages/Tools/TriggerTool forMeasuringAdverseDrugEvents.aspx (accessed Sep. 23, 2011).

106. Rozich J.D., Haraden C.R., Resar R.K.: Adverse drug event trigger tool: A practical methodology for measuring medication related harm. *Qual Saf Health Care* 12:194–200, Jun. 2003.

107. Classen D.C., et al.: "Global Trigger Tool" shows that adverse events in hospitals may be ten times greater than previously measured. *Health Aff (Millwood)* 30:581–589, Apr. 2011.

108. Institute for Healthcare Improvement: *IHI Global Trigger Tool Guide,* Version 7. Dec. 2006. http://www.unmc.edu/rural/patient-safety/tool-time/TT13-040207-5 MillionLives/IHIGlobalTrigger ToolGuideDec06.pdf (accessed Sep. 23, 2011).

109. U.S. Office of Personnel Management: 5 CFR PART 724 RIN 3206–AJ93. Implementation of Title II of the Notification and Federal Employee Antidiscrimination and Retaliation Act of 2002. *Federal*

Register 69:Jan. 22, 2004. http://www.cms.gov/ AboutWebsite/Downloads/NoFearOPMRules.pdf (accessed Sep. 23, 2011).

110. Conway J.B., et al.: Key learning from the Dana-Farber Cancer Institute's 10-year patient safety journey. *American Society of Clinical Oncology 2006 Educational Book,* 42nd Annual Meeting, Atlanta, Jun. 2–6, 2006. http://www.asco.org/ASCOv2/ Home/Education%20&%20Training/Educational %20Book/PDF%20Files/2006/Practice01.pdf (accessed Sep. 23, 2011).

111. Pichert J.W., et al.: Communicating about unexpected outcomes and errors. In Carayon P. (ed.): *Handbook of Human Factors and Ergonomics in Healthcare and Patient Safety,* 2nd ed., Boca Raton, FL: CRC Press, forthcoming.

112. Edwards J.R., et al.: National Healthcare Safety Network (NHSN) Report: Data summary for 2006 through 2008, issued December 2009. *Am J Infect Control* 37:783–805, Dec. 2009.

113. American College of Surgeons: *National Surgical Quality Improvement Program (ACS NSQIP®).* http://www.acsnsqip.org/default.jsp (accessed Sep. 23, 2011).

114. World Health Organization: *European Health for All Database (HFA-DB).* http://www.euro.who.int/en/ what-we-do/data-and-evidence/databases/ european-health-for-all-database-hfa-db2 (accessed Sep. 23, 2011).

115. The Scottish Government: *Scotland Performs: NHS Scotland.* http://www.scotland.gov.uk/ About/scotPerforms/partnerstories/NHSScotland performance (accessed Sep. 23, 2011).

116. [Netherlands] National Institute for Public Health and the Environment (RIVM): *Home Page.* http://www.rivm.nl/en/ (accessed Sep. 23, 2011).

117. Nolte E.: International benchmarking of healthcare quality: A review of the literature. *Rand Europe Technical Report* 738, 2010. http://www.rand.org/ pubs/technical_reports/TR738.html (accessed Sep. 23, 2011).

118. CAHPS®: *HCAHPS Approved Survey Vendors as of June 1, 2011.* http://www.hcahpsonline.org/ app_vendor.aspx (accessed Sep. 23, 2011).

119. Studer Q., Robinson B.C., Cook K.: *The HCAHPS Handbook: Hardwire Your Hospital for Pay-for-Performance Success.* Gulf Breeze, FL: Fire Starter Publishing, 2010.

120. Croteau R.J., Schyve P.M.: Proactively error-proofing health care processes. In Spath P.L. (ed.): *Error Reduction in Health Care: A Systems Approach to Improving Patient Safety,* 2nd ed. San Francisco: Jossey-Bass, 2011, pp. 197–216.

121. American Society for Healthcare Risk Management: *Strategies and Tips for Maximizing Failure Mode & Effect Analysis in Your Organization.* Monograph. Jul. 2002. http://www.ashrm.org/ashrm/education/ development/monographs/FMEAwhitepaper.pdf

122. Marx D.A., Slonim A.D.: Assessing patient safety risk before the injury occurs: An introduction to socio-technical probabilistic risk modelling in health care. *Qual Saf Health Care* 12:ii33–ii38, Dec. 2003.

123. U.S. Department of Health & Human Services, Office of the Assistant Secretary for Planning and Evaluation: *Assessing Needs and Assets: Stories and Models from the Field.* http://aspe.hhs.gov/ezec/planning/ assessing.htm#story (accessed Sep. 23, 2011).

124. Blue Cross Blue Shield of Tennessee: *Reimbursement for Serious Reportable Adverse Events (Never Events).* http://www.bcbst.com/providers/administration/ Never_Events_2009.pdf (accessed Sep. 23, 2011).

125. Johns Hopkins Medicine, Human Resources: *Impact Analysis.* Jan. 11, 2006. http://www.hopkinsmedicine.org/jhhr/Organization DevelopmentandTraining/Leadership/impactanalysis (accessed Sep. 23, 2011).

126. Pronovost P.J., Lilford R.: Analysis & commentary: A road map for improving the performance of performance measures. *Health Aff (Millwood)* 30:569–573, Apr. 2011.

127. Murff H.J., et al.: Relationship between patient complaints and surgical complications. *Qual Saf Health Care* 15:13–16, Feb. 2006.

128. University HealthSystem Consortium: *Measure Performance.* https://www.uhc.edu/1244.htm (accessed Sep. 23, 2011).

129. VHA: *Comparative Clinical Measurement.* https://www.vha.com/Solutions/ClinicalImprovement/ Pages/ComparativeClinicalMeasurement.aspx (accessed Sep. 23, 2011).

130. Premier: *Home Page.* http://www.premierinc.com/ (accessed Sep. 23, 2011).

131. Institute for Healthcare Improvement: IHI Innovation Series white paper. *The Breakthrough Series: IHI's Collaborative Model for Achieving Breakthrough Improvement.* Cambridge, MA: Institute for Healthcare Improvement, 2003. http://www.ihi.org (accessed Sep. 23, 2011).

132. Greenberg P.B., et al.: Prevalence and predictors of ocular complications associated with cataract surgery in United States veterans. *Ophthalmology* 118:507–514, Mar. 2011.

133. Organisation for Economic Co-operation and Development (OECD): *Health Care Quality Indicators.* http://www.oecd.org/document/ 34/0,3746,en_2649_37407_37088930_1_1_1_ 37407,00.html (accessed Sep. 23, 2011).

134. IKAS, the Danish Institute for Quality and Accreditation in Healthcare: *The Danish Healthcare Quality Programme.* http://www.aalborgsygehus.rn.dk/ NR/rdonlyres/1172C002-F817-4597-AA9 D-DA0FB6F95A48/0/DDKMpjeceUKversion.pdf (accessed Sep. 23, 2011).

135. The National Coalition on Health Care and the Institute for Healthcare Improvement: Reducing

medical errors and improving patient safety: Success
stories from the front lines of medicine. *Accelerating
Change Today (A.C.T.).* Feb. 2000. http://www.ihi.org/
knowledge/Pages/Publications/Reducingmedicalerrors
andimprovingpatientsafetySuccessstoriesfromthefront
linesofmedicine.aspx (accessed Sep. 23, 2011).

136. McGaghie W.C., et al.: Lessons for continuing medical
education from simulation research in undergraduate
and graduate medical education: Effectiveness of
continuing medical education: American College of
Chest Physicians Evidence-Based Educational
Guidelines. *Chest* 135(3 suppl.):62S–68S, Mar. 2009.

137. Institute for Healthcare Improvement: *IHI Offerings.*
http://www.ihi.org/offerings/Pages/default.aspx
(accessed Sep. 23, 2011).

138. Wu A.W., Lipshutz A.K., Pronovost P.J.: Effectiveness
and efficiency of root cause analysis in medicine.
JAMA 299:685–687, Feb. 13, 2008.

139. Kaplan H.S., Fastman B.R.: Organization of event
reporting data for sense making and system improvement. *Qual Saf Health Care* 12:ii68–ii72, Dec. 2003.

140. Rex J.H., et al.: Systematic root cause analysis of
adverse drug events in a tertiary referral hospital. *Jt
Comm J Qual Improv* 26:563–575, Oct. 2000.

141. U.S. Department of Veterans Affairs National
Center for Patient Safety: *Root Cause Analysis.*
http://www.patientsafety.gov/vision.html#RCA
(accessed Sep. 23, 2011).

142. Percarpio K.B., Watts B.V., Weeks W.B.: The effectiveness of root cause analysis: What does the literature
tell us? *Jt Comm J Qual Patient Saf* 34:391–398, Jul.
2008.

143. Bagian J.P., et al.: The Veterans Affairs root cause
analysis system in action. *Jt Comm J Qual Improv*
28:531–545, Oct. 2002.

144. Heget J.R., et al.: John M. Eisenberg Patient Safety
Awards. System innovation: Veterans Health
Administration National Center for Patient Safety. *Jt
Comm J Qual Improv* 28:660–665, Dec. 2002.

145. Williams P.M.: Techniques for root cause analysis. *Proc
(Bayl Univ Med Cent)* 14, Apr. 2001.
http://www.ncbi.nlm.nih.gov/pmc/articles/PMC12929
97/ (accessed Sep. 23, 2011).

146. University HealthSystem Consortium (UHC): *Sentinel
Event Management and Prevention: Best Practice
Recommendations.* Chicago: UHC, 2007.

147. Skaggs L.: Hospital risk management programs in the
age of health care reform. *Kansas Journal of Law and
Public Policy* 4:89–108, Winter 1995.

148. Mills P.D., et al.: Actions and implementation
strategies to reduce suicidal events in the Veterans
Health Administration. *Jt Comm J Qual Patient Saf*
32:130–141, Mar. 2006.

149. European Medicines Agency: *Home Page.*
http://www.ema.europa.eu (accessed Sep. 23, 2011).

150. U.S. Food and Drug Administration: *Home Page.*
http://www.fda.gov (accessed Sep. 23, 2011).

151. European Medicines Agency: *Canada.*

http://www.ema.europa.eu/ema/index.jsp?curl=pages/
partners_and_networks/document_listing/document_
listing_000230.jsp&murl=menus/partners_and_
networks/partners_and_networks.jsp&mid=WC0b01a
c0580034f00&jsenabled=true (accessed Sep. 23,
2011).

152. European Medicines Agency: *Japan.*
http://www.ema.europa.eu/ema/index.jsp?curl=pages/
partners_and_networks/document_listing/document_
listing_000231.jsp&murl=menus/partners_and_
networks/partners_and_networks.jsp&mid=WC0b01a
c0580034f01 (accessed Sep. 23, 2011).

153. European Medicines Agency: *Switzerland.*
http://www.ema.europa.eu/ema/index.jsp?curl=pages/
partners_and_networks/document_listing/document
_listing_000262.jsp&murl=menus/partners_and_
networks/partners_and_networks.jsp&mid=WC0b01a
c058009b148 (accessed Sep. 23, 2011).

154. European Medicines Agency: *Australia.*
http://www.ema.europa.eu/ema/index.jsp?curl=pages/
partners_and_networks/document_listing/document_
listing_000309.jsp&murl=menus/partners_and_
networks/partners_and_networks.jsp&mid=WC0b01a
c05801e0897&jsenabled=true (accessed Sep. 23,
2011).

155. Deis J.N., et al.: Transforming the morbidity and
mortality conference into an instrument for system-
wide improvement. In Henriksen K., et al. (eds):
*Advances in Patient Safety: New Directions and
Alternative Approaches,* vol. 2. U.S. Agency for
Healthcare Research and Quality, 2008.
http://www.ahrq.gov/downloads/pub/advances2/vol2/
Advances-Deis_82.pdf (accessed Sep. 23, 2011).

156. Szekendi M.K., et al.: Using patient safety morbidity
and mortality conferences to promote transparency
and a culture of safety. *Jt Comm J Qual Patient Saf*
36:3–9, Jan. 2010.

157. Kauffmann R.M., et al.: The use of a multidisciplinary
morbidity and mortality conference to incorporate
ACGME general competencies. *J Surg Educ*
68:303–308, Jul.–Aug. 2011.

158. Gawande A.: *Complications: A Surgeon's Notes on an
Imperfect Science.* New York City: Metropolitan Books,
Henry Holt and Co., 2002.

159. Gordon L.A.: Can Cedars-Sinai's "M+M Matrix" save
surgical education? *Bull Am Coll Surg* 89:16–20, Jun.
2004.

160. Prince J.M., et al.: Increased interactive format for
Morbidity & Mortality conference improves educational value and enhances confidence. *J Surg Educ*
64:266–272, Sep.–Oct. 2007.

161. Ishikawa K.: *Guide to Quality Control.* White Plains,
NY: Asian Productivity Organization, Kraus
International Publications, 1982.

162. Ray E.M., et al.: Family alert: Implementing direct
family activation of a pediatric rapid response team. *Jt
Comm J Qual Patient Saf* 35:575–580, Nov. 2009.

163. Landsman S.: The risk of risk management. *Fordham*

Law Review 78:2315–2327, Jan. 2010.

164. Landsman S.: Reflections on juryphobia and medical malpractice reform. *DePaul Law Review* 57:221–241, Winter 2008.

165. Braithwaite J., et al.: Experiences of health professionals who conducted root cause analyses after undergoing a safety improvement programme. *Qual Saf Health Care* 15:393–399, Dec. 2006.

166. Miller A., et al.: Clinical communication in a trauma intensive care unit (ICU): A case study. *Proceedings of the Human Factors and Ergonomics Society 52nd Annual Meeting* 52:835–839, Jan. 2008.

167. White A.A., et al.: Cause and effect analysis of closed claims in obstetrics and gynecology. *Obstet Gynecol* 105:1031–1038, May 2005.

168. Pichert J.W., et al.: Understanding the etiology of serious medical events involving children: Implications for pediatricians and their risk managers. *Pediatr Ann* 26:160–164, 167–168, 170–172, Mar. 1997.

169. Hain P.D., et al.: Using risk management files to identify and address causative factors associated with adverse events in pediatrics. *Ther Clin Risk Manag* 3:625–631, Aug. 2007.

170. White A.A., et al.: Cause-and-effect analysis of risk management files to assess patient care in the emergency department. *Acad Emerg Med* 11:1035–1041,

Oct. 2004.

171. Morris J.A. Jr., et al.: Surgical adverse events, risk management and malpractice outcome: Morbidity and mortality review is not enough. *Ann Surg* 237:844–852, Jun. 2003.

172. Kesselheim A.S., et al.: Using malpractice claims to identify risk factors for neurological impairment among infants following non-reassuring fetal heart rate patterns during labour. *J Eval Clin Pract* 16:476–483, Jun. 2010.

173. Weingart S.N., et al.: Process of care failures in breast cancer diagnosis. *J Gen Intern Med* 24:702–709, Jun. 2009.

174. Kachalia A., et al.: Missed and delayed diagnoses in the emergency department: A study of closed malpractice claims from 4 liability insurers. *Ann Emerg Med* 49:196–205, Feb. 2007.

175. Meadows S., Baker K., Butler J.: The incident decision tree: Guidelines for action following patient safety incidents. In Henriksen K., et al. (eds.): *Advances in Patient Safety: From Research to Implementation,* vol. 4. Bethesda, MD: U.S. Agency for Healthcare Research and Quality, 2005, pp. 387–399.

176. Morath J.M., Turnbull J.E.: *To Do No Harm: Ensuring Patient Safety in Healthcare Organizations.* San Francisco: Jossey-Bass, 2005.

CHAPTER 2

Identifying and Responding to Patient Safety Problems

Christine Goeschel, Sc.D., M.P.A., M.P.S., R.N.; Michael A. Rosen, Ph.D.; Lisa Lubomski, Ph.D.; David A. Thompson, D.N.Sc., M.S., R.N.; Julius Cuong Pham, M.D., Ph.D.; Peter J. Pronovost, M.D., Ph.D.; Sean Berenholtz, M.D., M.H.S.

The rapid expansion of advances in biomedical science holds the potential for decreasing chronic disease burdens, reducing acute care costs, and increasing productive longevity. Yet actualized benefits do not begin to achieve what is possible. Estimates at the beginning of the century suggested that more than 100,000 people die annually in the United States from health care–associated infections,[1] as many as 98,000 die from mistakes of commission,[2] and thousands more succumb as a result of diagnostic errors[3-5] or the failure to receive evidence-based therapies.[6] In spite of significant investment in efforts to change those statistics, a recent study by the U.S. Office of the Inspector General affirmed that hospitalized Medicare patients continue to suffer iatrogenic harm; nearly 14% of the patients experienced an adverse event, and almost half of those were deemed preventable.[7] Moreover, many studies suggest that preventable health care harm is a leading cause of death around the world.[8-10]

Although it has been more than 10 years since the U.S. Institute of Medicine (IOM) report *To Err Is Human*[2] described this crisis, evidence that outcomes are improving is sporadic and uneven across delivery systems in developed and developing countries.[11,12] The inability to broadly ameliorate patient safety hazards does not reflect lack of active effort. At all levels in the chain of accountability for quality, activities to improve quality and patient safety abound.[13]

Collectively, these initiatives are resource intensive and well intentioned but are often neither locally efficient nor effective.[14] Identifying and responding to patient safety problems is complex. In our experience, programs that are scientifically sound, use robust measurement, address problems deemed important by frontline caregivers, and allow for flexibility to incorporate local wisdom offer the greatest potential for success. Yet organizations eager to identify and respond to patient safety problems often struggle to decide where to focus, how to begin, and how to measure progress.[15,16]

In this chapter, we identify some of the key challenges to identifying and responding to patient safety problems, offer strategies to address these challenges, and discuss emerging knowledge that is likely to expedite evolution of this important area of health care delivery.

KEY MESSAGES FROM THE LITERATURE

The importance and necessity of developing systems to identify and to learn from patient safety problems is well accepted.[17,18] A variety of potential sources of information are available to facilitate the identification of adverse events and near misses (or *close calls*), including mal-practice claims, investigations of sentinel events* by risk managers, morbidity and mortality conferences, and patient safety reporting systems (PSRSs), which are also referred to in some settings as *incident reporting systems.* International agreement is strong regarding the need for patient safety data, and the development of PSRSs has been widespread. Research reports regarding these systems indicate their value in improving patient safety culture, increasing awareness of patient safety, and focusing efforts to prevent errors.[19–22] Yet the literature also suggests that health care organizations often fail to fully realize the benefits of these systems for a variety of reasons,[23,24] as follows:

- Reporting systems may be complex, tedious, and time-consuming and have little face validity—that is, staff see no value in reports that are generated or no actions are taken based on reporting.

- Silos often exist within and between PSRSs. That is, unit-specific information is not shared with other units in the same system,

system-level information is not shared outside the health care organization with "like" organizations, or data collection systems are limited to reports of a particular type of adverse event, such as an adverse drug event.

- Health care providers fail to report adverse incidents.

- A single standard taxonomy to characterize adverse events is not yet universally endorsed.

- Organizations often fail to meet caregiver needs for timely feedback.

- Methods to analyze, prioritize, and learn from a large number of incidents are underdeveloped.

- Strategies to help health care organizations prioritize where their greatest hazards lie are underdeveloped.

- The challenges of identifying and implementing effective strategies to address the prevention of events like those reported are often daunting.[23,24]

- The ability to evaluate risk reduction in the wake of improvement efforts is limited.

The need to capture and to learn from patient safety errors is at the root of U.S. legislation supporting peer review–protected Patient Safety Organizations (PSOs).[25] Standard formats for PSO event reporting and the promise of aggregated national data on the type, frequency, and severity of errors offer hope for focusing and expediting national improvement efforts. Although PSO data are not yet available to help focus national efforts, developers and end users of successful systems are sharing strategies to increase the use and utility of electronic reporting structures.[24,26,27] Yet simultaneous with the need to learn from errors through standard formats is the challenge of not losing error context. Dekker warns as follows:

---

* A sentinel event is an unexpected occurrence involving death or serious physical or psychological injury, or the risk thereof. *Serious injury* specifically includes loss of limb or function. The phrase "or the risk thereof" includes any process variation for which a recurrence would carry a significant chance of a serious adverse outcome (The Joint Commission: *Sentinel Event Policy and Procedures.* Jan. 4, 2011. http://www.jointcommission.org/Sentinel_Event_Policy_and_Procedures/ [accessed Jun. 17, 2011]). Joint Commission International requires its accredited organizations to establish which unanticipated events are considered "sentinel" but establishes at minimum that the following events are subject to review: unanticipated death unrelated to the natural course of the patient's illness or underlying condition; major permanent loss of function unrelated to the natural course of the patient's illness or underlying condition; and wrong-site, wrong-procedure, wrong-patient surgery (Joint Commission International: *Joint Commission International Accreditation Standards for Hospitals*, 4th ed. Oak Brook, IL: Joint Commission Resources, 2010).

Classification disembodies data. It removes the context that helped produce the close call in its particular manifestation. This disables understanding because by excising performance fragments away from their context, classification destroys the local rationality principle.[28(p. 31)]

It is essential to motivate health care providers to report events into the system. Factors found to encourage provider reporting include ensuring confidentiality of reports, focusing outputs on addressing system problems associated with event occurrence rather than punishing staff, and providing timely feedback regarding the reported adverse events and subsequent interventions. Although the majority of reports may represent authentic risks for patient harm, it is not possible to simultaneously address every identified hazard.[21,27,29]

It is important, therefore, to develop and implement standard processes for prioritizing hazards and implementing interventions to mitigate those hazards, as well as to include a diverse range of staff positions when assessing whether the identified risks have been reduced.[30–32] The organization should broadly promulgate its adopted strategies to address the risks identified through the PSRS. This meets the goals of making the commitment to safety real and visible and showing providers the value of reporting.

The evidence base for use of PSRSs is maturing throughout the world. Organizations wishing to implement improvements in care that make patients safer have multiple sources, some of which are cited in this chapter, to which they may turn for guidance. When organizations develop and implement PSRSs and share their reporting and improvement experiences—whether successful or not—with the broader health care community, they help all patients, not just their own. Critical challenges to developing and implementing systems to maximize safe health care delivery exist, as we describe in the following section.

ADDRESSING CRITICAL CHALLENGES
Creating a Culture Conducive to Patient Safety

What Is Safety Culture and Why Is It Important? In many ways, "safety culture" is a unifying concept for patient safety and quality improvement (QI) efforts. Many health care organizations first became acquainted with the term through the 1999 IOM report, which recommended that hospitals improve their cultures of safety.[2] Yet understanding what a culture of safety is or knowing how to achieve such a culture is still embryonic in health care. The Joint Commission requires that hospitals regularly evaluate safety culture using valid and reliable tools to meet accreditation,[33,34] and Joint Commission International accreditation standards[35] address aspects of a safety culture. Methods to assess safety culture in hospitals and other health care settings are still being developed and implemented. Yet culture-assessment tools vary widely, methods of survey administration are often unreliable, and evidence regarding how to use culture results effectively is scant.[36–40] Although safety culture is still a relatively a new concept for health care, other high-risk industries have a long history from which we can learn.

Organizations capable of maintaining nearly failure-free operations in highly complex industries, such as aviation and nuclear power, have been termed high-reliability organizations.[41,42] One of the primary mechanisms underlying this capacity is a strong safety culture—a set of shared values and beliefs among members of that organization that include the following[42,43]:

- Sensitivity to operations (vigilant monitoring and evaluation of system processes and states)

- Reluctance to simplify (avoiding simplistic explanations of failure)

- Preoccupation with failure (near misses are treated as opportunities to learn about and to improve the system)
- Deference to expertise (respect for input from all team members, regardless of power status)
- Resilience (preparedness to respond to failures and novel situations)

Other high-risk domains have documented strong associations between the safety culture of a facility and the behaviors of workers (for example, unsafe acts) and important organizational outcomes, such as accidents and incidents of harm.[44] Recent studies indicate similar patterns in health care. Specifically, several dimensions of patient safety culture, as measured by the U.S. Agency for Healthcare Research and Quality (AHRQ) Hospital Survey on Patient Safety Culture,[45] significantly correlate with AHRQ Patient Safety Indicators (PSIs—composite measures derived from administrative data[46]), such as staff perceptions of the quality of handoffs and transitions (r = −.50), teamwork across units (r = −.42), and teamwork within units (r = −.32, $p < .001$ for all).[47] In addition to these direct associations, safety culture can contribute to the effectiveness of interventions. For example, in a recent study, teamwork and safety climate scores positively correlated with the degree of improvement in mortality and morbidity achieved in the implementation of a surgical checklist, such that units with better safety culture realized more benefit from the intervention.[48]

In sum, safety culture matters. Facilities with positive safety cultures are more likely to provide better care and to harm fewer patients. Consequently, safety culture can be an important diagnostic tool for understanding how safe a unit is and what safety needs it may have. In addition, interventions directly or indirectly targeting the improvement of safety culture are worthwhile pursuits.

How Can You Measure and Improve Safety Culture? Interventions to improve safety culture are tightly intertwined with measurement approaches, and, in some senses, the act of measuring is an intervention on its own, as it sends signals to staff members about the values of the organization. Interventions that directly target safety culture are rare. The Comprehensive Unit-Based Safety Program (CUSP), however, is the one widely applied exception. CUSP uses multiple strategies, including education to build awareness of patient safety and systems science, staff empowerment to take ownership of patient safety issues on their units, building of relationships between executive leadership and unit improvement teams, and provision of tools for learning from errors and improving teamwork. This approach improves safety culture and decreases length of stay and medication errors in ICUs.[49] In addition, CUSP has been coupled with the Translating Evidence into Practice (TRIP) model as a means of implementing standardized evidence-based protocols.[50]

Team training interventions are also viewed as ways to improve safety culture. These programs, such as TeamSTEPPS®,[51] target teamwork competencies of staff members for improvement, the knowledge, skills, and attitudes that underlie effective communication, coordination, and collaboration. Team training interventions have been shown to successfully improve safety culture, teamwork behaviors, and staff satisfaction,[52] as well as the efficiency of clinical processes,[53] patient safety event rates,[54] and clinical outcomes.[55]

A number of survey-based safety culture or climate tools have been developed for use in the health care domain,[56,57] including, as previously mentioned, the widely used Hospital Survey on Patient Safety Culture,[45] which features a comparative database and has promising predictive validity at the facility level.[47]

Although measuring safety culture is a necessary first step toward improvement, it alone is insufficient. Safety culture data can be used diagnostically to understand potential system vulnerabilities (for example, What are staff perceptions of handoffs? Are the handoffs improving or getting worse?) and to prioritize interventions. Feedback and goal-setting strategies (for example, setting a certain threshold score or a goal for improvement) can also be important for driving improvement in culture.[58,59]

Identifying Hazards

Identifying and mitigating safety risks are important domains of patient safety research and practice. Efforts to identify hazards may take place at multiple levels (unit, department, hospital, health system, state, region, country) to determine where potential or known risks of patient harm can occur. Analyses can focus on adverse events (retrospective) or on the potential for harm (prospective assessment).

Measurement is critical for driving systematic change in organizations. Shojania[59] has provided a thorough review and critique of the patient safety measurement systems currently available in health care. His analysis leads to the practical conclusion that each method and type of data has relative strengths and weaknesses and that, consequently, organizations should not rely on a single metric or measurement system for all their varying measurement needs. The most accurate picture of a system's level of safety will come from looking across multiple measures, as shown in Table 2-1 (pages 42–47). In addition, different measures may be suited for different

purposes. In the following sections, we discuss the key tasks in managing patient safety issues (for example, prospective and retrospective identification of hazards, learning from mistakes, and monitoring and evaluating improvement over time) and practical measurement approaches for each.

Identifying Hazards in Hindsight. Many organizations allocate the majority of their patient-safety resources to learning from problems or medical errors that have already occurred. On a unit or departmental (microscopic) level, this may involve analysis of sentinel events, incident reports, or patient complaints about quality of care. Analyses may be formal (for example, root cause analysis) or informal (for example, discussion at staff meetings) and involve teams or individuals. At the unit level, just as at the institutional level, the basic intent of analysis is to explore the causes and contributing factors associated with a patient safety problem and then to plan and to implement strategies to prevent the event from recurring. A case involving medication mix-up in the emergency department provides an example of how unit-level analyses involving diverse team members can result in problem resolution (*see* Sidebar 2-1, page 47).

On an institutional or regional level (macroscopic), retrospective analysis of medical errors can occur through PSRSs, which constitute one important method of identifying hazards. The collective objectives of these reporting systems are to detect events; to disseminate information about medical errors; and to assist health care organizations, given their limited resources, in prioritizing safety efforts. For example, The Joint Commission's Sentinel Event Database is used to identify hazards and their relative incidence, root cause, setting, source of identification (self-reported or not), and outcome.[60]

Table 2-1. Methods for Hospitals to Monitor for Internal Patient Safety Problems

Method*	Advantages	Disadvantages
Traditional incident reporting	• Process already ubiquitous • Can identify latent errors ("system problems")	• Underreporting of serious incidents • Frequent reporting of events not suited to individual analysis (e.g., falls†) • Can be demoralizing when staff do not perceive meaningful improvements resulting from incidents they have reported • Cannot assess changes in safety (over time)
Stimulated/facilitated incident reporting[1–3]	• Builds on an existing process • Improves frequency of events and broadens range of events • Can contribute to improvements in culture	• More labor intensive than traditional incident reporting • Greater engagement of staff increases importance of making meaningful improvements (i.e., even more demoralizing than usual if improvements not made) • Cannot assess changes in safety
Patient complaints	• Process/data already exist • Highlights important problems about patient experience often not captured elsewhere	• May be dismissed by clinicians as "service problems" • May require more up-front work (compared with incident reporting) to identify incidents worth analyzing in detail for potential safety improvements • Cannot assess changes in safety
Malpractice claims	• Process/data already exist • Details about causes of the event and its impact on the patient usually collected as part of medicolegal process • Complements incident reporting for capturing rare but serious events (e.g., wrong-site surgery)	• Heavily biased toward detecting diagnostic issues and procedural complication (though these are usually not detected by other systems) • Cannot assess changes in safety
Risk management reports	• Probably similar to malpractice claims, but not clear	• Probably similar to malpractice claims, but not clear

(continued on page 43)

Table 2-1. Methods for Hospitals to Monitor for Internal Patient Safety Problems (continued)

Method*	Advantages	Disadvantages
Executive walk-arounds	• Engages frontline staff without requiring much work for them • Provides a human face to problems management usually learns about through impersonal pie charts and time trends • Alerts management to problems faced daily by frontline staff	• Demoralizing to frontline staff if management focuses only on improved public relations ("management cares") and does not seriously address the problems identified • Tempting for management to focus on easy fixes (e.g., related to equipment) not deeper problems or those requiring substantial investments of resources (e.g., staffing, skill mix, or workload problems)
Chart audits (commonly operationalized with "trigger tools"[4–6])	• Types of events captured may be more likely to engage frontline clinicians (particularly physicians) • Produce rates that can be monitored over time, not just counts or frequencies susceptible to changes in reporting biases	• Requires willing clinicians to participate • Many important events not documented in charts, and contributing factors for documented events typically unclear • Many triggers have low specificity
Electronic triggers[7] (e.g., drug–lab combinations, use of "antidotes" suggestive of medication errors)	• Very efficient • Potentially high-sensitivity capture for the events captured	• Captures only certain types of events (small subset of events involving medications or laboratory tests) • Trade-offs between sensitivity and specificity
Performance indicators derived from administrative data[8,9]	• Data easily available • In principle, event rates can be tracked over time, but in practice probably applies only for frequent event types in large health care systems[10]	• Low signal-to-noise ratio • Various methodologic problems[11] that can result in misleading characterizations of performance • Managers and clinicians tend to distrust these data (often with good reason) • Requires intensive effort to investigate if poor performance is real and requires further effort to determine causes

(continued on page 44)

Table 2-1. Methods for Hospitals to Monitor for Internal Patient Safety Problems (continued)

Method*	Advantages	Disadvantages
Data warehouses[12,13]	• Richness of detail (e.g., from medications data, laboratory results, time stamps) addresses many of the limitations of administrative data • Can generate data that will engage both managers and clinicians • Event rates can be followed over time	• Requires substantial up-front investments and appropriate clinical and methodological expertise[14] • Requires organizational culture and management structures conducive to driving change on the basis of these novel data
Modifying traditional morbidity and mortality rounds with modern patient safety framework[15]	• Builds on format familiar to clinicians • Types of events captured and richness of detail more likely to engage physicians	• Care required to avoid traditional focus on individual errors and blaming other departments[16] • New processes required to follow up systematically on issues identified (traditional rounds heavy on discussion, with follow-up occurring only haphazardly) • Addressing problems identified often requires host department to engage and collaborate with other departments—departures from traditional norm
Discrepancies between clinical and autopsy diagnoses[17]	• Builds on a traditional process of improvement • Detects problems likely to engage clinicians	• Likely to succeed only in select hospitals because of low autopsy rates and decreased interest in autopsies among clinicians and pathologists at most hospitals[18]
Monitoring pathologic discrepancies (e.g., between cytology and histology[19] or ante-mortem biopsies and autopsies[20])	• Relatively efficient • Can identify patterns of problems amenable to substantial improvement projects[19] • Event rates can be followed over time	• Requires interest on the part of pathologists to undertake this nontraditional form of quality assurance and willingness of clinical departments to collaborate in improvement projects
Corrected laboratory results/reports[21]	• Relatively efficient • Event rates can probably be followed over time	• Fairly narrow focus • Requires interested laboratory medicine personnel

(continued on page 45)

Table 2-1. Methods for Hospitals to Monitor for Internal Patient Safety Problems (continued)

Method*	Advantages	Disadvantages
Natural language screening of electronic portions of medical records[22]	• Relatively efficient once implemented • Reasonable sensitivity and specificity for certain types of events	• Requires appropriate technical expertise and initial investment of time to develop and refine combinations of search terms with acceptable sensitivity and specificity for safety problems
Direct observation (e.g., audits of hand hygiene compliance, medication administration,[23] operating room procedures,[24,25] daily rounds[26])	• Richer, more accurate data than by many other methods • Identifies problems particularly difficult to detect by other means • Event rates can be followed over time	• Somewhat labor intensive (but short periods of measurement may provide ample data) • Requires appropriately trained observers • Care must be taken not to create mistrust among frontline staff
Active surveillance[27,28] (combination of chart-based trigger tool applied in quasi–real time, stimulated reporting, and other interactions with frontline staff)	• Rich data that are more likely to include information about causal factors than record review alone • Process can engage frontline staff and stimulate them to participate in subsequent improvement efforts • Event rates can be followed over time	• Somewhat labor intensive (but short periods of measurement may provide ample data) • Requires appropriately trained observers • Care must be taken not to create mistrust among frontline staff
Telephone calls to patients[29] (can be automated[30,31])	• Identifies problems typically not captured by other methods (e.g., postdischarge adverse events[30] and problems occurring between ambulatory visits[31])	• Requires appropriate technology and, even with automation, still requires investment of personnel time (e.g., at least one nurse case manager and a physician) to respond in real time to clinical problems

* References are not provided for the first five methods because they were among those evaluated in the study by Levtzion-Korach et al.[32] A more complete discussion of the advantages and disadvantages of many of the strategies listed in the table can be found in the review by Thomas and Petersen.[33]

† Falls occur with such frequency that they require epidemiologic study of the main contributing factors in order to identify effective methods of prevention (akin to infection control), not case-by-case root cause analyses.

(continued on page 46)

Table 2-1. Methods for Hospitals to Monitor for Internal Patient Safety Problems (continued)

References

1. Weingart S.N., Ship A.N., Aronson M.D.: Confidential clinician-reported surveillance of adverse events among medical inpatients. *J Gen Intern Med* 15:470–477, Jul. 2000.
2. Wu A.W., Holzmueller C.G., Lubomski L.H.: Development of the ICU safety reporting system. *J Patient Saf* 1:23–32, Mar. 2005.
3. Evans S.M., et al.: Evaluation of an intervention aimed at improving voluntary incident reporting in hospitals. *Qual Saf Health Care* 16:169–175, Jun. 2007.
4. Takata G.S., et al.: Development, testing, and findings of a pediatric-focused trigger tool to identify medication-related harm in US children's hospitals. *Pediatrics* 121:e927–e935, Apr. 2008.
5. Griffin F.A., Classen D.C.: Detection of adverse events in surgical patients using the Trigger Tool approach. *Qual Saf Health Care* 17:253–258, Aug. 2008.
6. Resar R.K., et al.: A trigger tool to identify adverse events in the intensive care unit. *Jt Comm J Qual Patient Saf* 32:585–590, Oct. 2006.
7. Raschke R.A., et al.: A computer alert system to prevent injury from adverse drug events: Development and evaluation in a community teaching hospital. *JAMA* 280:1317–1320, Oct. 21, 1998. Erratum in: *JAMA* 281:420, Feb. 3, 1999.
8. Romano P.S., et al.: Validity of selected AHRQ Patient Safety Indicators based on VA National Surgical Quality Improvement Program data. *Health Serv Res* 44:182–204, Feb. 2009.
9. Jarman B., et al.: Explaining differences in English hospital death rates using routinely collected data. *BMJ* (7197)318:1515–1520, Jun. 5, 1999.
10. West A.N., Weeks W.B., Bagian J.P.: Rare adverse medical events in VA inpatient care: Reliability limits to using patient safety indicators as performance measures. *Health Serv Res* 43:249–266, 2008.
11. Shojania K.G., Forster A.J.: Hospital mortality: When failure is not a good measure of success. *CMAJ* 179:153–157, Jul. 15, 2008.
12. Horvath M.M., et al.: Sharing adverse drug event data using business intelligence technology. *J Patient Saf* 5:35–41, Mar. 2009.
13. Lowe H.J., et al.: STRIDE—An integrated standards-based translational research informatics platform. *AMIA Annu Symp Proc* 2009:391–395, Nov. 14, 2009.
14. van Walraven C., et al.: The usefulness of administrative databases for identifying disease cohorts is increased with a multivariate model. *J Clin Epidemiol* 63:1332–1341, Dec. 2010.
15. McDonnell C., Laxer R.M., Roy W.L.: Redesigning a morbidity and mortality program in a university-affiliated pediatric anesthesia department. *Jt Comm J Qual Patient Saf* 36:117–125, Mar. 2010.
16. Pierluissi E, et al.: Discussion of medical errors in morbidity and mortality conferences. *JAMA* 290:2838–2842, Dec. 3, 2003.
17. Shojania K.G., et al.: Changes in rates of autopsy-detected diagnostic errors over time: A systematic review. *JAMA* 289:2849–2856, Jun. 4, 2003.
18. Shojania K.G., Burton E.C.: The vanishing nonforensic autopsy. *N Engl J Med* 358:873–875, Feb. 28, 2008.
19. Raab S.S.: Improving patient safety through quality assurance. *Arch Pathol Lab Med* 130:633–637, May 2006.
20. Burton E.C., Troxclair D.A., Newman W.P. III: Autopsy diagnoses of malignant neoplasms: How often are clinical diagnoses incorrect? *JAMA* 280:1245–1248, Oct. 14, 1998.
21. Yuan S., et al.: Clinical impact associated with corrected results in clinical microbiology testing. *J Clin Microbiol* 43:2188–2193, May 2005.
22. Murff H.J., et al.: Electronically screening discharge summaries for adverse medical events. *J Am Med Inform Assoc* 10:339–350, Jul.–Aug. 2003.
23. Kopp B.J., et al.: Medication errors and adverse drug events in an intensive care unit: Direct observation approach for detection. *Crit Care Med* 34:415–425, Feb. 2006.
24. Greenberg C.C., et al.: The frequency and significance of discrepancies in the surgical count. *Ann Surg* 248:337–341, Aug. 2008.
25. Smith A.F., et al.: Interprofessional handover and patient safety in anaesthesia: Observational study of handovers in the recovery room. *Br J Anaesth* 101:332–337, Sep. 2008.
26. Andrews L.B., et al.: An alternative strategy for studying adverse events in medical care. *Lancet* 349:309–313, Feb. 1, 1997.

(continued on page 47)

Table 2-1. Methods for Hospitals to Monitor for Internal Patient Safety Problems (continued)

References (continued)

27. Forster A.J., et al.: Adverse events detected by clinical surveillance on an obstetric service. *Obstet Gynecol* 108:1073–1083, Nov. 2006.
28. Forster A.J., et al.: The impact of adverse events in the intensive care unit on hospital mortality and length of stay. *BMC Health Serv Res* 8:259, Dec. 17, 2008.
29. Dudas V., et al.: The impact of follow-up telephone calls to patients after hospitalization. *Am J Med* 111:26S–30S, Dec. 2001.
30. Forster A.J., et al.: Identifying patients with post-discharge care problems using an interactive voice response system. *J Gen Intern Med* 24:520–525, Apr. 2009.
31. Sarkar U., et al.: Use of an interactive, telephone-based self-management support program to identify adverse events among ambulatory diabetes patients. *J Gen Intern Med* 23:459–465, Apr. 2008.
32. Levtzion-Korach O., et al.: Integrating incident data from five reporting systems to assess patient safety: Making sense of the elephant. *Jt Comm J Qual Patient Saf* 36:402–410, Sep. 2010.
33. Thomas E.J., Petersen L.A.: Measuring adverse events in health care. J Gen Intern Med 18:61–67. Jan. 2003.

Source: Shojania K.G.: The elephant of patient safety: What you see depends on how you look. *Jt Comm J Qual Patient Saf* 36:399–401, Sep. 2010.

Sidebar 2-1. Medication Mix-up in the Emergency Department

A 45-year-old man presented to the emergency department with a myocardial infarction. Instead of receiving metoprolol, as ordered, the patient received terbutaline, which resulted in profound tachycardia instead of the intended bradycardia. Investigation of the event revealed that terbutaline was found in the "pocket" of the automated medication dispensing system (AMDS) designated for metoprolol. Displacement of terbutaline, located next to metoprolol in the AMDS, had been caused by physical migration of the medication under the weak storage barrier, incorrect restocking of the AMDS, and/or incorrect returning of medications to the AMDS. Interventions to reinforce the storage barriers, to minimize use of "open matrix" AMDS, to create a pharmacy "return bin," and to standardize the stocking process reduced medication displacements by 37%. More importantly, the collaboration between nurses, physicians, and pharmacists to tackle this defect instilled a culture of teamwork, mutual support, and safety throughout the departments of emergency medicine and pharmacy.

Source: Adapted from Gripper S., et al.: Emergency medicine: Medication displacement in an automated medication dispensing system. In Wu A.W. (ed.): *The Value of Close Calls in Improving Patient Safety: Learning How to Avoid and Mitigate Patient Harm.* Oak Brook, IL: Joint Commission Resources, 2011, pp. 139–143.

The National Reporting and Learning System (NRLS), a PSRS developed by the United Kingdom's National Patient Safety Agency, is intended to quantify, to characterize, and to prioritize safety issues to support the National Health Service (NHS) in making health care safer. The NRLS is one of the largest repositories of medical errors (more than two million) reported by frontline staff (from more than 500 participating trusts [public-sector corporations that provides services on behalf of the NHS]) in a single country. The NRLS initially focused on identifying hazards to patients. However, to mitigate those hazards, the reports must be analyzed, priority areas identified, and interventions that unite multiple stakeholders implemented.[4,61] Risk prioritization in health care is underdeveloped compared with other industries with more-sophisticated mathematical models and methods of processing high-risk or harmful events. When leaders of large safety reporting systems were asked how they filtered and prioritized reported data, respondents suggested a matrix of simple but often subjective methods, including (1) severity of harm, with unanticipated deaths or catastrophic harm receiving immediate priority, and (2) events classified as high harm with a high probability of recurrence. Other considerations included the frequency of occurrence or probability of future recurrence of the event, risk to the organization's reputation, events that could serve as teachable moments on a broad scale, and systemwide problems that were resource intensive and could yield broad financial and patient safety dividends.[20,62]

An example from the NRLS, as provided in Sidebar 2-2 (page 49), highlights the potential for shared learning.

This example illustrates the urgent need for a global mechanism to act quickly and efficiently on patient safety problems. Disseminating patient safety issues found in one system via an international announcement may reduce risks to all patients. In direct response to this concept, the Canadian Patient Safety Institute (CPSI), working with the World Health Organization Patient Safety Programme[63] and PSRS leaders from around the world, launched its Global Patient Safety Alerts system in February 2011.[64] Global Patient Safety Alerts is an open-access Web site and information-sharing resource dedicated to helping "individuals prevent and mitigate patient safety incidents in their organizations and help others succeed." The site contains more than 800 patient safety incident advisories, alerts, and recommendations as well as customizable, evidence-based tools available to help patient safety leaders mitigate harm.[64]

Patient safety leaders should consider two well-known limitations when retrospectively identifying problems. First, by definition, retrospective analysis means that the event, error, or harm has taken place. In highly reliable organizations, a systemwide preoccupation with failure leads to a culture that averts harm. ("Highly reliable care delivery" is what the IOM, in its 1999 report, called on all providers to achieve.[2]) Second, hindsight bias (a type of judgment bias) may cause memory distortion. Hindsight bias reflects the human tendency to overestimate our ability to have predicted or foreseen an event after learning about the outcome and may result in problems while trying to analyze, interpret, and learn from mistakes.[65] Ideally, therefore, organizations correct system flaws before they affect patients.

Prospective Identification of Hazards. Ideally, identification of hazards in the medical system is prospective—before patient harm occurs. Failure mode and effects analysis (FMEA),

---

Sidebar 2-2. Investigation of Hospitalization of Hemodialysis Patients for Acute Hemolysis

In September 2008, a trust in the United Kingdom reported a small cluster of hemodialysis patients being hospitalized for acute hemolysis (destruction of red blood cells leading to anemia and risk of severe hyperkalemia). An initial investigation revealed that silver-stabilized hydrogen peroxide had recently been added to the hospital's water system to reduce the bacterial load. This additive was not effectively communicated to the renal unit that uses the same water supply. The hydrogen peroxide precipitated acute hemolysis, from which one patient died while four others required transfusions. Hemodialysis patients worldwide who are at risk for this type of adverse event are generally unaware of the National Patient Safety alert. In this case, clinical and published information suggests similar acute hemolysis cases have occurred in Scotland (four adults) and Israel (nine children).

Source: Adapted from National Patient Safety Agency, Central Alerting System: Risks to haemodialysis patients from water supply (hydrogen peroxide). *Rapid Response Report NPSA/2008/RRR007.* Sep. 30, 2008. https://www.cas.dh.gov.uk/ViewandAcknowledgment/ViewAlert.aspx?AlertID=50472 (accessed Sep. 23, 2011).

---

which originated in other industries, is one method to prospectively identify hazards that is increasingly used in health care.[66–68] *A failure mode* is any error or defect in a process, design, or item, particularly one that affects the customer, and can be potential or actual. *Effects analysis* refers to studying the consequences of those failures. The process typically involves assessing processes of care and identifying potential hazards. Hazard ranking considers severity of harm, likelihood of occurrence, and the ability to detect the hazard. The potential hazards with the highest risk-priority number are targets for mitigation.

Simulation of high-risk events or procedures that occur infrequently may also be used to identify hazards.[69–71] Simulation is increasingly used in clinical education but is available primarily as a venue for formal training in academic programs and teaching hospitals. The investment in equipment and personnel required to establish a state-of-the-art simulation center limits the feasibility for routine competency assessment and training at the local level.

One of the most powerful and least expensive methods to identify hazards is to train caregivers on the science of safety and then ask them how they believe patients are likely to be harmed in their care areas. This is one of two questions on the safety assessment survey that comprise Step 2 of the Johns Hopkins CUSP intervention.[58] All staff and physicians are encouraged to complete the survey. The unit leaders review survey responses and categorize them by type of system issue (for example, teamwork). The leaders share results with the executive supporting the unit and the entire CUSP team. Using group-consensus methods, the team decides which safety hazards pose the greatest threats and work on them first. In a recent example at Johns Hopkins, results from the staff safety assessment identified communication as a major patient safety risk—a variety of communication problems were identified by physicians, nurses, and ancillary staff. On close examination, however, the team recognized that it was communication regarding patient laboratory tests and values that seemed to be a frequent concern. Accordingly, the team agreed to work on communication, with a particular "all-caregiver" focus on communication about laboratory testing and reporting.[58]

Mitigating Hazards. In the United States, state laws; regulatory bodies; and accreditation agencies, such as The Joint Commission and its international accreditation "arm," Joint Commission International, expect and often require institutions and governing bodies to thoroughly investigate sentinel events (*see* page 38 for definition).[35,72] Yet the extent to which these investigations lead to safer care is not clear. Many organizations have multiple systems capturing data on real or potential hazards but limited mechanisms or resources to prioritize hazards, develop and implement interventions, and evaluate the impact of interventions for improving safety. Moreover, the tendency is to implement interventions that are weak and have a low probability of mitigating risk, such as reeducation or encouraging vigilance, because these activities involve few resources. At the institutional level, it is important to develop a formal infrastructure for supporting patient safety improvement.[73,74]

PSOs in the United States, and reporting and learning communities on a global basis (which focus on creating venues where larger groups, such as countries, can collectively share what they are learning and work collaboratively to design strong interventions that have a high probability of preventing errors and reducing risks to patients),[75] represent recent efforts to mitigate ubiquitous hazards.

Learning from Mistakes

A core behavior of a safe culture is the ability to learn, not just to recover, from mistakes. Proactive patient safety happens in many ways. One of the most frequent methods used to anticipate potential hazards attached to new protocols, equipment, or procedure is through FMEA, as previously described. Yet every patient care area is a world of inherited risks, hidden in the protocols, procedures, and common practices of the people who work there. Mistakes happen. Near misses are an everyday occurrence. The Learning from Defects tool[76] provides one way to increase the number of events investigated and mitigated. Teams investigate unit-based system problems (a process called second-order problem solving) that they perceive to pose the greatest risk. The tool guides staff through four questions: What happened? Why did it happen? What can you do to reduce the risk that it will recur? and How do you know the extent to which the risk was actually reduced? A written summary answering these questions is the measure of learning. We encourage teams to share these one-page summaries throughout their organizations. For example, an ICU team found that "a protocol to guide therapy" was a negative contributor because a weaning protocol was not available for difficult airway cases. As a result, the patient was extubated prematurely, could not breathe, and required emergency intubation. "Communication during a crisis" was checked as a positive contributor because the anesthesia team was provided with the appropriate information needed to make an informed decision regarding the best method of reintubation. To evaluate subsequent risk reduction, periodic audits could be done on all difficult airway cases to determine whether a cuff-leak test was performed before extubation.[76]

When working with teams to achieve the targets set for the national central line–associated bloodstream infection (CLABSI) effort in the United States,[1] we ask teams to investigate CLABSIs as a defect.[77] This helps change the culture from one in which infections are thought to be inevitable to one in which they are understood to be preventable. In identifying opportunities to further reduce infections, many CLABSI teams have found that they could improve their central-line maintenance practices. While reviewing hand hygiene efforts, some hospital observers found that hand hygiene practices were good when alcohol gel dispensers were full. When the dispensers were empty, the frequency of hand cleansing deteriorated significantly. The learning included suggestions for how to easily make "dispenser-empty" notifications.

Building Capacity

There are currently few people with the training required to conduct rigorous health care QI research, or to develop, implement, and evaluate quality and safety improvement programs at an organizational level. Most clinical quality and safety leaders have "inherited" this responsibility as a byproduct of a strategic planning effort rather than through a period of skill development. Yet the need for quality and safety leadership has exploded as public, payer, and policy demands for measurable health care improvements have become the norm.

Quality and patient safety leaders from the boardroom to the bedside require formal training and mentoring to become proficient at identifying and responding to patient safety.[78] In our experience, at the highest levels of the organization, it helps to have specific tools and checklists that support boards and executives in their patient safety leadership roles.[16,77,79] There are also a growing number of role-specific programs available through professional societies, academic organizations (degree-granting and nondegree programs), and PSOs. Short training programs in patient safety may provide some concepts and basic skills needed to lead improvement projects, but they generally do not provide the evaluation skills necessary to manage hospital programs. The Plan-Do-Study-Act (PDSA) method was embraced early by health care clinicians eager to improve care. Unfortunately, PDSA oversimplifies the process of improvement. Although it is useful as an easy-to-learn method for making incremental improvements, it is not a good methodology for large-scale change, particularly in complex organizations. It does not reflect the various activities required for successful improvement activities, such as executive support, leadership, coordination, communication, education, rigorous data collection and analysis, and investment of the financial and human resources needed to modify processes.

Organizations committed to identifying and resolving patient safety problems increasingly seek individuals with advanced project management training and advanced degrees in public health, biostatistics, economics, human factors, and organizational psychology to lead their patient safety departments or activities. In addition to scientific knowledge and technical skills, patient safety leaders need communication and teamwork skills to assess, convey, and resolve patient safety challenges. Increased financial support is needed for developing the basic science of QI research, for training in design and evaluation methods for individuals working in the field, and for reporting of QI studies.[80]

How Will We Know We Have Improved?

Developing a Meaningful Scorecard. Many hospitals have responded to the heightened focus on patient safety by creating scorecards to evaluate—and often to publicly report—their progress in improving quality and patient safety. Despite this growing interest in scorecards, the science of measuring patient safety is immature. One framework to help health care organizations develop and evaluate the validity of their scorecards uses the term *safety scorecard* to acknowledge the overlap between quality and safety.[81] This framework assumes that the goal of the scorecard is to monitor progress in patient safety over time or relative to a benchmark.

The Joint Commission, the National Quality Forum, and many professional societies provide important and detailed technical criteria for valid measures. To select safety measures for local use, however, we suggest leaders consider three key questions: Is the measure important, is the measure valid, and can the measure be used to improve safety in your health care organization?

Is the Measure Important? When selecting a measure for a safety scorecard, an organization should ensure that it addresses an issue that is important to the organization. This could be a strategic priority for the organization or a measure that is required by an external agency, such as Joint Commission heart failure core measures.[82] Scorecard measures are inherently high profile, and organizations typically invest great energy to ensure that the results achieved are positive. Consequently, the measures must be worth the concentration of effort that will be devoted to them. Furthermore, it is essential that the measures selected are salient to the workers who will be required to improve the associated care processes. Internal ownership of scorecard measures requires leadership to select outcome or process measures that represent the improvement objectives of frontline workers.

Is the Measure Valid? To evaluate validity, the organization should assess (1) the level of evidence supporting the measure, (2) the face validity of the measure, and (3) the risk for bias. A valid safety measure has strong empiric evidence demonstrating that the intervention improves safety and concisely evaluates the effectiveness of the intervention on its intended outcome. The validity of a given measure depends on context—thus, the same measure may be valid for one patient safety issue in one unit but not valid for a different patient safety issue in a different unit. To illustrate, consider a safety measure that is used to evaluate smoking cessation counseling after acute myocardial infarction. An organization should evaluate the evidence linking smoking cessation to improved patient outcomes after myocardial infarction and to how it measures smoking cessation counseling. Yet organizations frequently measure only whether a nurse documented the provision of counseling to the patient. Little evidence demonstrates that this method of measuring the intervention will accurately evaluate the patient's understanding of smoking risks or behavior change. Consequently, but not surprisingly, reports of increased performance of smoking cessation counseling do not correlate with reduced patient mortality.[83] An organization should also evaluate whether the measure has face validity—for example, by asking the people who will use the data whether they believe that improving performance on the measure (as it is defined and assessed) will improve patient outcomes. If they do not believe that the measure will improve patient outcomes, they are not likely to use it.

After considering validity, an organization should evaluate the extent to which bias (a systematic departure from the truth)—selection, measurement, and analytic biases—can influence a measure, particularly when assessing the organization's performance over time or benchmarking against peer organizations.[80] In our experience, measurement bias or systematic error introduced in the process of data collection is extensive in the field of patient safety. The problem of missing data (which often account for 60% or more of the available data), for example, plagues many patient safety efforts and makes it impossible to estimate progress or to make accurate inferences about improvements in safety.[84]

Can We Use the Measure to Improve Safety in Our Health Care Organization? Discussion among relevant internal stakeholders can help organizations determine whether the benefits are worth the investments required to collect data completely and accurately and with minimal bias for the candidate measure. Furthermore, organizations should collect data for given measures only if they will use the data to guide improvement efforts. For example, if an organization decides to measure infection rates, it must then implement interventions to improve its rates. If no plan to implement interventions to improve performance on the measure is developed, then the scarce resources dedicated to collecting data are wasted. Similarly, organizations should examine existing measures and discontinue those that have been shown to have little or no benefit. Yet organizations interested in efficient and effective ways to monitor their quality and safety performances are hampered by the absence of national standards for how to collect and report quality and safety data (*see* Sidebar 2-3, page 54)

CONCLUSION

Preventable health care harm is a leading cause of death around the world. Despite significant effort, evidence that outcomes are improving is sporadic at best. Improving patient safety in health care organizations is exceedingly complex and requires commitment and engagement from the boardroom to the bedside. To improve patient safety, health care organizations need efficient and effective strategies to identify and mitigate patient safety problems; create a culture conducive to patient safety; learn from mistakes; build capacity, including patient safety experts with training in the design and evaluation of patient safety improvement efforts; and measure progress. Nevertheless, many challenges exist within health care organizations, and broad improvements in patient safety require additional efforts to advance our understanding of the science of health care delivery.

WHAT IS ON THE HORIZON?

The benefits from global investments in biomedical research fall far short of the possibilities. Measurable improvement in patient safety is disappointing, largely because researchers, policy makers, and providers have failed to coordinate efforts to reduce preventable harm. Technical advancements in pharmacotherapeutics, information technologies, and diagnostics are likely to continue unabated. Demands for cost-effective, clinically current, and culturally sensitive care are not likely to subside. Thus, the complexity of identifying and resolving patient-safety problems is likely to expand.

Emerging work in the social sciences may provide important insights regarding how to more effectively identify and resolve patient safety issues in the future.[85,86] For example, medical sociologist Dixon-Woods and colleagues attributed success of the Michigan Intensive Care Unit project, which attracted international attention by successfully reducing rates of central venous catheter bloodstream infections, to (1) use of a combination of interventions, each of which functioned in different ways to shape a culture of commitment to doing better at the sharp end of practice, and (2) the creation of a

---

Sidebar 2-3. Using Board Quality Scorecards to Measure Improvement

A recent study looked at how hospital boards address their fiduciary responsibilities to monitor and to improve quality and safety of care in their organizations. Wide variations were exhibited in the training provided to boards to administer this duty and in the ways that boards assessed improvement. A review of 22 distinct board quality and safety scorecards suggested that the unique value of qualitative versus quantitative data may not be clear and that knowledge regarding how to select measures that are useful for improving care may be limited. The scorecards included 273 unique process measures, which accounted for 61% of the total number of measures; outcome measures accounted for the remaining 39%. The individual hospital scorecards contained from 16 to 163 measures. Moreover, many of the scorecard data were accompanied by color coding (red, yellow, green), up-and-down arrows, or stars, suggesting that deciding how to interpret and to use the data provided is challenging.

Source: Adapted from Goeschel C.A., et al.: Board quality scorecards: Measuring improvement. *Am J Med Qual* 26:254–260, Jul.–Aug. 2011.

---

densely networked community with strong horizontal links that exerted normative pressures on members.[85] The literature increasingly acknowledges the importance of *context* in the successful implementation of patient safety practices, perhaps driven, at least in part, by the SQUIRE reporting guidelines, which draw attention to the "context factors that helped determine the intervention's effectiveness (or lack thereof)."[87] Yet we know very little about what and how contextual factors influence patient safety and mitigation of identified harm. Similarly, patient safety culture, as an overarching construct identified by the IOM,[2] is an area in which providers would benefit from additional work to develop and to validate culture measures for many non–acute care settings and to assess relationships between culture and patient safety practices.

Learning how to develop and leverage "clinical" social networks to resolve patient problems is also likely to expedite improvement. Many organizations currently use intranet services to link their caregiver communities, but advancements in how to organize and to tap the tacit knowledge of the community are rapidly opening new opportunities for patient safety learning. Social networks have great potential for facilitating change, particularly among professional groups. Understanding how to build, to support, and to use them to identify and to resolve patient safety problems is an area of promising new exploration.

Expanding patient safety teams to include organizational sociologists and psychologists, human factors engineers, medical anthropologists, and others from the social sciences will bring important scientific insights to what have heretofore been intensive but often myopic efforts to identify and to resolve patient safety issues.

References

1. U.S. Department of Health & Human Services: *HHS Action Plan to Prevent Healthcare-Associated Infections.* http://www.hhs.gov/ash/initiatives/hai/actionplan/ (accessed Sep. 23, 2011).

2. Institute of Medicine: *To Err Is Human: Building a Safer Health System.* Washington, DC: National Academy Press, 2000.

3. Newman-Toker D.E., Pronovost P.J.: Diagnostic errors: The next frontier for patient safety. *JAMA* 301:1060–1062, Mar. 11, 2009.

4. Sevdalis N., et al.: Diagnostic error in a national incident reporting system in the UK. *J Eval Clin Pract* 16:1276–1281, Dec. 2010.

5. Wachter R.M.: Why diagnostic errors don't get any respect—And what can be done about them. *Health Aff (Millwood)* 29:1605–1610, Sep. 2010.

6. McGlynn E.A., et al.: The quality of health care delivered to adults in the United States. *N Engl J Med* 348:2635–2645, Jun. 26, 2003.

7. Levinson D.R.: *Adverse Events in Hospitals: National Incidence Among Medicare Beneficiaries.* Washington, DC: U.S. Department of Health & Human Services, Office of the Inspector General, Nov. 2010. Report No. OEI-06-09-00090. http://psnet.ahrq.gov/resource.aspx?resourceID=19811&sourceID=1&emailID=19328 (accessed Sep. 23, 2011).

8. Donaldson L.: When will health care pass the orange-wire test? *Lancet* 364(9445):1567–1568, Oct. 30–Nov. 5, 2004.

9. Landrigan C.P., et al.: Temporal trends in rates of patient harm resulting from medical care. *N Engl J Med* 363:2124–2134, Nov. 25, 2010.

10. Pronovost P.J., et al.: A research framework for reducing preventable patient harm. *Clin Infect Dis* 52:507–513, Feb. 15, 2011.

11. Rosenthal V.D., et al.: Device-associated nosocomial infections in 55 intensive care units of 8 developing countries. *Ann Intern Med* 145:582–591, Oct. 17, 2006.

12. Jha A.K., et al.: Patient safety research: An overview of the global evidence. *Qual Saf Health Care* 19:42–47, Feb. 2010.

13. Berwick D.M.: A user's manual for the IOM's "Quality Chasm" report. *Health Aff (Millwood)* 21:80–90, May–Jun. 2002.

14. Wachter R.M.: Patient safety at ten: Unmistakable progress, troubling gaps. *Health Aff (Millwood)* 29:165–173, Jan.–Feb. 2010.

15. Shekelle P.G., et al.: Advancing the science of patient safety. *Ann Intern Med* 154:693–696, May 17, 2011.

16. Goeschel C.A., Wachter R.M., Pronovost P.J.: Responsibility for quality improvement and patient safety: Hospital board and medical staff leadership challenges. *Chest* 138:171–178, Jul. 2010.

17. Institute of Medicine: *Patient Safety: Achieving a New Standard of Care.* Washington, DC: National Academies Press, 2004.

18. World Alliance for Patient Safety: *WHO Draft Guidelines for Adverse Event Reporting and Learning Systems.* World Health Organization, 2005. http://www.who.int/patientsafety/events/05/Reporting_Guidelines.pdf (accessed Sep. 23, 2011).

19. Runciman W.B.: Lessons from the Australian Patient Safety Foundation: Setting up a national patient safety surveillance system—Is this the right model? *Qual Saf Health Care* 11:246–251, Sep. 2002.

20. Pham J.C., et al.: Establishing a global learning community for incident-reporting systems. *Qual Saf Health Care* 19:446–451, Oct. 2010.

21. Edwards J.R., et al.: National Healthcare Safety Network (NHSN) report: Data summary for 2006 through 2008, issued December 2009. *Am J Infect Control* 37:783–805, Dec. 2009.

22. Levtzion-Korach O., et al.: Integrating incident data from five reporting systems to assess patient safety: Making sense of the elephant. *Jt Comm J Qual Patient Saf* 36:402–410, Sep. 2010.

23. Bennett C.L., et al.: The Research on Adverse Drug Events and Reports (RADAR) project. *JAMA* 293:2131–2140, May 4, 2005.

24. Benn J., et al.: Feedback from incident reporting: Information and action to improve patient safety. *Qual Saf Health Care* 18:11–21, Feb. 2009.

25. U.S. Agency for Healthcare Research and Quality: *Patient Safety Organizations.* http://www.pso.ahrq.gov/index.html (accessed Sep. 23, 2011).

26. Farley D.O., et al.: Adverse-event-reporting practices by U.S. hospitals: Results of a national survey. *Qual Saf Health Care* 17:416–423, Dec. 2008.

27. Pronovost P.J., et al.: Improving the value of patient safety reporting systems. In Henriksen K., et al. (eds): *Advances in Patient Safety: New Directions and Alternative Approaches,* vol. 1. U.S. Agency for Healthcare Research and Quality, 2008. http://www.ahrq.gov/downloads/pub/advances2/vol1/Advances-Pronovost_95.pdf (accessed Sep. 23, 2011).

28. Dekker S.W.A.: Promoting meaningful close-call reporting: Lessons from aviation. In Wu A.W. (ed.): *The Value of Close Calls in Improving Patient Safety: Learning How to Avoid and Mitigate Patient Harm.* Oak Brook, IL: Joint Commission Resources, 2011, pp. 25–37.

29. Winters B.D., Berenholtz S.M., Pronovost P.: Improving patient safety reporting systems. *Crit Care Med* 35:1206–1207, Apr. 2007.

30. Miller M.R., Clark J.S., Lehmann C.U.: Computer based medication error reporting: Insights and implications. *Qual Saf Health Care* 15:208–213, Jun. 2006.

31. Pham J.C., et al.: ReCASTing the RCA: An improved model for performing root cause analyses. *Am J Med Qual* 25:186–191, May–Jun. 2010.

32. Berenholtz S.M., Hartsell T.L., Pronovost P.J.: Learning from defects to enhance morbidity and mortality conferences. *Am J Med Qual* 24:192–195, May–Jun. 2009.

33. The Joint Commission: Behaviors that undermine a culture of safety. *Sentinel Event Alert* 40, Jul. 9, 2008. http://www.jointcommission.org/assets/1/18/SEA_40.pdf (accessed Sep. 23, 2011).

34. JCAHO issues call to improve liability system and promote culture of safety. *Qual Lett Healthc Lead* 17:13–14, Apr. 2005.

35. Joint Commission International: *Joint Commission International Accreditation Standards for Hospitals,* 4th ed. Oak Brook, IL: Joint Commission Resources, 2009.

36. Singer S., et al.: Relationship of safety climate and safety performance in hospitals. *Health Serv Res* 44:399–421, Apr. 2009.

37. Singer S.J., et al.: Patient safety climate in 92 U.S. hospitals: Differences by work area and discipline. *Med Care* 47:23–31, Jan. 2009.

38. Bognár A., et al.: Errors and the burden of errors: Attitudes, perceptions, and the culture of safety in pediatric cardiac surgical teams. *Ann Thorac Surg* 85:1374–1381, Apr. 2008.

39. Deilkås E.T., Hofoss D.: Psychometric properties of the Norwegian version of the Safety Attitudes Questionnaire (SAQ), Generic version (Short Form 2006). *BMC Health Serv Res* 8:191, Sep. 22, 2008.

40. Mannion R., Konteh F.H., Davies H.T.: Assessing organisational culture for quality and safety improvement: A national survey of tools and tool use. *Qual Saf Health Care* 18:153–156, Apr. 2009.

41. Roberts K.H.: Managing high reliability organizations. *California Management Review* 32:101–113, Summer 1990.

42. Weick K.E.: Organizational culture as a source of high reliability. *California Manage Rev* 29:112–127, Winter 1987.

43. Luria J.W., et al.: Reliability science and patient safety. *Pediatr Clin North Am* 53:1121–1133, Dec. 2006.

44. Hofmann D.A., Stetzer A.: A cross-level investigation of factors influencing unsafe behaviors and accidents. *Personnel Psychology* 49:307–339, Jun. 1996.

45. U.S. Agency for Healthcare Quality and Research: *Hospital Survey on Patient Safety Culture.* http://www.ahrq.gov/qual/patientsafetyculture/hospsurvindex.htm (accessed Sep. 23, 2011).

46. U.S. Agency for Healthcare Quality and Research: *Patient Safety Indicators Overview.* http://www.qualityindicators.ahrq.gov/Modules/psi_overview.aspx (accessed Sep. 23, 2011).

47. Mardon R.E., et al.: Exploring relationships between hospital patient safety culture and adverse events. *J Patient Saf* 6:226–232, Dec. 2010.

48. Haynes A.B., et al.: Changes in safety attitude and relationship to decreased postoperative morbidity and mortality following implementation of a checklist-based surgical safety intervention. *BMJ Qual Saf* 20:102–107, Jan. 2011.

49. Pronovost P., et al.: A practical tool to reduce medication errors during patient transfer from an intensive care unit. *Journal of Clinical Outcomes Management* 11(1):26, 29–33, 2004.

50. Pronovost P.J., Berenholtz S.M., Needham D.M.: Translating evidence into practice: A model for large scale knowledge translation. *BMJ* 337:1714, Oct. 6, 2008.

51. U.S. Agency for Healthcare Research and Quality: *TeamSTEPPS®: National Implementation.* http://teamstepps.ahrq.gov/ (accessed Sep. 23, 2011).

52. Weaver S.J., et al.: The anatomy of health care team training and the state of practice: A critical review. *Acad Med* 85:1746–1760, Nov. 2010.

53. Capella J., et al.: Teamwork training improves the clinical care of trauma patients. *J Surg Educ* 67:439–443, Nov.–Dec. 2010.

54. Deering S., et al: On the front lines of patient safety: Implementation and evaluation of team training in Iraq. *Jt Comm J Qual Patient Saf* 37:350–356, Aug. 2011.

55. Neily J., et al.: Association between implementation of a medical team training program and surgical mortality. *JAMA* 304:1693–1700, Oct. 20, 2010.

56. Colla J.B., et al.: Measuring patient safety climate: A review of surveys. *Qual Saf Health Care* 14:364–366, Oct. 2005.

57. Singla A.K., et al.: Assessing patient safety culture: A review and synthesis of the measurement tools. *J Patient Saf* 2:105–115, Sep. 2006.

58. Paine L.A., et al.: Assessing and improving safety culture throughout an academic medical centre: A prospective cohort study. *Qual Saf Health Care* 19:547–554, Dec. 2010.

59. Shojania K.G.: The elephant of patient safety: What you see depends on how you look. *Jt Comm J Qual Patient Saf* 36:399–401, Sep. 2010.

60. The Joint Commission: *Sentinel Event Data Summary.* Aug. 15, 2011. http://www.jointcommission.org/sentinel_event_statistics_quarterly/ (accessed Sep. 23, 2011).

61. U.K. National Patient Safety Agency, National Reporting and Learning Service: *Quarterly Data Summaries.* http://www.npsa.nhs.uk/nrls/patient-safety-incident-data/quarterly-data-reports/ (accessed Sep. 23, 2011).

62. Pham J.C., et al.: The harm susceptibility model: A method to prioritise risks identified in patient safety reporting systems. *Qual Saf Health Care* 19:440–445, Oct. 2010.

63. World Health Organization: *Patient Safety: About Us.* http://www.who.int/patientsafety/about/en/ (accessed Sep. 23, 2011).

64. Canadian Patient Safety Institute: *Global Patient Safety Alerts.* http://www.globalpatientsafetyalerts.com/English/Pages/default.aspx (accessed Sep. 23, 2011).

65. Henriksen K., Kaplan H.: Hindsight bias, outcome knowledge and adaptive learning. *Qual Saf Health Care* 12(suppl. 2):ii46–ii50, Dec. 2003.

66. Coles G., et al.: Using failure mode effects and criticality analysis for high-risk processes at three community hospitals. *Jt Comm J Qual Patient Saf* 31:132–140, Mar. 2005.

67. Joint Commission Resources: Using RCA and FMEA to improve patient safety. *Joint Commission: The Source* 4:1–11, Nov. 2006.

68. Kimehi-Woods J., Shultz J.P.: Using HFMEA to assess potential for patient harm from tubing misconnections. *Jt Comm J Qual Patient Saf* 32:373–381, Jul. 2006.

69. Perkins G.D.: Simulation in resuscitation training. *Resuscitation* 73:202–211, May 2007.

70. Smith H.M., et al.: Simulation education in anesthesia training: A case report of successful resuscitation of bupivacaine-induced cardiac arrest linked to recent simulation training. *Anesth Analg* 106:1581–1584, May 2008.

71. Herzer K.R., et al.: A practical framework for patient care teams to prospectively identify and mitigate clinical hazards. *Jt Comm J Qual Patient Saf* 35:72–81, Feb. 2009.

72. The Joint Commission: *Sentinel Event Policy and Procedures.* Jan. 4, 2011. http://www.jointcommission.org/Sentinel_Event_Policy_and_Procedures/ (accessed Sep. 23, 2011).

73. Pronovost P.J., et al.: Paying the piper: Investing in infrastructure for patient safety. *Jt Comm J Qual Patient Saf* 34:342–348, Jun. 2008.

74. Pronovost P.J., et al.: Creating high reliability in health care organizations. *Health Serv Res* 41:1599–1617, Aug. 2006.

75. Runciman W.B., et al.: An integrated framework for safety, quality and risk management: An information and incident management system based on a universal patient safety classification. *Qual Saf Health Care* 15(suppl. 1):i82–i90, Dec. 2006.

76. Pronovost P.J., et al.: A practical tool to learn from defects in patient care. *Jt Comm J Qual Patient Saf* 32:102–108, Feb. 2006.

77. Goeschel C.A., et al.: Executive/Senior Leader Checklist to improve culture and reduce central line–associated bloodstream infections. *Jt Comm J Qual Patient Saf* 36:519–524, Nov. 2010.

78. Conway J.: Getting boards on board: Engaging governing boards in quality and safety. *Jt Comm J Qual Patient Saf* 34:214–220, Apr. 2008.

79. Goeschel C.A., et al.: Hospital Board Checklist to improve culture and reduce central line–associated bloodstream infections. *Jt Comm J Qual Patient Saf* 36:525–528, Nov. 2010.

80. Berenholtz S.M., et al.: Improving the quality of quality improvement projects. *Jt Comm J Qual Patient Saf* 36:468–473, Oct. 2010.

81. Pronovost P.J., Berenholtz S.M., Needham D.M.: A framework for health care organizations to develop and evaluate a safety scorecard. *JAMA* 298:2063–2065, Nov. 7, 2007.

82. The Joint Commission: *Heart Failure.* Feb. 7, 2011. http://www.jointcommission.org/heart_failure/ (accessed Sep. 23, 2011).

83. Bradley E.H., et al.: Hospital quality for acute myocardial infarction: Correlation among process measures and relationship with short-term mortality. *JAMA* 296:72–78, Jul. 5, 2006.

84. Needham D.M., et al.: Improving data quality control in quality improvement projects. *Int J Qual Health Care* 21:145–150, Apr. 2009.

85. Dixon-Woods M., et al.: Explaining Michigan: Developing an ex post theory of a quality improvement program. *Milbank Q* 89:167–205, Jun. 2011.

86. Pronovost P.J., Marsteller J.A., Goeschel C.A.: Preventing bloodstream infections: A measurable national success story in quality improvement. *Health Aff (Millwood)* 30:628–634, Apr. 2011.

87. SQUIRE: *Standards for Quality Improvement Reporting Excellence.* http://www.squire-statement.org/guidelines (accessed Sep. 23, 2011).

CHAPTER 3

Training Physician and Nursing Leaders for Performance Improvement

Paul Convery, M.D., M.M.M.; Carl E. Couch, M.D., M.M.M.; Rosemary Luquire, R.N., Ph.D., F.A.A.N., N.E.A.-B.C.

Physician and nurse leadership is vitally important in health care today, given all the challenges and changes on the horizon facing organizations. Core aspects in the global imperative of improving health care—whether driven by market forces or a national policy of health care reform[1,2]—include improved value; greater efficiency; higher levels of quality and safety; higher reliability in the care that is delivered; and the increased need for an educated, motivated, and committed workforce. Such a workforce consists of not only physicians and nurses but many other health care professionals and administrators. It will be important for health care organizations, health care systems, hospitals, and medical groups (and, in the United States, accountable care organizations—newly designed structures intended to improve the integration and coordination of care[3]) to have well-defined strategies and approaches to align and engage clinical leaders and to develop clinical leadership within their workforces.

Physicians were founders of the first hospitals in the United States, and even 100 years ago, one third of hospitals were physician led.[4] During the early 1900s, hospital administrators were frequently either physicians or nurses, but by the middle of the century, many hospitals had turned to nonclinicans for management of day-to-day operations. In 2008 only 3% of the approximately 5,000 hospitals in the United States were managed by physician CEOs,[4] and in 2010 only 5% of the chief executives in the United Kingdom's National Health Service (NHS) were physicians.[5] Furthermore, a 2002 poll found that 56% of hospital administrators in the United States had difficulty filling vacant medical staff leadership positions.[4] However, the number of clinician leaders is increasing,[4] stimulated by pressure to improve the quality and safety of patient care. Driving forces behind this pressure include reports of medical error–associated patient harm[6] and of poor delivery of evidence-based care[7] and the increased scrutiny of institutional leadership in the wake of the Enron, WorldCom, and the Allegheny Health, Educational and Research Foundation scandals early this century, making hospital boards more directly accountable for oversight of the quality and safety of patient care.[8] New Zealand, for example, saw an increased role for clinician leaders last decade, stemming from the need for greater collaboration between clinicians and managers to meet financial challenges and from the formation of integrated district health boards, contracted by the government to focus on health outcomes rather than on resource management as the "bottom line" of an organization.[9]

Clinical leaders, who bring dual training and experience in medical care and leadership/managerial competencies to the table, can (1) provide the technical knowledge about health care quality and safety that most hospital boards and nonclinician executives lack[8] and (2) bridge the communication gap between hospital leaders and frontline clinicians. They can also give a voice to the largest constituencies responsible for health care quality and safety—nurses and physicians—in organizational and policy decisions. These are all critical factors for any health care organization seeking to achieve high reliability because bidirectional communication is essential to identifying and to prioritizing opportunities to improve quality of care and implement best-practice solutions. Such communication will not be achieved without strong physician and nursing leaders at the center of the organizational culture.

As Chassin and Loeb recently stated, to achieve and sustain consistent excellence in safety and quality, health care organizations must focus on three components necessary to achieving high reliability: leadership, a safety culture, and robust process improvement.[10] Physician and nurse leadership can be an important tool for health care organizations seeking to become highly reliable organizations and to embrace a true culture of patient safety. This chapter describes various programs, approaches, and courses that can be used in developing physician and nursing leadership and collaboration between physician and nursing leaders for performance improvement, with a focus on Baylor Health Care System's approach.

PHYSICIAN LEADERSHIP
Why We Need Physician Leaders

Leaders who are trained in medicine play the following leadership and medical staff management roles[11]:

- Strategy development, including taking a medical advisory role to the executive
- Clinical governance, particularly related to quality, risk management, and regulatory requirements
- Oversight of operational areas that benefit from clinical and management skills

The combination of medical expertise and leadership competencies can help address some of the special leadership challenges that health care organizations face, including organizational complexity (characterized by many professional workforces operating within their own isolated silos while simultaneously providing care to the same patients); physician characteristics and training that make physicians resist the collaboration and "followership" necessary for effective teamwork; and the pressing need to improve access, affordability, and quality of health care.[12,13] Other special challenges in health care leadership that these leaders can help surmount are the complexity and variability of the external environment (insurance, reimbursement, regulation), the constantly evolving technology and the need to evaluate its effectiveness, the difficulties in managing the multiple professional workforces, and the multiple and competing goals of service.[14] An additional challenge lies in the multiple models in which physicians are associated with hospitals. Physicians may be independent members of the medical staff (and often members of competing hospitals' medical staffs), may be employed by the hospital or contracted for specific services, or may be involved in joint ventures with the hospital. This complex environment requires specialized skills and leadership.

As health care organizations throughout the world face the many changes needed to improve health care, clinical expertise and leadership skills are imperative to ensure that their policy decisions (1) enhance rather than compromise care and (2) are implemented to maximize physician buy-in and to minimize the perception that institutional changes are driven by financial rather than patient care concerns. The latter is important, because such a perception can induce physician resistance, which is in turn a barrier to delivery of safe, high-quality, and affordable health care. Because physicians are responsible for 75% of the cost incurred by health care organizations, they are key players in any initiative targeting improvements in quality and efficiency of care.[15] Physicians are well-suited to addressing "value" problems—the need to increase quality while decreasing costs[16]—because they can influence both sides of the equation.[17]

Why Physicians Need Training to Become Leaders in Complex Organizations

Falcone and Santiani expressed the need for training as follows:

> Most physicians . . . are bright, intuitive, optimistic, and hardworking. They are almost always successful in their practice and in their community. They may hold a variety of medical staff responsibilities and may, in fact, be quite comfortable with the concept of leadership and management within their scope of activities. It would be normal to feel that this success could be easily translated into the success of managing (or leading) a large institution; however, nothing could be further from the truth.[4(p. 89)]

Physicians typically possess a number of leadership strengths—in particular, acute intelligence, quick learning, and strong decision-making skills.[18] Their leadership weaknesses tend to lie in the areas of consensus building and decision making related to personnel.[18] Physicians are trained in a rigorous scientific discipline that "inculcates a value for autonomous decision-making, personal achievement, and the importance of improving their own performance, rather than that of any institution."[19(p. 170)] Specific aspects of medical training that present

barriers to physicians' easy transition to leadership roles are as follows[13]:

- The long, hierarchical training with extended subordination
- The extensive emphasis on individual performance
- The potential for "extrapolated leadership," in which physicians extend their clinical authority to settings in which it is irrelevant
- Physicians' focus on "deficit-based" thinking (diagnosis requires identification of a problem [deficit] followed by problem solving to remove that deficit) rather than "appreciative" thinking (building momentum for change based on achieving a vision of best possible performance rather than remedying current individual shortcomings)

Research has not yet investigated the traits that best discriminate between poor and great physician leaders in the same way that it has for general leadership.[12] However, expert opinion, reported failures of existing physician leaders, and surveys of current and aspiring physician leaders led Stoller to identify several common core competencies, as follows[12(p. 311)]:

- Technical knowledge and skills (of operations, finance and accounting, information technology and systems, human resources [including diversity], strategic planning, legal issues in health care, and public policy)
- Knowledge of health care (reimbursement strategies, legislation and regulation, quality assessment and management)
- Problem-solving prowess (around organizational strategy and project management)
- Emotional intelligence (the ability to evaluate oneself and others and to manage oneself in the context of a group)
- Communication (in leading change in groups and in individual encounters, such as in negotiation and conflict resolution)
- Commitment to lifelong learning

Historically, physicians have been promoted to leadership positions on the basis of clinical and/or academic skill rather than any demonstration of leadership competencies.[12] Furthermore, a change in role from clinical practice to leader/administrator (crossing to "the dark side"[4[p. 91]]) was frequently viewed as retirement by clinical colleagues, leading to the loss of peer relationships and respect,[20] thereby making it more difficult for the physician leader to fulfill his or her role.

Two important changes are altering this pattern. First, physicians are coming to view administrative roles as valid career choices and are showing an interest in developing leadership skills.[4,21] Second, physicians moving into leadership roles and health care organizations seeking physician leaders are recognizing the need for formal training in leadership and management skills.[22,23]

Different Types of Leadership in Which Physician Leaders Need Training

Because of the wide range of activities that physicians may lead within health care systems, physician leaders may need various types of leadership training, including training in classic leadership skills and training in quality improvement (QI), also often termed *performance improvement.*

Classic Leadership Training. Classic leadership training encompasses the core leadership competencies[12] and may be provided through formal training, as reflected in academic degrees, such as a master's in business administration (M.B.A.), a master's in hospital/health care administration (M.H.A.), or a master's in medical management (M.M.M.); customized, internally developed programs; or mentoring programs and targeted leadership assignments to develop individuals' skills. A 2005 survey of

hospital CEOs and presidents in the United States found that 71% of the respondents used formal education to develop physician leaders, 18% used coaching or mentoring, and 19% used targeted leadership assignments (with various combinations of the three being used in some cases).[22]

The Association of American Medical Colleges lists 38 National Leadership Development Programs targeted toward leaders in medicine, higher education, and health care and offered by various professional associations, medical schools, business schools, and graduate schools across the United States.[24] Physicians are also seeking traditional leadership and management training through M.B.A. programs concurrently with medical school education and later in their careers. At least 60 medical schools in the United States offer joint M.D.-M.B.A. programs,[18] as do some Canadian universities.[25] In the United Kingdom the Academy of Medical Royal Colleges and the NHS Institute for Innovation and Improvement have implemented an Enhancing Engagement in Medical Leadership project, which embeds management skills into physicians' careers from medical school to postspecialist registration using a three-tiered medical-leadership competency framework.[26] Although all physicians will be required to master the core competencies (such as self-awareness, teamwork, and understanding the health system as a business), a more advanced set of competencies (and related training) is applied to physicians wishing to become managers or executives.[26]

Executive M.B.A. programs have proliferated worldwide, and many institutions offer programs focusing on health care or specifically targeting physicians and physician executives. In the United States, these include the University of Texas at Dallas,[27] the University of Massachusetts Amherst Isenberg School of Management,[28] Auburn University,[29] and the University of Tennessee–Knoxville.[30] Programs in the United Kingdom include the Executive M.B.A. in Health Service Management offered by Greenwich College,[31] the M.B.A. in Hospital Administration at Anglia Ruskin University,[32] and Keele University's Health Executive M.B.A.[33] In Canada the Sauder School of Business at the University of British Columbia launched the country's first executive M.B.A. exclusively for health care careers in 2008,[34] and the Rotman School of Management at the University of Toronto offers an executive program in Advanced Health Leadership.[35] In India the University of Delhi offers a part-time M.B.A. in Health Care Administration[36]; and in Germany, European Business School (EBS) Universität für Wirtschaft und Recht[37] and Phillipps Universität Marburg offer executive M.B.A.s in Health Care Management.[38]

Outside the traditional university degrees, many health care organizations in the United States have chosen to create their own internal leadership training programs—for example, the Cleveland Clinic's Leading in Health Care and Cleveland Clinic Academy and the Mayo Clinic Foundation's Career and Leadership Development program.[12] Such internal programs can be tailored to the needs of the organization and local physicians and produce leaders well-versed in the organization's own philosophy.[39] They do, however, typically cover a similar set of core topics and skills to the courses offered in M.B.A. or M.M.M. programs: strategic planning, teamwork and team building, financial metrics, business planning, marketing, situational leadership, mentorship and people development, and expense management.[12] Where customized internal programs tend to differ is in such content as innovation, emotional intelligence, diversity issues, genera-

tional-cohort issues, health care policy, and time management.[12] Institutions may differ in terms of their programs' specific aims, such as developing a large cohort of leadership-trained recent medical graduates from which leaders can later be selected or focusing leadership training on a small cohort of future medical leaders identified through assessment of leadership potential and competitive recruitment.[21] Duration and intensity vary, with some programs following a long-term strategy, with workshops or classes spread over several months and interspersed with opportunities for participants to apply the information to their current positions or to group projects; other programs use high-intensity models in which all topics are addressed in several consecutive days.[21] Although the former model allows greater absorption and exploration of the material, as well the opportunity to form peer networks with other participants, the increased duration tends to increase cost.[21]

Although coaching and mentoring have been ranked by physician leaders, physician educators, and medical students as the most effective means of developing physician leaders[40] and play an important role in physician leader development,[41] they are used much less frequently than formal education programs.[22,41] Because observational learning is recognized as a common method of physician learning,[42] and mentoring is particularly apt for teaching aspects of interpersonal skills identified as typically weak in physician leaders,[12] the incorporation of mentors and coaching in formal physician leader development programs is recommended.[41]

Quality Improvement Leadership Training. Physician leaders, for whom the "patient first" attitude has been embedded through medical training, are ideally placed to promote and to ensure clinical quality and patient safety in a health care organization.[23] Physician leadership is particularly critical in creating a culture of safety within an organization and in helping a hospital or health care organization become a highly reliable organization. When change management is needed in these areas, physicians have two important roles to play: (1) devising improvement strategies and (2) using their insights into the clinical and managerial worlds to gain the medical staff buy-in that is critical to the success of any improvement strategy involving changes in physician practices.[23]

To effectively devise and lead QI initiatives, physicians (like other leaders) require training in the methods of QI. To meet this need, health care organizations, nonprofit organizations, universities, and national governments have developed relatively short, intensive programs providing foundation QI skills. Examples in the United States include the Advanced Training Program (ATP) in Health Care Delivery Improvement offered by the Institute for Healthcare Improvement, in partnership with Intermountain Health Care[43]; and the "Accelerating Best Care at Baylor" program (*see* page 68). The ATP trains senior leaders, middle management, and frontline health professionals to teach, to implement and to evaluate QI, outcome measurement, and management of clinical and nonclinical processes.[43] Topics covered include theory and techniques of guideline and protocol development and implementation, outcome measurement, health-services research, health policy and economics, cost-based accounting, medical informatics, severity of illness measurement and application, continuous QI, and teams and teamwork.[43] A mini–ATP is also offered for practicing clinicians, providing grounding in data-system design, outcome measurement and tracking, data management, clinical-cost accounting, information synthesis

and meta-analysis, severity of illness measurement and application, continuous QI, and leadership skills.[43] St. Joseph's Health Center in Toronto has also developed a program for physician leaders that uses a competency profile, personal development plans, self-directed learning, and action learning groups focused on current challenges within the health center to promote a culture of collaboration and shared accountability between medical staff and hospital administrators.[44]

In Germany the University of Heidelberg's Institute of Public Health offers a three-week course in Quality Management in International Health, which, drawing on case studies from low- and middle-income countries, covers the "general principles and frameworks for defining and promoting the quality of health systems and services including processes, models, and tools for assuring and evaluating quality."[45] In the United Kingdom the Health Foundation has developed "Generation Q," a part-time leadership program designed to develop leaders "who understand how complex health systems work and who inspire others to transform healthcare quality and bring about sustainable, system-wide change."[46] The course covers the four domains of improvement leadership— contextual, relational, technical, and personal—and participants learn to apply improvement science, leadership, and change theories to the challenges facing health care leaders.[46] The Australian Government's National Health and Medical Research Council offers a similar resource in its National Institute of Clinical Studies (NICS) Leadership Program,[47] which is intended to help physicians, nurses, and other health professionals early in their careers develop into "leaders in knowledge translation and implementation of evidence into the health system."

NURSING LEADERSHIP
Changing Role of Nurses

The 2010 Institute of Medicine (IOM) report *The Future of Nursing: Leading Change, Advancing Health* recognized that nurses have the potential to effect wide-reaching changes in the health care system—and likewise are a critical component to the success of any wide-reaching transformation.[48] The report's key messages were that (1) nurses should practice to the full extent of their education and training, (2) the nursing education system should be improved to promote seamless academic progression, (3) nurses should achieve higher levels of education, (4) nurses should be full partners with physicians and other health care professionals in redesigning the health care system, and (5) effective workforce planning and policy making require better data collection and improved information infrastructure.[48] The report also recommended an expanded role for nurses in leadership (in which nursing representatives should be included at all levels) and clinical practice (with registered nurses and advanced practice nurses taking on roles as care coordinators and primary care clinicians for certain services).[48,49] It further noted that nurses are being asked to provide increasingly complex care, insofar as they care for critically ill patients and patients with multiple chronic diseases, use advanced technology and information management systems, and collaborate with multidisciplinary teams whose other members hold master's or doctoral degrees.[49] To accommodate the recommended integration of leadership theory and business practices across the curriculum, the IOM report called for the proportion of nurses holding baccalaureate rather than associate degrees to be increased from the current 50% to 80% and for the number of nurses holding doctoral degrees to double by 2020.[48,49]

Nursing Leadership Roles

Nurses lead in many ways and in a variety of settings within health care organizations. Much of their leadership occurs unobtrusively through informal one-on-one mentoring relationships, which, while effective, are an "invisible" form of leadership that is generally overlooked by the broader health care system.[50] At the highest level of leadership—board membership—nurses are substantially underrepresented, with only 2% of hospital board positions being held by nurses, compared to 26% held by physicians.[51] They have, however, been making gains in the "corporate suites" in hospitals in the United States: Chief nursing officers (CNOs) often have expanded responsibility as chief clinical officers or chief quality officers, and many nurses have moved into chief operating officer and CEO roles in the past decade.[52] A growing number of hospitals led by nurse CEOs has also been reported in Canada.[53] In the United Kingdom the creation of trusts within the NHS led to increased leadership roles and representation for nurses in the 1990s; each trust was required to appoint a nurse executive to its board.[54] However, there is current concern that many of the nurse leaders will be lost in the effort to reach government targets for management cuts as the NHS transitions to general practitioner consortia.[55]

Research has identified several essential skills or qualities for nurse executives, including personal integrity, strategic vision/action orientation, team building/communication, management and technical competence, people skills, and personal survival skills.[56,57] Rankings of essential leadership skills show an interesting contrast between Europe and the United States. In one study, participants from 16 member countries of the World Health Organization European Region were asked to identify important attributes for chief nurses. They ranked communication first, followed by teamwork, leadership, strategic thinking, and political astuteness.[58] In contrast, in the United States, clinical knowledge was ranked first among the 14 attributes considered, and communication eighth—and teamwork was omitted entirely.[59] Qualitative studies that do not attempt to rank leadership skills have identified similar categories of effective leadership traits for nurse executives—core principles and values-based leadership (for example, leading to serve, striving for excellence, exhibiting a passion for nursing) and collaborative teamwork with patient care staff and with management—but also include the use of quantitative data in decision making.[57,60]

Nursing Leadership Programs

As Kaminski has stated, "No matter who an organization puts in a leadership role, without the proper preparation, skills development, and tools at hand, she or he will not be successful."[61(p. 32)] Nurses moving from clinical practice into administrative leadership and management positions face different sets of challenges from their physician colleagues. Although nursing education does not foster the autonomous approach typical of medical training and does introduce general leadership concepts and the mind-set of working collaboratively, its primary focus is nonetheless the science of human beings and patient care.[50] Thus, nursing leaders, like physician leaders, need training in leadership competencies to be effective in their new roles—but with emphasis on different areas based on physicians' and nurses' different "starting strengths."

Although M.B.A. and similar degree programs targeting nurses may not be as widely publicized as those targeting physicians, they are readily available. DeSales University offers a joint M.S.N./M.B.A. program, which "prepares graduates for employment in high level executive positions within the health care system" in administration, management, and health policy roles.[62] The University of Phoenix,[63] the University of Virginia School of Nursing,[64] and Johns Hopkins University School of Nursing[65] offer similar programs, while others, such as the University of Baltimore/Towson University[66] and the University of Pennsylvania, offer joint degrees combining an M.B.A. and a Ph.D. in nursing.[67] In addition, many schools in the United States and Canada offer master's of science degrees in nursing programs that focus on administration, leadership and management, health care administration, or health care systems management.[68,69] Executive programs for mid-career nurses, such as the New York University Wagner Executive Master of Public Administration: Concentration for Nurse Leaders program,[70] are also available.

Leadership programs for nurses have also been created outside the traditional academic setting. For example, Sigma Theta Tau has established an International Leadership Institute to prepare nursing leaders for board membership.[50] This two-year structured program addresses the key concepts of leadership styles, board versus staff responsibilities, development and fund-raising, relevant legal issues, stewardship, generative governance, and strategic thinking. It also incorporates a formal mentorship by presidents, vice presidents, and CEOs serving on national or international health care organization boards.[50] The American Association of Colleges of Nursing sponsors an executive fellowship for new and aspiring nurse leaders in academic settings[71] and, together with the American Organization of Nurse Executives, has identified core content for nursing programs, with a focus on a range of administration and management issues, including leadership, policy development, and continuous quality improvement.[72] Similar well-established programs include the Robert Wood Johnson program for nurse executives[73] and the Wharton School nursing leaders program at the University of Pennsylvania.[74] The Dorothy Wylie Nursing Leadership Institute in Canada offers a seven-day in-residence program centered on a mentorship model to identify emerging leaders and to begin the process of nurturing their development,[69,75] and the Registered Nurses Association of Ontario's Center for Professional Excellence has offered five-day clinical leadership programs for staff nurses for almost 30 years, reaching more than 75 organizational sites and more than 5,000 nurses.[69] In the United Kingdom the Royal College of Nursing provides a Clinical Leadership Programme through which it partners with health and social care organizations to develop practitioners' leadership skills.[76] This 15-day program (spread over 15 months) teaches the application of leadership and management skills through the development and implementation of a work-based service-improvement project.[76] In addition, the International Council of Nurses, which works closely with specialized agencies of the United Nations, such as the World Health Organization and the International Labour Organization, as well as international non-governmental organizations, such as Amnesty International and the International Red Cross,[77] offers "Leadership for Change," which aims "to prepare nurses for leadership roles in nursing and the broader health sector during these challenging times of health system change and reform."[78] This program uses a five-prong approach to leadership development—workshops, individual development planning, team projects, structured learning activities, and mentoring—and has been introduced in 50 countries throughout the world.[78]

Health care organizations have also developed internal nurse leadership programs, paralleling those offered for physician leadership development. For example, the Baylor Health Care System (BHCS) and Southern Methodist University (SMU) in Dallas have collaborated to develop the Nurse Executive Fellowship Program (*see* pages 76–77), and Georgetown University Hospital in Washington, D.C., offers clinical managers the opportunity to participate in Sigma Theta Tau's Web-based nursing management curriculum.

PHYSICIAN AND NURSING CO-LEADERSHIP

Interest in co-leadership of patient care by nurses and physicians is growing.[57] Although several studies show a positive relationship between increased collaboration between physicians and nurses in clinical care and improved patient outcomes, a 2008 review of the literature conducted by Jennings et al. revealed a paucity of research on the effect of collaborative leadership on patient care.[57] Nonetheless, co-leadership is not a new idea, having been recommended since the early 1980s.[57] Research interest appears to have peaked in the mid- to late 1990s; in a 1996 study, for example, Tjosvold and MacPherson reported that physician and nursing goals promoting collaboration increased task effectiveness and quality of care, but that goals promoting competition decreased productive interactions and patient outcomes, reflecting the leaders' inability to openly exchange ideas.[15] Jennings et al. called for additional research, which should include multisite interventional studies, and for the establishment of a consistent definition of *collaborative leadership*.[57]

One specific model of co-leadership that merits investigation is "whole systems shared governance," in which hospital management structures and processes are redesigned to engage all staff involved in providing care to improve the quality and efficiency of care.[79] Shared governance originated in nursing as a means to empower nurses and to coordinate their work across organizations, but it has been expanded in some settings to include all caregivers, with the hope that it will eventually create a more effective and broad-based hospital operational process.[79] Three psychiatric hospitals in Germany introduced a comprehensive co-leadership model in 1997, in which each hospital, department, and single ward was led by a team consisting of a physician, a psychologist or social worker, and a nurse.[80] Such co-leadership at all organizational levels can improve decision making in shared accountability areas and create a shared vision that spreads throughout the organization.[81] Approximately a decade after the introduction of the co-leadership model, all professional groups were generally satisfied with the model, although the nonphysician leaders viewed several aspects significantly more favorably and were more likely to believe that the model appropriately represented and recognized the physicians' role in care.[80] The nonphysician leaders were also more likely to believe the shared leadership model appropriately emphasized the importance of nursing.[80] Effective nurse-physician partnership can help create a high-reliability organization but requires clear understanding of domains of shared versus separate accountability; mechanisms for annual priority setting and designation of leaders for each priority; and professional support for the nurse and physician leaders that enables them to effectively perform their clinical practice, education, research, and administrative roles.[81] Organizations implementing co-leadership must recognize that establishing an effective systemwide model requires time, commitment, and financial resources.[81]

BAYLOR HEALTH CARE CASE STUDIES IN LEADERSHIP TRAINING

Baylor Health Care System (BHCS), an integrated not-for-profit health care delivery system based in Dallas, includes 15 owned, leased, and affiliated hospitals; 6 short-stay hospitals; more than 100 primary care, specialty care, and senior health centers; more than 500 physicians employed in HealthTexas Provider Network (HTPN); and more than 4,000 affiliated physicians. BHCS has a long-standing organizational commitment to quality, formalized in 2000 by the board of trustees' Quality Resolution, in which it "challenges itself and everyone involved in providing health care throughout the system to give patient safety and continuous improvement in the quality of patient care the highest priority in the planning, budgeting and execution of all activities in order to achieve significant, demonstrable and measurable positive improvement in the quality of patient care and safety."[82(p. 281)]

Among the QI strategies BHCS pursues is the active development of clinical leaders. This investment in leadership reflects (1) the critical need for physician and nurse expertise in the design of QI initiatives, patient safety strategies, and health care transformation; and (2) the ability of physician and nurse leaders, through peer-to-peer communication, to improve the likelihood of widespread adoption of innovations necessary for effective change. Many different kinds of leaders, with different levels and sets of leadership skills, are needed in large health care organizations (see Figure 3-1, pages 70–73), and BHCS has established a range of leadership development programs to meet these various needs. This is important for BHCS to achieve its goal of becoming a highly reliable organization.

"Accelerating Best Care at Baylor"

To equip clinicians and administrators with the skills necessary to lead change, BHCS introduced "Accelerating Best Care at Baylor" (ABC Baylor) in 2004, a QI education program based on the Intermountain Health Care ATP (*see* page 64). ABC Baylor teaches theory and techniques of rapid-cycle QI, "Lean" training, outcomes management, and staff development. In a five-day course, physicians, nurses, and administrators learn skills to design, implement, and evaluate QI efforts, with a focus on the Plan-Do-Check-Act cycle. To date, 250 physicians, more than 700 nurses, and 250 other administrative and QI leaders have completed the course. Multidisciplinary teams often attend the program with a specific area of focus that requires improvement. More than 90% of graduates report that they continue to use the tools of process improvement taught in ABC Baylor, and 50% lead another QI effort within one year of graduation. It is estimated that the 25 most recent ABC Baylor projects saved BHCS $1.5 million, including a project conducted in one hospital to increase the accurate entry of laboratory test orders, which was estimated to save $10,845 per year by decreasing errors in the tests run, and a project to improve the resource-management system in one hospital's surgery department, which reduced staff overtime and eliminated 3:00 to 11:00 P.M. contract labor, resulting in annual cost savings of $320,000.

The success of the ABC Baylor class led to its incorporation in a BHCS–led and U.S. Agency for Healthcare Research and Quality–funded randomized controlled trial testing the effects of health information technology and QI education on quality of care in 47 rural Texas hospitals.[83,84] In addition, the Commonwealth of Pennsylvania contracted with BHCS to provide a customized ABC Baylor course for QI leaders in Pennsylvania hospitals.[85] The program began with a demonstration project conducted in two community hospitals. The project teams at one hospital undertook five QI projects targeting heart failure discharge instructions, surgical antibiotic prophylaxis, care for stroke patients, timely administration of antibiotics for pneumonia, and pneumococcal vaccine administration, and they achieved 100% compliance in each of these areas.[86] Project teams at the second hospital targeted deep vein thrombosis prophylaxis and pneumococcal vaccination, and they not only achieved 100% compliance within the hospital units in which the projects were piloted but extended the improved protocols and processes throughout the hospital as a whole.[87] As a result of this success, a similar system for teaching and implementing rapid-cycle QI was successfully adopted and applied to additional projects.[87] Other adaptations of the ABC Baylor course include a one-day version to extend the knowledge needed to effectively participate in QI projects to frontline health care staff and a format suitable for medical students and residents during their training.

Leadership Development Institute

In 2006 BHCS introduced the Leadership Development Institute to provide its leaders with the necessary skills and tools to achieve system goals, divided into the following categories (with the associated goals):

- People ("be the best place to work")
- Quality ("deliver safe, timely, effective, efficient, equitable and patient-centered care supported by education and research")
- Service ("to both our patients and our community")
- Finance ("be responsible financial stewards")

Twice a year, BHCS gathers leaders at the manager level and above for a day-long workshop to do the following:

Figure 3-1. Physician Leadership Levels and Skills

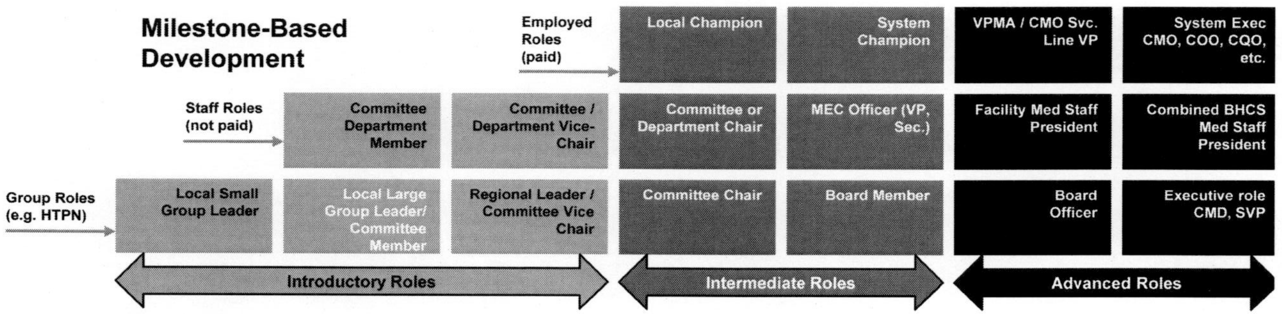

Leadership Skills	Introductory Roles	Intermediate Roles	Advanced Roles	
	Coaching & Developing Others	Coaching & Developing Others	Coaching & Developing Others	Coaching & Developing Others
	Sizing up Talent	Sizing up Talent	Building Organizational Talent	Building Organizational Talent
	Aligning Performance for Success	Aligning Performance for Success	Aligning Performance for Success	
	Building Successful Teams and Partnerships	Building Successful Teams and Partnerships	Building Successful Teams and Partnerships	Building a Successful Team
	Facilitating Change	Facilitating Change	Accelerating Change	Leading Change
	Leading Through Vision and Values	Leading Through Vision and Values	Leading Through Vision and Values	Inspiring a Common Vision
	Engaging and Influencing	Engaging and Influencing	Sharing Responsibility	Sharing Responsibility
	System Thinking	Gaining Commitment	Strategic Influence	

(continued on page 71)

Figure 3-1. Physician Leadership Levels and Skills (continued)

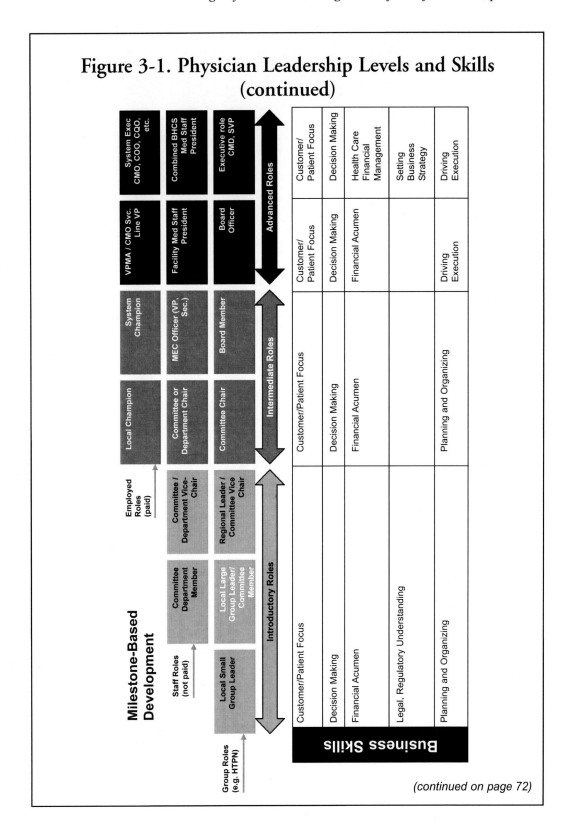

(continued on page 72)

Figure 3-1. Physician Leadership Levels and Skills (continued)

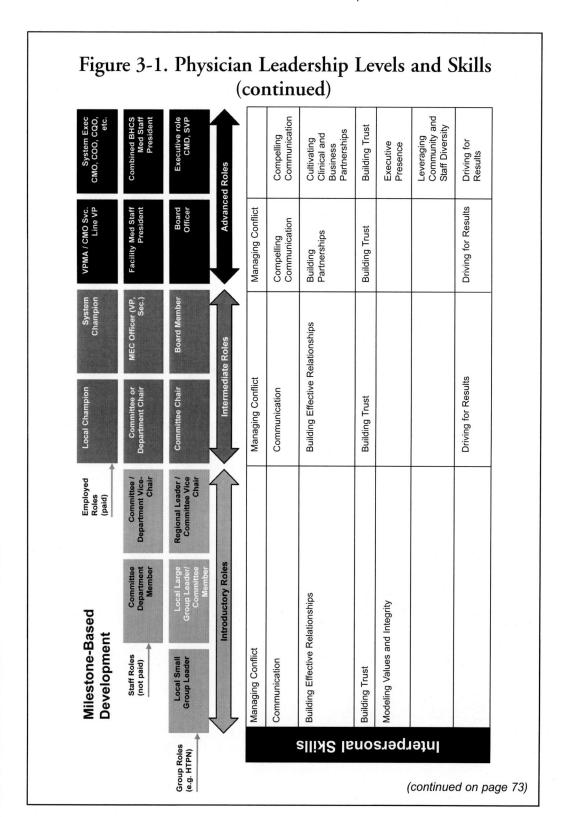

(continued on page 73)

Figure 3-1. Physician Leadership Levels and Skills (continued)

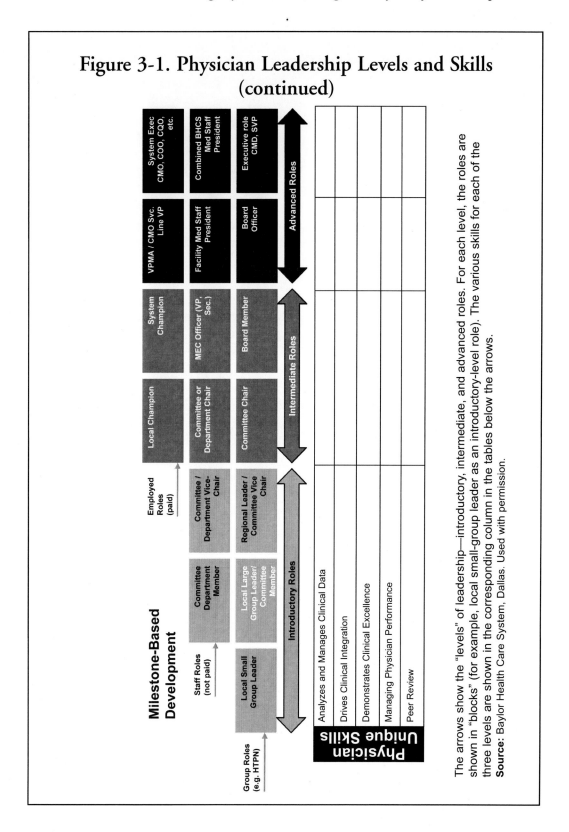

The arrows show the "levels" of leadership—introductory, intermediate, and advanced roles. For each level, the roles are shown in "blocks" (for example, local small-group leader as an introductory-level role). The various skills for each of the three levels are shown in the corresponding column in the tables below the arrows.
Source: Baylor Health Care System, Dallas. Used with permission.

- Communicate progress and future direction relative to the system goals
- Provide skills training
- Foster networking across BHCS
- Recognize and reward performance and behaviors
- Provide a structured framework for sharing lessons and training with staff

Topics addressed range from the Studer Group's Nine Principles for organizational success (*see* Sidebar 3-1, page 75) to candidate selection and interviewing techniques and techniques for holding an effective meeting. In addition, leaders receive (and are trained on) tools to support success, including communication methods, manager evaluation software, 90-day action plans, goal-setting tasks, and tools for staff recognition, such as thank-you notes to recognize service or success.

Introduction to Physician Leadership

Each year, BHCS senior leaders identify approximately 70 physicians showing leadership potential to attend a one-day leadership course co-taught by a physician from the American College of Physician Executives, a consulting firm, and senior BHCS physician leaders. The program introduces physicians to administrative and leadership issues, with such topics as "Moving from an Effective Clinician to an Effective Leader," "Medical Staff Management and the Board," "Managing Disruptive Physicians," and "The Importance of Physician Leadership to Baylor." This course, now in its fourth year, has been successful in engaging physicians to act in a collaborative manner and in helping them to understand their roles in medical staff or medical group leadership and within the context of the larger organization. For example, they learn to manage various physician behaviors that could be interpreted as "disruptive" and gain under-

standing of medical staff responsibilities and restrictions.[88] After The Joint Commission released the *Sentinel Event Alert* concerning the negative impact of disruptive physician behavior on patient safety,[89] each of the BHCS medical staffs approved identical "disruptive physician" policies and guidelines to address this issue. The history of leadership training made that approval much easier to implement.

Physician Advanced Leadership Development with Southern Methodist University

For more experienced physician leaders—directors of large medical groups, medical staff presidents, vice presidents of medical affairs, department chairs, and others in leadership roles—BHCS, in collaboration with the SMU Cox School of Business, developed a two-year course providing training in the more complex expertise required for higher levels of leadership.[88] This course is scheduled so that practicing physicians do not sacrifice an exorbitant amount of income-producing time. After applicants are nominated by their hospital presidents, they complete a short application form that acknowledges their commitment to a leadership role and to fulfilling the course's requirements.

The course's key curriculum elements fall into three broad categories, as shown in Sidebar 3-2 (page 76). The course is taught in six full-day sessions at SMU, spread out over two years. One month after each formal educational session, participants meet in small dinner-discussion groups to consider leadership and management topics. These topics are selected from leadership literature or case studies and are presented in a Journal Club format, a traditional medical education method with which physicians are familiar. Although these groups are led by senior BHCS physician leaders, senior

Sidebar 3-1. Nine Principles for Organizational Success

Principle 1: *Commit to excellence*—When excellence is reached, employees and physicians feel valued. It creates passion for associates and leaders by putting the "why" back into health care.

Principle 2: *Measure the important things*—Measurement holds people accountable and aligns resources to hit specific targets.

Principle 3: *Build a culture around service*—Connecting service to organizational values elevates service excellence from a program to a culture.

Principle 4: *Create and develop great leaders*—Leadership development creates effective leaders, sustains results, enhances skill sets, and raises the bar. It is also an agent of cultural change.

Principle 5: *Focus on employee satisfaction*—Employee satisfaction depends on patient and physician satisfaction. Increased employee satisfaction means decreased cost and less employee turnover.

Principle 6: *Build individual accountability*—Motivate leaders and employees to act like "owners" rather than "renters." This is accomplished by emphasizing the importance of the hiring process, communicating information, and generating employee ideas.

Principle 7: *Align behaviors with goals and values*—Integrate the vision, values, and goals into daily decisions and actions.

Principle 8: *Communicate at all levels*—Communication within an organization must travel in all directions and impart positive as well as negative information. This is often referred to as "Managing Up."

Principle 9: *Recognize and reward success*—Recognizing and rewarding success provides real-life examples for staff. Positive behaviors are reinforced, and role models are created.

Source: Adapted from Studer Group: *Nine Principles*®. http://www.studergroup.com/dotCMS/knowledgeAssetDetail?inode=109972 (accessed Sep. 23, 2011). Used with permission.

Sidebar 3-2. Key Curriculum Elements in Baylor Health Care System, Advanced Physician Leadership Course (with Southern Methodist University)*

Leadership
- Analyze individual leadership styles and develop management effectiveness
- Develop personal awareness and conflict resolution skills
- Lead effective organizational initiatives
- Manage through influence
- Learn about the art of leadership

Corporate Finance
- Health care costs and financial management
- Managerial accounting: planning, controlling, and decision making
- Financial analysis to select projects and investments

Strategy
- Strategic management: competing on the leading edge
- Corporate strategy: leading upward
- Human capital strategy: managing performance to evaluate and to develop employees

* The course is scheduled over 6 days across a 2-year period.

Source: Baylor Health Care System, Dallas. Used with permission.

---

administrators—CEOs and chief operating and financial officers—also attend.[88] The classroom and dinner-discussion activities have promoted the intermingling of physician leaders from all BHCS hospitals and physicians from different medical staffs to exchange ideas and strategies. This attitude has contributed to the creation of a common culture across the system.

Several graduates of this program have subsequently pursued M.B.A. or M.M.M. degrees,[88] many of the physicians who have participated in the various leadership programs have gone on to more formal leadership roles within the system, and all have become more engaged leaders within BHCS. For the past two consecutive years, BHCS has chosen a physician leader to participate in the Executive M.B.A. program at the SMU Cox School of Business; the first of these physicians will graduate in 2012. The designation of the physician leader entails nomination from a senior executive and the candidate's submission of an application and essay, with a selection committee making the final determination.

Nursing Leadership Development with Southern Methodist University

BHCS and the SMU Cox School of Business have also developed a year-long Nurse Executive Fellowship Program. Fellows must apply for the program via a written process (with their CNO's endorsement) and must already hold a master's degree. In 2009–2010, 22 nurses participated in this leadership development program.

Participants choose from recommended SMU courses that match the identified BHCS nursing leadership competencies in the categories of "Business Acumen: Managing the Business," "Leading and Managing People," and "The Leader Within," as shown in Table 3-1 (pages 78–79).

Fellows also complete 360-degree feedback tools and individual development plans and work with individually assigned mentors who guide their development during the year. In the final portion of the program, participants must complete capstone projects that draw together the skills and information learned through the preceding coursework. In addition to the fellows' goals of improving delivery of care, patient outcomes, or operating efficiency, capstone projects must demonstrate a financial return on investment (ROI). Examples of capstone projects completed in the 2009–2010 year include "Decreasing the length of stay for percutaneous coronary intervention patients," "Going 'green' in the operating room," and "Reducing use of agency RNs." Improvements in quality of care and patient safety achieved through the capstone projects include the following:

- A decreased rate of patient falls with injury, accompanied by increased use of patient and medication scanning and decreased nursing turnover and vacancies, in the bone marrow transplantation unit
- Implementation of a program to identify patients eligible for same-day discharge (with telephone follow-up to ensure no complications) following percutaneous coronary intervention (PCI), which achieved a 4.96 patient approval rating on a 5-point scale, with no identified complications, while relieving bed overcrowding that followed an increase in the hospital's PCI volume.

In addition, several of the individual capstone projects have demonstrated cost savings in excess of $100,000, with a total ROI of the program of more than $950,000. The program's impact on participants is reflected in the 71% increase in the fellows' perception of their readiness for promotion by the program's end. Several fellows have subsequently moved into new roles with expanded responsibilities.

Quality Champion Model

Since 2005 BHCS has driven QI through the Best Care Physician Champion model. Both systemwide and local hospital physician champions have been identified in several specialties—obstetrics, cardiology, patient safety, clinical preventive services, in-hospital care, surgery, and geriatrics. Physician champions provide motivation, encouragement, and clinical expertise to collaboratively improve quality in their respective fields and practice areas. Recently, BHCS has expanded this model to include nursing champions, who perform the complementary role of motivating and catalyzing process improvements among nursing staff.

Clinical champions were key contributors to success in the implementation of a standardized order set for heart failure admissions at all BHCS hospitals. Through the appointment of a heart failure physician champion at each hospital, mobilization of hospitalist champions, and other strategies to engage frontline care providers, use of the order set reached 73% within 15 months of implementation. In addition, compliance with publicly reported heart failure processes of care increased, and inpatient mortality and direct costs for care were significantly reduced.[90] Clinical champions were also involved in promoting and implementing a community-acquired pneumonia order set, use of which was associated with an unadjusted 3% reduction in in-hospital mortality.[91]

Table 3-1. Baylor Health Care System (BHCS) Nursing Leadership Academy: Competencies and Recommended Southern Methodist University (SMU) Courses

BHCS Competencies	Recommended SMU Courses		
Business Acumen: Managing the Business			
Financial Management	Manager's Guide to Financial Statements	Financial Analysis, Earnings and Cash Flows	
Human Resource Management	Human Capital Strategy	Leveraging Human Resources	Assessing Talent
Performance Improvement	Coaching for Improved Performance	Motivating Others	Writing Effective Performance Plans
Foundational Thinking Skills	Problem Solving		
Technology	Business Process Management	Logistics and Supply Chain	
Strategic Management	Balanced Scorecard	What Good Managers Do	
Making Operational Decisions	Business Process Management	Financial Budgeting: Allocation of Resources	
Patient Relations	The Patient as the Customer	Marketing: Branding and Messages	
Leading and Managing People			
Leadership Skills	Leading from the Center	Leadership Styles	Cross-Generational Leadership
Relationship Management	Courageous Conversations		
Influencing Behaviors	Influencing Across the Organization		
Diversity	Leveraging Individual Differences		
Shared Decision Making	Decision Making		
Building Trust	Speed of Trust		
Cultivating Partnerships	Building High-Performance Teams	Negotiating to the Top: A Gain-Gain Approach	Creating High-Performance Culture
Sharing Responsibility	The Language of Accountability		

(continued on page 79)

Table 3-1. Baylor Health Care System (BHCS) Nursing Leadership Academy: Competencies and Recommended Southern Methodist University (SMU) Courses (continued)

BHCS Competencies	Recommended SMU Courses		
The Leader Within			
Personal and Professional Accountability	Values (Ethics, Personal, Vision)	The Language of Accountability	Leadership Styles
Career Planning	360° Feedback	Action Plan	
Personal Journey Disciplines	Accountability Trios		
Reflective Practice	The Learning Journal		
Executive Presence	Speaking as a Leader®	Taking the Stage®	
Capstone Project	Case Study Presentations	Build It Experience	

Source: Baylor Health Care System, Dallas. Used with permission.

Boot Camp for New Nursing Leaders

Boot Camp for New Nursing Leaders, which pioneered at the Heart Hospital at Baylor Plano (Texas) in February 2009, addresses the knowledge gap for new nursing leaders, who are typically promoted for excellent clinical skills but lack formal management and leadership skills. Boot Camp is a four-day course that provides the necessary survival skills to make the transition to leadership. The curriculum is customized to BHCS, centering on the "Baylor Circle of Care" goals of People, Quality, Finance, and Service, as well as BHCS's Professional Nursing Practice Model: skilled communication, collaboration, effective decision making, adequate staffing, authentic leadership, and meaningful recognition (as adapted from the American Association of Critical-Care Nurses Synergy Model for Patient Care[92]). The curriculum covers the major organizational structure and the use of process and outcomes reports, among other issues, and provides hands-on training in, for example, accessing resources (policies and procedure) and reports for a particular topic on the BHCS intranet.[93] Approximately 400 nursing leaders also attend development programs tailored to their needs at least twice a year.

Nursing Quality Summit

BHCS holds an annual day-long Nursing Quality Summit organized by the Staff Nurse Council. The purpose is to share best practices in QI, with a focus on nursing-sensitive outcomes, to encourage the spread of those best practices across the system. The 2010 summit, attended by 600 BHCS nurses, featured 32 presentations of nurse-led rapid-cycle improvement projects. By exposing more nurses to what can be achieved through the rapid-cycle improvement process, the Nursing Quality Summit also stimulates participation in ABC Baylor. This, in turn, gives BHCS a strong cadre of nurses with knowledge of and trained in QI, particularly in the use and value of quality indicators. Feedback on the summit has been positive, with 98% of nurses reporting that they had acquired information applicable to their practices.

Physician and Nurse Co-Leadership

BHCS has had marked success with physician and nurse co-leadership. For example, implementation of the heart failure order set (*see* page 77) was led at each hospital not only by the local physician champion but also by the CNO, who ensured that the order sets were promoted and readily available for physician use. Physicians and nurses also co-lead the Baylor Best Care Committee, which oversees the planning, budgeting, execution, and reporting of activities to improve the quality and safety of care throughout BHCS, and the BHCS clinical councils. These councils, which represent such clinical areas as critical care, emergency services, women's health, and surgery, drive quality and safety initiatives throughout the system.

RECOMMENDATIONS

The shift from nonclinican leadership in health care to senior clinician leaders is well under way. Hospitals and other health care organizations should not be asking *whether* they should include nurse and physician executives and board members but rather *how to prepare* their clinicians for leadership roles. On the basis of the literature and our experience in implementing clinical leadership models and training, we offer the following recommendations:

- Develop a strategic plan for hiring and training physician and nursing leaders.
- Consider multiple formats and approaches to physician and nurse leadership develop-

ment. As described earlier, options include external academic-degree programs, the use of leadership development consulting firms, and internally tailored programs (possibly developed and/or provided in partnership with a local university), any of which can be supplemented by mentoring relationships. The BHCS approach has combined these options, with formats ranging from formal educational sessions to dinner-discussion groups, to better prepare hospital and health system clinicians for leadership roles. In determining training options, organizations should consider the number of leaders and future leaders whom they desire to train, the organizational resources for developing and sustaining internal leadership programs, and the relative costs of formal academic programs for nurses and physicians. Partnering with the business school of a local university, as BHCS has done with the SMU Cox School of Business, provides the external credibility of a recognized degree, diploma, or certificate while offering the opportunity to tailor the training to target the organization's particular needs. In this way, the organization fosters future leaders with the generally applicable leadership skills and the institutional knowledge that can aid a smooth transition of leadership and achieve effective improvement and transformation.

- Tailor training to individuals according to their career stage and aspirations. Physicians and nurses are interested in different levels of leadership training, depending on their career stages and goals. Many BHCS physicians take only the ABC Baylor QI course and lead only specific activities. A new medical staff officer may find the one-day Introduction to Leadership course all that is needed at the time, but after progressing to the medical staff president role, he or she may find the two-year Advanced Leadership course to be more suitable. On the other hand, several nurses and physicians are actively interested in official leadership roles and seek formal degrees.

- Be aware of legal and regulatory restrictions on education (nonmonetary benefits) given to physician members of the medical staff. It is advisable to consult with legal experts regarding how to address this issue. BHCS does not pay—or charge—physicians to participate in its leadership-development activities. Physicians do sign agreements that state that they are participating on the basis of their roles as organizational leaders and that they are expected to continue to lead quality, patient safety, and other improvements across BHCS. It is helpful to clarify at the outset of clinician leadership classes that the participants are there *as leaders* and that they are expected to be leaders within the organization in the future.

- To justify continued investment in leadership training, measure and track the work and progress of the participants after the completion of each session or course. At BHCS, physician and nursing leaders participate in committees and improvement projects that capitalize on their learning, which we track through such mechanisms as participant surveys and postcompletion promotions. For example, a survey of the first group of physicians who completed the Advanced Leadership course revealed that in the subsqent two years, more than 70% of the physicians had moved into positions of greater responsibility. Tracking of the first cohort of 20 Nurse Executive Fellows showed that 3 of the participants had been promoted within six months of completing the fellowship. Monitoring such metrics provides some sense of the ROI for the organization and substantiates the value of

leadership training, which will be particularly important in the future as budgets become more constrained.

SUMMARY

Formal physician and nursing leadership training is essential to health care if it is to become an industry of highly reliable organizations. We must have leaders with clinical experience and administrative expertise who understand the complexity of the environment and system models of health care organizations and who "speak the language" of frontline care staff.

The formal clinical education that physicians and nurses currently receive provides little in the way of leadership or management training. However, in our experience, they generally are receptive to learning these skills and tools. Many programs teaching these skills are available to physicians and nurses through academic institutions and professional organizations, but an organization seeking to establish a corps of clinician leaders will likely gain the greatest benefit from having its clinicians learn the necessary leadership and management skills within the context of the organization itself. This allows for a tailored program and relevant hands-on experience. Developing and implementing such programs should be viewed as an organizational investment rather than as an expenditure. The organization benefits when its leaders are conversant with the complex factors affecting frontline care, as it enhances their effectiveness in setting relevant priorities and in motivating frontline care providers to participate in QI efforts that will help provide the best health care to the greatest possible number of patients. Teaching clinicians new skills and facilitating their transitions to new leadership roles also moves physicians and nurses from the role of "victim" in an ever-changing health care environment to the role of "leader," able to take charge of the future. Finally, leadership appeals to individuals' best instincts and can provide interested nurses and physicians with an alternative, "bigger picture" means of improving patients' health and the health care experience.

The authors thank Briget da Graca, M.S., E.L.S., for assistance with researching and writing this chapter.

References

1. H.R. 3590. Patient Protection and Affordable Care Act (PPACA) of 2010, Pul. L. No. 111-148, Mar. 23, 2010. http://www.gpo.gov/fdsys/pkg/ PLAW-111publ148/pdf/PLAW-111publ148.pdf (accessed Sep. 23, 2011).

2. United Kingdom Department of Health: *Equity and Excellence: Liberating the NHS*. 2010. http://www.dh.gov.uk/en/Publicationsandstatistics/ Publications/PublicationsPolicyAndGuidance/DH_11 7353 (accessed Sep. 23, 2011).

3. Berwick D.M.: Launching accountable care organizations—The proposed rule for the Medicare Shared Savings Program. *N Engl J Med* 364:e32, Apr. 21, 2011.

4. Falcone R.E., Satiani B.: Physician as hospital chief executive officer. *Vasc Endovascular Surg* 42:88–94, Feb.–Mar. 2008.

5. Ham C., et al.: *Medical Chief Executives in the NHS: Facilitators and Barriers to Their Career Progress.* Coventry, UK: NHS Institute for Innovation and Improvement, 2010.

6. Institute of Medicine: *To Err Is Human: Building a Safer Health System.* Washington, DC: National Academy Press, 2000.

7. Institute of Medicine: *Crossing the Quality Chasm: A New Health System for the 21st Century.* Washington, DC: National Academy Press, 2001.

8. Goeschel C.A., Wachter R.M., Pronovost P.J.: Responsibility for quality improvement and patient safety: Hospital board and medical staff leadership challenges. *Chest* 138:171–178, Jul. 2010.

9. Malcolm L., et al.: Improving the doctor-manager relationship: Building a successful partnership between management and clinical leadership: Experience from New Zealand. *BMJ* 326(7390):653–654, Mar. 22, 2003.

10. Chassin M.R., Loeb J.M.: The ongoing quality improvement journey: Next stop, high reliability. *Health Aff (Millwood)* 30:559–568, Apr. 2011.

11. Dwyer A.J.: Medical managers in contemporary healthcare organisations: A consideration of the literature. *Aust Health Rev* 34:514–522, Nov. 2010.

12. Stoller J.K.: Developing physician-leaders: Key competencies and available programs. *J Health Adm Educ* 25:307–328, Fall 2008.

13. Stoller J.K.: Developing physician-leaders: A call to action. *J Gen Intern Med* 24:876–878, Jul. 2009.

14. Leatt P., Porter J.: Where are the healthcare leaders? The need for investment in leadership development. *Healthc Pap* 4:14–31, Jul. 2003.

15. Tjosvold D., MacPherson R.C.: Joint hospital management by physicians and nursing administrators. *Health Care Manage Rev* 21:43–54, Summer 1996.

16. Porter M.E., Teisberg E.O.: *Redefining Health Care: Creating Value-Based Competition on Results.* Boston: Harvard Business Press, 2006.

17. Swensen S.J., et al.: Controlling healthcare costs by removing waste: What American doctors can do now. *BMJ Qual Saf* 20:534–537, Jun. 2011.

18. Huff C.: Are your docs management ready? *Hosp Health Netw* 84:20–23, 22, Apr. 2010.

19. Weisbord M.R: *Organizational Diagnosis: A Workbook of Theory and Practice.* New York City: Perseus Books, 1978.

20. Schwartz R.W., Pogge C.: Physician leadership: Essential skills in a changing environment. *Am J Surg* 180:187–192, Sep. 2000.

21. Warren O.J., Carnall R.: Medical leadership: Why it's important, what is required, and how we develop it. *Postgrad Med J* 87:27–32, Jan. 2011.

22. Epstein A.L.: The state of physician leadership in medical groups: A study of leaders and leadership development among AMGA organizations. *Group Practice Journal* 54:24–31, Feb. 2005.

23. Sinclair D.G., Carruthers C., Swettenham J.: Healthcare and physician leadership. *Healthc Q* 14:6–8, Jan. 2011.

24. Association of American Medical Colleges: *Leadership Development.* https://www.aamc.org/initiatives/ leadership/ld/ (accessed Sep. 23, 2011).

25. Hecterra Publishing Inc.: *Health and Medical MBA Degree Programs in Canada.* http://www.canadian-universities.net/MBA/Health_and_Medical_MBA.html (accessed Sep. 23, 2011).

26. Hunt L.: Medical leaders: The long engagement. *Health Serv J* 117:30–31, Aug. 2007.

27. University of Texas at Dallas: *Professional/Executive Programs* http://www.utdallas.edu/admissions/ professional/ (accessed Sep. 23, 2011).

28. University of Massachusetts, Isenberg School of Management: *Press Release: MBA Program for Physician Executives Ranked 12th in the Nation .* May 8, 2008. http://www.isenberg.umass.edu/undergrad/ news/MBA_Program_for_Physician_Executives_ Ranked_12th_in_the_Nation_528/ (accessed Sep. 23, 2011).

29. Auburn University: *The Physicians Executive MBA.* http://business.auburn.edu/emba/PEMBA/index.cfm (accessed Sep. 23, 2011).

30. University of Tennessee–Knoxville: *Physician Executive MBA.* http://pemba.utk.edu/ (accessed Sep. 23, 2011).

31. Greenwich School of Management: *Weekend EMBA in*

Health Service Management. http://www.greenwich
-college.ac.uk/programmes-courses/postgraduate/
emba/executive-master-of-business-administration
-exec-mba-health-services-management-london.asp
(accessed Sep. 23, 2011).

32. Anglia Ruskin University, Faculty of Health & Social
Care: *MBA in Hospital Administration.*
http://www.anglia.ac.uk/ruskin/en/home/faculties/
fhsc/international_students/mba_in_hospital_
administration.html (accessed Sep. 23, 2011).

33. Keele University: *Postgraduate Taught: Health Executive
MBA.* http://www.keele.ac.uk/pgtcourses/
coursedetails/healthexecutivemba/ (accessed Sep. 23,
2011).

34. University of British Columbia, Sauder School of
Business: *UBC Executive MBA in Health Care.*
http://webcontent.sauder.ubc.ca/Home/Programs/
Executive%20Education/~/media/Files/Executive%20
Education/EMBAProgramBrochure2009.ashx
(accessed Sep. 23, 2011).

35. University of Toronto, Rotman School of Management: *Rotman Executive Programs: Advanced Health
Leadership Program.* http://ep.rotman.utoronto.ca/
open/health_leadership/ (accessed Sep. 23, 2011).

36. University of Delhi, Faculty of Management Studies:
*Master of Business Administration—Health Care Admin-
istration (Part Time).* http://www.fms.edu/?q=node/27
(accessed Sep. 23, 2011).

37. European Business School: *Executive MBA Health Care
Management.* http://www.ebs.edu/index.php?id=
2946&L=1 (accessed Sep. 23, 2011).

38. Phillipps Universität Marburg: *Executive MBA-
Programme.* http://www.uni-marburg.de/fb02/mba/
programme/mba_hcm_home (accessed Sep. 23,
2011).

39. McAlearney A.S., et al.: Developing effective physician
leaders: Changing cultures and transforming organizations. *Hosp Top* 83:11–18, Spring 2005.

40. McKenna M.K., Gartland M.P., Pugno P.A.: Development of physician leadership competencies: Perceptions of physician leaders, physician educators and
medical students. *J Health Adm Educ* 21:343–354,
Summer 2004.

41. Nowill D.P.: Lessons of experience: Key events and
lessons learned of effective chief medical officers at
freestanding children's hospitals. *J Healthc Manag*
56:63–79; discussion 79–80, Jan.–Feb. 2011.

42. Taylor C.A., Taylor J.C., Stoller J.K.: The influence
of mentorship and role modeling on developing
physician-leaders: Views of aspiring and established
physician-leaders. *J Gen Intern Med* 24:1130–1134,
Oct. 2009.

43. Intermountain Healthcare, Institute for Health Care
Delivery Research: *20-Day Course for Executives &
QI Leaders—Advanced Training Program (ATP).*
http://www.intermountainhealthcare.org/qualityandres
earch/institute/courses/atp/Pages/home.aspx (accessed
Sep. 23, 2011)

44. Vimr M.A., Thompson G.G.: Building physician
capacity for transformational leadership. *Healthc
Manage Forum* 24(1 suppl.):S49–S61, Spring 2011.

45. University of Heidelberg, Institute of Public Health:
Quality Management in International Health.
http://www.klinikum.uni-heidelberg.de/
QualManagement.8021.0.html (accessed Sep. 23,
2011).

46. Health Foundation: *Generation Q.*
http://www.health.org.uk/areas-of-work/
programmes/generationq/ (accessed Sep. 23, 2011).

47. Australian Government, National Health and Medical
Research Council: *National Institute of Clinical Studies
(NICS) Leadership Program.* http://www.nhmrc.gov.au/
node/113 (accessed Sep. 23, 2011).

48. Institute of Medicine: *The Future of Nursing: Leading
Change, Advancing Health.* Washington, DC:
National Academies Press, 2010. http://www.nap.edu/
openbook.php?record_id=12956&page=R1 (accessed
Sep. 23, 2011).

49. Kuehn B.M.: IOM: Boost nurses' role in health care.
JAMA 304:2345–2346, Dec.1, 2010.

50. Carlson E.A., et al.: Board leadership development:
The key to effective nursing leadership in the 21st
century. *J Contin Educ Nurs* 42:107–113; Mar. 2011.

51. Prybil L.D.: Nursing involvement in hospital
governance. *J Nurs Care Qual* 22:1–3, Jan.–Mar. 2007.

52. Hughes J.E.: *Does a Nurse Make a Good CEO?* Mar. 4,
2010. http://www.phoenix.edu/uopx-knowledge
-network/articles/industry-viewpoints/nurse-make
-a-good-ceo.html (accessed Sep. 23, 2011).

53. Scrivener L.: At local hospitals, nurses' time has come.
Toronto Star, Nov. 15, 2009. http://www.healthzone.ca/
health/newsfeatures/healthcaresystem/article/726007
--at-local- (accessed Sep. 23, 2011).

54. MacPherson W.R.: Nursing in the NHS: The executive nurse director. *Br J Hosp Med* 55:522–524, Apr.
17–30, 1996.

55. Ford S.: Minister warned over loss of nurse leaders.
Nursing Times, Apr. 4, 2011.
http://www.nursingtimes.net/nursing-practice/
clinical-specialisms/management/minister-warned
-over-loss-of-nurse-leaders/5028105.article (accessed
Sep. 23, 2011).

56. Carroll T.L.: Leadership skills and attributes of women
and nurse executives: Challenges for the 21st century.
Nurs Adm Q 29:146–153, Apr.–Jun. 2005.

57. Jennings B.M., Disch J., Senn L.: Chapter 20: Leadership. In Hughes R.J. (ed.): *Patient Safety and Quality:
An Evidence-Based Handbook for Nurses.* U.S. Agency
for Healthcare Research and Quality, 2008.
http://www.ahrq.gov/qual/nurseshdbk/docs/
JenningsB_L.pdf (accessed Sep. 23, 2011).

58. Hennessy D., Hicks C.: The ideal attributes of
chief nurses in Europe: A Delphi study. *J Adv Nurs*
43:441–448, Sep. 2003.

59. Byers J.F.: Knowledge, skills, and attributes needed
for nurse and non-nurse executives. *J Nurs Adm*

30:354–356, Jul.–Aug. 2000.

60. Upenieks V.V.: What constitutes successful nurse leadership? A qualitative approach utilizing Kanter's theory of organizational behavior. *J Nurs Adm* 32:622–632, Dec. 2002.

61. Kaminski V.: "Just because a nurse is a really good nurse doesn't mean she will be a good manager!" *Nurs Leadersh (Tor Ont)* 23:31–32, Dec. 2010.

62. DeSales University: *MSN Nurse Executive at DeSales University.* http://www.desales.edu/default.aspx?pageid=810 (accessed Sep. 23, 2011).

63. University of Phoenix: *Master of Science in Nursing/Master of Business Administration/Health Care Management.* https://schools.collegedegrees.com/forms/university-of-phoenix/publisher/ rncentral/program-id/86 (accessed Sep. 23, 2011).

64. University of Virginia School of Nursing: *Master's of Science in Nursing/Master's of Business Administration.* http://www.nursing.virginia.edu/programs/msnmba/ (accessed Sep. 23, 2011).

65. Johns Hopkins University School of Nursing: *MSN/MBA.* http://www.son.jhmi.edu/academics/academic_programs/masters/msn-mba/ (accessed Sep. 23, 2011).

66. University of Baltimore/Towson University: *M.B.A./Ph.D. in Nursing.* http://mba.ubalt.towson.edu/programs/dual-degree-programs/mba-phd-nursing.html (accessed Sep. 23, 2011).

67. University of Pennsylvania School of Nursing: *Joint Degree Options.* http://www.nursing.upenn.edu/admissions/doctoral/Pages/Joint_Degree_Options.aspx (accessed Sep. 23, 2011).

68. GradSchools.com: *Nurse Administration Graduate Programs.* http://www.gradschools.com/search-programs/nurse-administration (accessed Sep. 23, 2011).

69. Kitty H.L.: *Nursing Leadership Development in Canada.* Ottawa: Canadian Nurses Association, 2005.

70. NYU Wagner: *Meet Tomorrow's Nurse Leaders.* http://wagner.nyu.edu/executivempa/nurseleaders/ (accessed Sep. 23, 2011).

71. American Association of Colleges of Nursing: *AACN Leadership for Academic Nursing Program.* http://www.aacn.nche.edu/Education/LANP.htm (accessed Sep. 23, 2011).

72. Kenner C., Androwich I.M., Edwards P.A.: Innovative educational strategies to prepare nurse executives for new leadership roles. *Nurs Adm Q* 27:172–179, Apr.–Jun. 2003.

73. Robert Wood Johnson Foundation: *Executive Nurse Fellows.* http://www.executivenursefellows.org/ (accessed Sep. 23, 2011).

74. Wharton School, University of Pennsylvania: *Wharton Nursing Leaders Program.* http://executiveeducation.wharton.upenn.edu/open-enrollment/health-care-programs/nursing-leaders-program.cfm (accessed Sep. 23, 2011).

75. Dorothy M. Wylie Nursing Leadership Institute: *Healthcare Leadership Development.* http://dwnli.ca/

76. Royal College of Nursing: *The RCN Clinical Leadership Programme.* http://www.rcn.org.uk/development/practice/leadership (accessed Sep. 23, 2011).

77. International Council of Nurses: *Professional Practice.* http://www.icn.ch/pillarsprograms/professional-practice/ (accessed Sep. 23, 2011).

78. International Council of Nurses: *Leadership for Change™.* http://www.icn.ch/pillarsprograms/leadership-for-change/leadership-for-change.html (accessed Sep. 23, 2011).

79. Casanova J.: Medical staffs and nursing staffs: The need for joint leadership. *Physician Exec* 34:24–27, Nov.–Dec. 2008.

80. Steinert T., Goebel R., Rieger W.: A nurse-physician co-leadership model in psychiatric hospitals: Results of a survey among leading staff members in three sites. *Int J Ment Health Nurs* 15:251–257, Dec. 2006.

81. Ponte P.R.: Nurse-physician co-leadership: A model of interdisciplinary practice governance. *J Nurs Adm* 34:481–484, Nov. 2004.

82. Ballard D.J., Spreadbury B., Hopkins R.S., III: Health care quality improvement across the Baylor Health Care System: The first century. *Proc (Bayl Univ Med Cent)* 17:277–288, Jul. 2004.

83. Filardo G., et al.: A hospital-randomized controlled trial of an educational quality improvement intervention in rural and small community hospitals in Texas following implementation of information technology. *Am J Med Qual* 22:418–427, Nov.–Dec. 2007.

84. Filardo G., et al.: A hospital-randomized controlled trial of a formal quality improvement educational program in rural and small community Texas hospitals: One year results. *Int J Qual Health Care* 21:225–232, Aug. 2009.

85. Haydar Z., et al.: Accelerating Best Care in Pennsylvania: Adapting a large academic system's quality improvement process to rural community hospitals. *Am J Med Qual* 23:252–258, Jul.–Aug. 2008.

86. Andrews A., Valente A.: Accelerating Best Care in Pennsylvania: The Hazleton General Hospital experience. *Am J Med Qual* 23:259–265, Jul.–Aug. 2008.

87. Dickey S.J., McNamara D.E.: Meadville Medical Center's experience with the Accelerating Best Care in Pennsylvania project: Lessons learned and future directions. *Am J Med Qual* 23:266–270, Jul.–Aug. 2008.

88. Dillon P.H., Nye J., Rice J.A.: *Programs of Promise: A Resource for the Development of Physician Leadership Academies.* Kansas City: Integrated Healthcare Strategies, 2009.

89. The Joint Commission: Behaviors that undermine a culture of safety. *Sentinel Event Alert* 40, Jul. 9, 2008. http://www.jointcommission.org/assets/1/18/SEA_40.pdf (accessed Sep. 23, 2011).

90. Ballard D.J., et al.: Impact of a standardized heart failure order set on mortality, readmission, and quality

and costs of care. *Int J Qual Health Care* 22:437–444, Dec. 2010.

91. Fleming N.S., Ogola G., Ballard D.J.: Implementing a standardized order set for community-acquired pneumonia: Impact on mortality and cost. *Jt Comm J Qual Patient Saf* 35:414–421, Aug. 2009.

92. American Association of Critical-Care Nurses: *The AACN Synergy Model for Patient Care.* http://www.aacn.org:88/wd/certifications/content/syn model.pcms?pid=1&&menu=http://www.aacn.org/ (accessed Sep. 23, 2011).

93. Baylor Health Care System (BHCS): *The Future of Nursing Starts Here.* Nursing Annual Report. Dallas: BHCS, 2009.

CHAPTER 4

The Role of Health Information
Technology in Quality and Safety

David W. Bates, M.D., M.Sc.; Gilad J. Kuperman, M.D., Ph.D.

The costs of health care in the United States are the highest of any country, yet the level of quality and safety in the care its patients receive is mediocre at best. There is a strong will to change this, in part because the high costs of health care are affecting the country's economic performance. Many believe that one of the keys to lowering costs and improving quality and safety will be increasing the adoption of health care information technology (HIT). Through the 2009 Health Information Technology for Economic and Clinical Health (HITECH) Act passed as part of the American Recovery and Reinvestment Act of 2009 (ARRA),[1] the United States is making an unprecedented investment in HIT, and the federal government has allocated nearly $30 billion[2] in incentives for providers and hospitals that adopt electronic health records (EHRs) and use them in "meaningful ways."[3] The concept of *meaningful use* is an important one because it has been demonstrated that simply adopting EHRs does not result in improved quality of care.[4]

We have focused on this legislation because it represents a sea change in terms of the national level of investment in HIT in the United States, although the use of HIT and the need for it were growing well before the legislation passed. In fact, in many other countries, particularly in Europe, use of EHRs is already routine in primary care. Thus, use of HIT would apply regardless of the requirements, and nearly all developed nations are making major investments in HIT and widely increasing its use. Furthermore, the policy approaches used in the United States are being tracked with great interest by those in many other countries, although it is not certain yet how successful they will be.

The U.S. Centers for Medicare & Medicaid Services (CMS) has had a strong focus on patient safety, and patient safety will be targeted by reimbursement measures outlined in the Affordable Care Act.[5] Even before the reimbursement measures go into effect, another effort, called the Partnership for Patients, as announced in early 2011,[6] will provide technical assistance to hospitals in improving safety. The two key goals of the partnership are to reduce the frequency of (1) preventable harm in hospitalized patients by 40% and (2) readmissions by 20% by 2013. HIT, linked with meaningful use, will be a key foundational tool for CMS to achieve these aims.

PROBLEMS WITH SAFETY

It is clear that health care throughout the world could be safer, as shown by a multinational study by Jha et al.[7] In one study, Nolte and McKee estimated that the preventable mortality rate in the United States was the highest of any country studied—nearly twice as high as that of France, for example.[8] Much of this difference does not relate to HIT; with the exception of primary care, France's HIT systems are not better than those in the United States. Still, in terms of HIT, the United States, as compared with other developed countries, has substantial room for improvement. A recent survey from the U.S. Office of the Inspector General estimated that approximately one in seven Medicare beneficiaries suffered an adverse event as the result of the care received,[9] with a total estimated cost of $4.4 billion. Some of the major causes of harm are health care–associated infections, adverse drug events, falls, pressure ulcers, and deep venous thromboses. Many of these causes are preventable, and specific interventions could have reduced their likelihood. Some of those interventions involve HIT, and measurement of the frequency of all types of harm will involve the use of HIT in the future.

PROBLEMS WITH QUALITY

In the most ambitious study of quality of care in the United States, McGlynn and colleagues found that the chances of receiving high-quality health care were little better than a coin flip.[10] They evaluated 439 indicators of quality for 30 acute and chronic conditions and found that patients received only 54.9% of recommended care. This proportion was relatively similar for acute conditions, chronic conditions, and preventive care. Care did vary substantially by condition, with 79% of patients getting recommended care for cataracts, for example, versus only 11% for alcohol dependence. The problem of poor quality has been relatively resistant to change, particularly for outcome measures as opposed to process measures, and several studies have demonstrated that simple use of EHRs is not associated with improved quality,[4] although other approaches have been more beneficial. For example, Shojania et al., who

evaluated the impact of a variety of approaches for improving the care of patients with diabetes,[11] found that of 11 different quality improvement (QI) strategies evaluated, 2 were associated with reductions in glycolated hemoglobin (A1C): team changes and case management. Mangione et al., who also evaluated disease management programs with respect to diabetes care,[12] found that these programs were associated with modest improvements in process measures but not with improved intermediate outcomes or levels of medication management.

Thus, it appears clear that simply using EHRs results in little improvement in quality measures. Shojania et al. performed a meta-analysis of clinical decision support for improving quality[13] and found a median improvement of 4.2% of improved adherence to care for process measures, which is a fairly small improvement. Another hypothesis suggested that after providers had used EHRs for a long period, they would eventually use them to improve care. However, a study that empirically evaluated this hypothesis for a seven-year period found no improvement.[14]

In this chapter, we survey recent trends and government efforts to speed adoption, discuss the evidence indicating the potential for HIT to improve safety and quality, and then provide messages for leaders.

TRENDS IN HEALTH INFORMATION TECHNOLOGY
Meaningful Use of Electronic Health Records

Levels of adoption of EHRs have been fairly low in the United States in the inpatient and outpatient settings, and, compared with other nations, the differences in the outpatient setting are great—particularly in primary care.[7] Many

Figure 4-1. HITECH Will Advance the Tipping Point

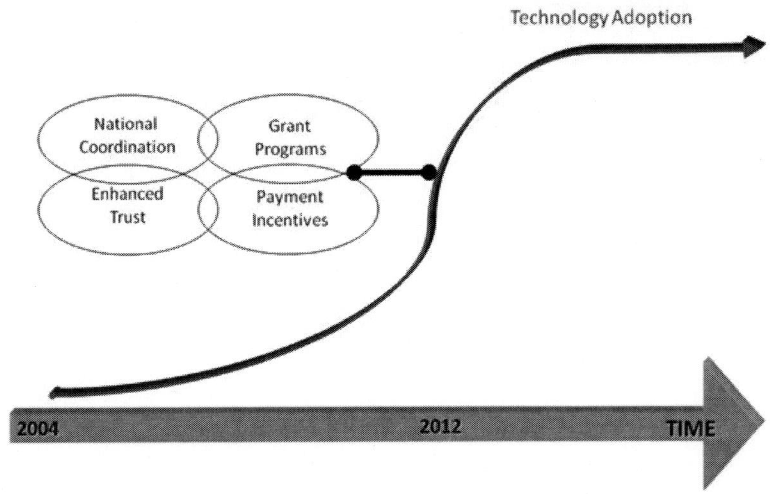

National coordination, grant programs, payment incentives, and enhanced trust are all intended to enable the Health Information Technology for Economic and Clinical Health (HITECH) Act to advance the tipping point for technology adoption.

Source: Personal communication to author [D.W.B.] from Charles P. Friedman, Ph.D., Deputy National Coordinator, Office of the National Coordinator for Health Information Technology, U.S. Department of Health & Human Services, Washington, DC.

other developed countries demonstrate very high levels of adoption of EHRs in primary care.

In the first comprehensive national survey of the adoption of EHRs across hospitals in the United States, the rate was estimated to be 1.5% for comprehensive systems and 7.6% for basic systems, on the basis of a panel's definition of what constituted a basic or comprehensive system in 2010.[15] However, these rates are somewhat misleading insofar as they include computerized laboratory and radiology reports, which were used by 77% of the respondents. Larger hospitals, teaching hospitals, and those located in urban areas were more likely to have EHRs. Another study estimated that the proportion of hospitals that had adopted EHRs increased from 8.7% in 2008 to 11.9% in 2009.[16]

In the outpatient setting, the adoption rate in 2008, as reported by DesRoches et al., was 4% for an extensive system and 13% for a basic system.[17] The most important barrier to adoption, particularly in that setting, has been financial; providers must pay for these records, but approximately 89% of the benefits accrue to payers and purchasers. To address this, incentives were included in the HITECH Act for adoption of EHRs for hospitals as well as for providers in the outpatient setting. The aim was to use a variety of stimuli, including national coordination and incentives, to advance the "tipping point" (*see* Figure 4-1, above).

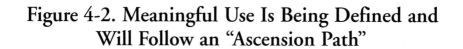

Figure 4-2. Meaningful Use Is Being Defined and Will Follow an "Ascension Path"

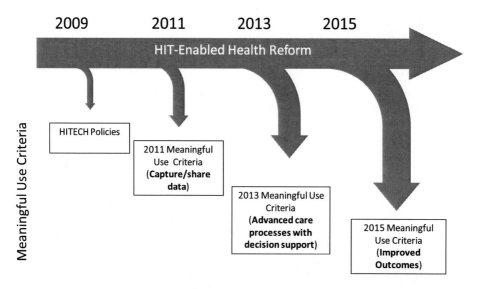

The incentives for meaningful use of electronic health records are spread out over multiple years, from getting providers started on the adoption curve in 2011 to improving outcomes by 2015.

Source: Personal communication to author [D.W.B.] from Charles P. Friedman, Ph.D., Deputy National Coordinator, Office of the National Coordinator for Health Information Technology, U.S. Department of Health & Human Services, Washington, DC.

In addition, the concept of meaningful use was coined to express that it is important not simply to have EHRs but to use EHRs in ways that improve safety, quality, and efficiency if society is to receive the desired benefits. The legislation had three specific requirements—that providers (1) use certified EHRs, (2) engage in clinical data exchange, and (3) agree to supply quality measurement data.

The incentives are spread out in stages over multiple years. The notion has been to get providers started on the adoption curve (Stage 1), with relatively limited systems in 2011, then to ask them to add more advanced care processes in 2013 (Stage 2), and then to move to improving outcomes by 2015 (Stage 3) (*see* Figure 4-2, above). The rules for Stage 1 have been approved by the U.S. government. The proposed rule for Stage 2 is not yet available; however, it appears that Stage 2 of meaningful use may be delayed from 2013 to 2014.

To date, the 2011 criteria have been released. Although in general they have received broad support, much of the debate has been about how fast to proceed, with vendors and providers wanting to go more slowly, and "consumers"—patients, purchasers, health plans, and disease management organizations—encouraging a faster pace. The vendors have been stretched with respect to adopting new functionalities, such as developing the ability to allow patients to download copies of their records, capturing the cause of death in the record, and capturing smoking status in eight specified categories; the issue is compounded by the length of their product cycles, which tend to be every 6 or 12 months.

International Efforts to Implement HIT

Countries around the world are making efforts to promote the implementation of HIT. Most developed countries already have fairly high levels of EHR implementation in primary care, but implementation in hospitals has lagged behind, and clinical data exchange is very limited in most countries.[7] For example, among seven countries, four (the United Kingdom, the Netherlands, Australia, and New Zealand) had nearly universal use of EHRs in ambulatory care among general practitioners, and Germany was also far along, while Canada and the United States lagged far behind. In contrast to the ambulatory setting, fewer than 10% of hospitals in all these countries had fully implemented EHRs, although a substantial proportion in some countries used computerized laboratory and radiology results.

Countries have used an array of approaches to encourage adoption. Most developed nations have single-payer systems, and some have taken the approach of paying for all EHRs in a particular setting, while others have used more incentive-based approaches. A few countries have achieved substantial success. For example, Denmark has implemented EHRs in a very high proportion of general practitioner (GP) offices, is achieving relatively high rates of adoption in hospitals, and has established the beginnings of data exchange. Other countries, including Canada and the United Kingdom,

have struggled more. One of the most ambitious and controversial efforts has been the United Kingdom program Connecting for Health, as described in Case Study 4-1 (below).

CASE STUDY 4-1. THE UNITED KINGDOM AND CONNECTING FOR HEALTH

The Connecting for Health program was established in 2002 following reports on HIT. The general approach was to centrally support linkages between EHRs and a number of key functionalities, which several vendors were selected to implement in a number of regions. Key efforts included the integrated care records service, which struggled throughout; electronic prescribing, which as of 2009 was in place in 70% of GP practices and pharmacies, though only 40% of prescriptions were issued with bar codes; electronic appointments' booking, which had slow uptake; and underpinning information technology (IT) infrastructure (sometimes called the "spine"), which was more successful, with 98% of GP practices connected by 2007. Thus, successes included high levels of HIT adoption in primary care, the linkage of practices enabling transfer of clinical information, and also electronic prescribing, although hospital implementations went poorly. The costs were high, with the original expectation being £2.3 billion for 3 years, but an assessment by the National Audit Office in 2006 showed that the costs had been £12.4 billion for 10 years, with some subsequent estimates even higher. Overall, the assessment of the program has been that the "value for money from services deployed is poor."[1] Criticisms of the program have included failure to deliver clinical benefit and concerns about data security risks, and medical staff have had important reservations about it. It is not clear what will be done next.[2]

References

1. British Computer Society, Health Informatics Forum Strategic Panel: *The Way Forward for NHS Health Informatics: Where Should NHS Connecting for Health (NHS CHF) Go from Here?* Dec. 15, 2006. London. http://www.bcs.org/upload/pdf/BCS-HIF-report.pdf (accessed Sep. 23, 2011).
2. National Health Service: *NHS Connecting for Health.* http://www.connectingforhealth.nhs.uk (accessed Sep. 23, 2011).

In 2001, Canada Health Infoway, the central group for HIT in Canada, released a plan intended to promote the adoption of interoperable EHRs,[18] as described in Case Study 4-2 (pages 92–94).

CASE STUDY 4-2. CANADA AND CANADA HEALTH INFOWAY

In 2001 Canada Health Infoway introduced a model including interprovincial and territorial collaboration, with the aim of building a national framework. Substantial progress has been made in some areas, including funding, agreement about HIT standards, patient registries, and picture-archiving (or PACS) systems, all of which has been perceived to be very beneficial. However, adoption rates remain low in Canada in primary and in secondary care. A recent evaluation by key stakeholders identified a number of critiques of the Canadian approach to date, including insufficient development of an e-health policy, inadequate engagement of clinicians, failure to establish a business case for EHRs, and a focus on national rather than regional interoperability. The investment to date—C$1.6 billion—has been much more modest than in the United Kingdom, and the program continues to move forward.

A number of cross-national efforts are under way. For example, the U.S. Department of Health &

Human Services and the European Commission have signed a memorandum related to health activities to promote the overall benefits for patients, health systems, and companies.[19] This is a large step forward to advance interoperability. In addition, the European Commission's eHealth Governance Initiative's Health Action Plan in 2004 marked the beginning of work to implement and to deploy interoperable eHealth services within and among member states.[20] It remains to be seen what effect these international efforts will have, but it will likely be considerable, particularly in Europe.

Health Information Exchange

Having access to the most complete data set about the patient enables the physician to take optimal care of the patient. In the absence of complete information, there is a risk (1) that the physician will order an incorrect treatment or make an incorrect therapeutic decision, (2) that unnecessary duplicative resources may be expended, and (3) that the patient may suffer avoidable harm. Even sophisticated EHRs that have computerized provider order entry (CPOE) systems, automated clinical documentation, and clinical decision support capabilities may not provide the physician with access to the patient's complete data set.

Evidence suggests that lack of access to complete patient data can be problematic in the clinical setting. Smith et al. found that clinical information that would have been relevant to the care of the patient was not available to the treating clinician in 13% of visits in a primary care setting.[21] The missing data were present in electronic form in some other system 52% of the time, and physicians said that the missing data was at least somewhat likely to have adversely affected care 44% of the time. In an emergency setting, Stiell et al. found that information gaps were present in 32% of visits.[22] The gaps were more common in sicker patients, for whom the missing data would have been considered "essential to care" 48% of the time. The inability to access data across care settings also inhibits key health care processes, such as transitions of care (involving handoffs or "handovers"), longitudinal analyses, public health reporting, and biosurveillance. The following factors represent hurdles to the easy exchange of health care data:

- Discrepancies in the structure and representation of health care data across health care organizations
- Challenges in matching patients across institutions
- The absence of a robust, efficient, and practical privacy framework to govern the exchange of health data across settings
- The lack of leadership and organizational frameworks to help advance interoperability and exchange of data across health care settings
- The absence of universal language representing safety concepts to exchange health care data within countries and across the world[23]

In 2001, in recognition of the limitations caused by the lack of interoperability, the U.S. National Committee for Vital and Health Statistics called for the creation of a National Health Information Infrastructure and recommended that the U.S. Department of Health & Human Services take a leadership role. In 2004, the U.S. Office of the National Coordinator (ONC) advocated "connected care" as part of its strategy to advance adoption of EHRs and advocated for the development of "regional health information organizations" (RHIOs) to address the financial, governance, technical, privacy, and sustainability issues associated with health information exchange. In 2010 the eHealth Initiative, a not-for-profit entity that focuses on eHealth, reported the existence of

234 RHIO initiatives, of which 73 were operational and 18 were sustainable.[24] For example, NYCLIX, Inc., is a RHIO that connects major medical centers and other health care providers in Manhattan and other parts of New York City. Through this RHIO, emergency physicians are able to access data from other facilities in the exchange. NYCLIX is also developing capabilities to notify primary care physicians when their patients are seen in emergency departments (EDs) or are admitted to member hospitals. NYCLIX is supported by grant funds and member dues. An initial favorable technology licensing arrangement is allowing NYCLIX to be sustainable for the time being; however, the current technology pricing model is time-limited, and the model for future sustainability and growth still is uncertain. Although the ultimate sustainability of RHIOs as a model for interoperability has been called into question, they represent a substantial amount of work and investment.[25]

The HITECH Act and the incentive program for meaningful use have substantially advanced the interoperability of health care data. Certainly, with the increased adoption of EHRs, more electronic data will be available. In addition, several of the Stage 1 meaningful use objectives promote the concept of interoperability (see Table 4-1, page 94).[26] One of the meaningful use themes—care coordination—targets interoperability directly, and the Stage 1 objectives require a demonstration of the direct exchange of data among providers. However, interoperability-related components—such as e-prescribing, providing data to patients, integrating laboratory data into an EHR, reporting public health data, and reporting quality data—all reflect the exchange of health information. The proposed Stage 2 and Stage 3 objectives would require increased support for care coordination and other aspects of interoperability.[28]

Table 4-1. Summary of Stage 1 Meaningful Use Measures*

Eligible Hospital Meaningful Use Core Objectives
1. Use computerized provider order entry for medication orders.
2. Implement drug–drug and drug–allergy interaction checks.
3. Maintain an up-to-date problem list of current and active diagnoses.
4. Maintain active medication list.
5. Maintain active medication allergy list.
6. Record patient demographics (language, gender, date of birth, etc.) electronically.
7. Record vital signs electronically.
8. Record smoking status for patients 13 years old and older.
9. Report hospital clinical quality measures.
10. Implement one clinical decision support rule related to a high-priority condition.
11. Provide patients with an electronic copy of their health information upon request.
12. Provide patients with an electronic copy of their discharge instructions at time of discharge, upon request.
13. Develop the capability to exchange key clinical information (for example, problems, medications, allergies, test results) among providers.
14. Protect electronic health information created or maintained by the certified EHR technology through the implementation of appropriate technical capabilities.

Eligible Hospital Menu Set Objectives
1. Implement drug formulary checks.
2. Record advance directives for patients 65 years old or older.
3. Incorporate clinical lab-test results into EHR as structured data.
4. Generate lists of patients by specific conditions to use for quality improvement, reduction of disparities, research, or outreach.
5. Use certified EHR technology to identify patient-specific education resources and provide resources to the patient.
6. The eligible hospital or critical access hospital that receives a patient from another setting should perform medication reconciliation.
7. The eligible hospital or critical access hospital that transitions its patient to another setting should provide summary care record for each transition of care or referral.
8. Capability to submit electronic data to immunization registries.
9. Capability to submit electronic data on reportable lab results to public health agencies.
10. Capability to submit electronic syndromic surveillance data to public health agencies.

* Core objectives are required; 5 objectives may be chosen from the list of 10 menu set objectives. EHR, electronic health record.

Source: Adapted from EHR Incentive Program: *Eligible Hospital and CAH Meaningful Use Table of Contents: Core Objectives and Menu Set Objectives.* http://www.cms.gov/EHRIncentivePrograms/Downloads/Hosp_CAH_MU-TOC.pdf (accessed Sep. 23, 2011).

In addition to the meaningful use incentive program for EHRs, the ONC has created other programs to advance interoperability—notably, the three-year, $564 million State Health Information Exchange Cooperative Agreement Program.[28] This program funds states to build capacity for exchanging health information across the health care system. The overall goal is to increase connectivity and to enable patient-centric information flow to improve quality and efficiency. The program calls on "state-designated entities" to advance governance, policies, technology, operations, and financing related to health information exchanges. State activities vary, but the states are obliged to build on existing efforts and coordinate with their respective Medicaid activities. Each state was required to submit a strategic and operational plan in 2010.

The ONC has also sponsored the Direct project,[29] which is intended to enable one provider to send data to another provider. This would enable many interoperability use cases—for example, a primary care provider sending data to a specialist as part of a referral, a hospital sending a discharge summary to a primary care physician, or a laboratory sending results to an ordering provider. The Direct project will not solve the problem of "get me all the patient's data" but will address Stage 1 meaningful use objectives. The vision is that Direct protocols could be built directly into the physicians' and hospitals' EHRs. Several issues remain to be addressed, such as creating an "address book" of providers who can receive messages and ensuring the privacy and security of the messages. Having Direct capabilities would be an important intermediate interoperability goal.

Case Study 4-3 (right) illustrates the challenges of establishing a clinical data exchange, even under relatively idealized circumstances.

CASE STUDY 4-3. CLINICAL DATA EXCHANGE IN THE MASSACHUSETTS eHEALTH COLLABORATIVE

The Massachusetts eHealth Collaborative[1] was established in 2004 with $50 million in support provided by the health insurer Blue Cross of Massachusetts to galvanize improvement in safety, quality, and efficiency across the state. Three communities were selected from around the state to participate. The aim of the collaborative was to get the providers to adopt EHRs in the ambulatory setting and to establish clinical data exchanges in the three communities with the goal of improving care.

The first practice went "live" in March 2006, and in the subsequent 18 months, 97% of the nearly 600 participating physicians were using EHRs. However, implementing a health information exchange was more challenging, particularly for two of the communities, Brockton and Newburyport. These two communities selected three EHR vendors, all of whom had agreed to represent key categories of data in standard ways. The communities also brought in another vendor to establish the data exchanges, but the vendors struggled in those efforts. Although they eventually succeeded (with considerable assistance from the collaborative itself), funding had run out, and the communities were unwilling to provide support to keep the exchange running. The greatest challenge was differences among vendors in how key data elements were working. In the third community, North Adams, all providers elected to use the same EHR, and the data exchange was successful, with more than 95% of patients opting in. However, levels of use even in this setting were modest.

Reference

1. The Massachusetts eHealth Collaborative: *Home Page.* http://www.maehc.org/ (accessed Sep. 23, 2011).

Getting Value from Health Information Technology

EHRs offer significant potential for improving the quality, safety, and efficiency of health care because they affect the day-to-day and "minute-to-minute" work of physicians and other clinicians, as reflected in the following examples:

- *Clinicians need to access patient data to make diagnostic and therapeutic decisions.* An EHR can provide data access in a timelier manner than a paper-based system and can also organize the data in a way that effectively supports decision making.

- *Physicians document many of their decisions as orders.* Whereas paper-based ordering systems are relatively unconstrained environments, computer order entry applications can help ensure legibility, completeness, rapid communication to ancillary departments, and other features to facilitate optimal care.

- *Clinicians document their findings in clinical notes.* Paper-based notes are available at only one location at a time and may be lost or have other limitations. Notes entered through an interactive application have the potential to be more complete, to be available in multiple locations, and to include data for analysis. Clinical documentation is complex, with myriad issues, and the transition from paper to computerized notes—although it solves the legibility issue and makes notes easier to find—also presents problems with finding information. The potential for clinical notes to improve care has recently been addressed,[30] although software for many EHR systems does not yet include many of the features that will eventually be helpful.

- *Health care is information intensive, but it is also communication intensive.* Examples of communications needs in health care include primary care physician to specialist, physician to nurse, nurse to pharmacist, and even physician to patient. Paper-based medical records do little to support communication among members of the health care team, whereas EHRs can significantly facilitate communication.

Also, EHRs can provide clinical decision support, which paper-based medical records systems cannot support at all. Wright et al. have laid out a framework for clinical decision support[31] that consists of the following:

- *Work-flow support to support standardization and reliability*—as in order sets and support for medication reconciliation

- *Real-time (synchronous) data-entry checking*—as in drug–drug and drug–allergy checking, ensuring that baseline laboratory tests have been ordered when a medication is ordered, and dosing decision support (such as dose-range checking)

- *Flags to clinicians about important abnormal laboratory results*—as in automated notification for low-potassium and low-glucose results

- *Health maintenance alerts to support primary- and secondary-disease prevention*—as in reminders when the patient is due for a Pap smear, mammogram, cholesterol, or A1C test.

- *"Hot links" to reference information*—as in linking to a monograph describing indications, side effects, and other medication information.

Despite the potential benefits from HIT, and particularly EHRs, they are from automatic. The literature has shown conflicting results about the impact of EHRs on the cost and quality of care, as illustrated in the following examples:

- In 2006 Chaudhry et al. reviewed the literature to assess the impact of HIT on the quality, efficiency, and cost of medical care.[32] In their assessment of 257 studies, the authors noted modest quality and efficiency benefits but minimal impact on costs. Approximately 25% of the studies were from four academic institutions that implemented internally developed systems; only 9 studies evaluated multifunctional, commercially developed systems.

- In 2009 a survey of 41 hospitals in Texas found an association between the adoption of technology and lower mortality rates, costs, and complications.[33]

- In 2011 a systematic review of 53 other studies found a "gap between the postulated and demonstrated benefits" of HIT.[34] The authors noted that evidence for cost-effectiveness was weak and, even when present, might not be generalizable.

- In 2011 an analysis of claims data in the ambulatory setting found minimal association between EHRs and improved quality, regardless of whether the EHRs included clinical decision support.[35]

- In 2011 a systematic review of the literature found that 92% of the recent articles on HIT "were positive overall."[36]

These conflicting results highlight some of the challenges in deriving lessons from the research on the impact of EHRs on quality and cost. Yet studies on the impact of EHRs often have important methodological limitations, such as the following:

- Many studies look at correlation rather than causality.[37]

- The measures that have been examined might not have been amenable to the interventions being studied. For example, if the clinical decision support was not targeting the quality measures that were the focus of the study, it would not be surprising that it was not shown to have an impact on those measures.[37]

- For many studies relating to the impact of EHRs on quality, information regarding the extent to which the EHR was actually used by the clinician, the extent of system training the clinician received, what kind of clinical decision support was built into the system, and whether that clinical decision support was in fact being used may not be available.[37]

- The studies did not take into account to what extent data from external sources are available to the physician as part of the EHR.[38]

- It may be the "human element" rather than the technology per se that leads to benefits from HIT. Buntin et al.[36] noted the importance of strong leadership and staff buy-in if benefits from health IT are to be realized.

Finally, care must be taken to ensure that the technology itself does not introduce new risks into the health care environment. Ash et al. have noted that unintended consequences may arise from the implementation of EHRs, and these need to be monitored and managed.[39] Examples of such unintended consequences include the following:

- Changes in work patterns, such as the need to enter data, respond to alerts, and deal with passwords, which include potential mismatches between the EHR and the extant work flow

- The need to address requests for enhancements on an ongoing basis

- The persistence of paper and the need to manage a mixed paper and automated environment

- Changes in communication patterns, such as a decreased need for a clinician to physically come to the floor, thereby reducing the opportunities for informal communication among members of the care team

- Frustration and other negative emotions

associated with the requirement to work with technology that may not always be functioning optimally

- The possibility of new kinds of errors, such as "juxtaposition" errors resulting from picking the wrong item off a drop-down list
- A decrease in physicians' sense of autonomy, reflecting the requirement that they follow standardized processes
- A dependence on technology requiring data backups

Sittig and Singh have noted that implementations of HIT should pay attention to the quality of the software, the hardware, the clinical content of the system, the user interface, the personnel who are implementing the system, the organizational characteristics (that is, the leadership structures and the approach to project management), and the monitoring of the system.[40] The regulatory environment also has an impact on the quality of the implementation.

The U.S. Agency for Health Care Research and Quality has recognized that human–computer interaction is an important contributor to obtaining the potential benefits of HIT. Toward that end, it chartered two analyses of EHR usability,[41,42] which yielded the following main principles:

- Well-designed systems are more likely to lead to care improvement.
- Existing efforts to evaluate EHR systems for best practices in information design are insufficient, and more work is needed in this area.
- Usability is a critical issue.
- Standards and guidelines for human–computer interaction are not available but would help contribute to user satisfaction with EHRs.

Problems HIT Can Create

Not only must the benefits that can accrue from HIT be considered, but also its unintended consequences. A number of studies have demonstrated that HIT can create many new problems as well as improve systems. For example, in one of their studies evaluating the unintended consequences of CPOE, Ash et al. found that unintended consequences relating to new work, more work, work-flow issues, system demands, communication, emotions, and dependence on the technology appeared most important.[43] Koppel et al., reporting about the role of CPOE in creating errors, found that a widely used CPOE system facilitated 22 different types of medication error risks.[44] However, they did not evaluate whether implementation of the system had increased or decreased the error rate. The key takeaway finding from this report is that any new technology can create new errors as well as prevent them and that it is essential to devote resources to tracking these errors and then systematically engineer them out. However, this may not be done effectively in all too many institutions.

As illustrated by the experience described in Case Study 4-4 (beginning below), it is essential for organizations implementing technologies such as CPOE to handle the sociotechnical issues associated with implementation as well as the technical ones.

CASE STUDY 4-4. APPLICATION OF COMMERCIAL COMPUTER ORDER ENTRY AT PITTSBURGH CHILDREN'S HOSPITAL

Pittsburgh Children's Hospital (Pittsburgh) implemented a commercial computerized provider order entry (CPOE) application.[1] Following implementation, providers in the pediatric ICU became concerned that implementation of the application had caused delays in care. They performed an analysis of data regarding children transferred in for special care and found that the mortality rate increased from 2.8% to 6.3% (odds ratio = 3.3) after introduction of the CPOE application. The authors' examination of the implementation revealed a number of issues. CPOE was introduced very rapidly—in six days, as opposed to a much more gradual implementation at many other institutions. After implementation, order entry was not allowed until the patient had actually entered the hospital and been logged into the system. Previously, the orders for many patients were written when they were en route to the hospital. After CPOE implementation, all the drugs, including the vasoactive drugs, were moved to the central pharmacy, yet the pharmacy was not allowed to process medication orders until after the patients' admissions were processed. Finally, many order sets—which are very quick to write—were not initially available. The net result was substantial delays in care delivery, which may have been responsible for the higher mortality rate. The institution's implementation process violated many of the standard principles for CPOE implementation. Notably, several other organizations have subsequently implemented CPOE and have found trends toward a lower mortality rate.[2]

References

1. Han Y.Y., et al.: Unexpected increased mortality after implementation of a commercially sold computerized physician order entry system. *Pediatrics* 116:1506–1512, Dec. 2005. Erratum in *Pediatrics* 117:594, Feb. 2006.
2. Del Beccaro M.A., et al.: Computerized provider order entry implementation: No association with increased mortality rates in an intensive care unit. *Pediatrics* 118:290–295, Jul. 2006.

In addition to these issues, a number of investigators have expressed other concerns about HIT and how they might be addressed. Many of the concerns relate to the failure of many systems to sufficiently address issues relating to cognitive support—that is, they do not address issues of data overload and do not optimally support decision making in data-intensive settings.[45] Other concerns relate to human factors: engineering and development. For example, Karsh et al. presented 12 HIT fallacies and their implications for design and implementation, which, if addressed, would help HIT result in desired quality and safety benefits more broadly.[46] Their key conclusion was that much more attention needs to be devoted to human factors issues in all systems if vendor systems in particular are to achieve the desired benefits. This might be accomplished in many ways, with the authors' suggestions ranging from incorporating human factors routinely into system design to prohibiting clauses in contracts that can prevent sharing of safety problems identified post-implementation ("hold harmless" clauses), which are clearly a problem. Karsh et al. implied that more regulation of HIT software might be beneficial, as is the case in the device industry; we, among others, disagree about the degree to which regulation would be helpful to versus stifling innovation.[47] The U.S. Food and Drug Administration is actively considering this issue,[48] and an Institute of Medicine panel is expected to make its recommendations soon concerning the potential effects of government policies and private-sector actions in maximizing patient safety and avoiding medical errors through HIT.[49]

HOW HEALTH INFORMATION TECHNOLOGY CAN BE USED TO IMPROVE SAFETY

HIT can improve safety in a variety of ways. Although the evidence is strongest for improvement of medication safety, HIT can also be helpful for improving handoffs and for ensuring that laboratory results receive appropriate follow-up.[50] Some of the specific technologies that can improve safety include CPOE; bar coding; smart monitoring, which is monitoring that the computer performs with notification to a provider when appropriate; computerized notification about critical test results; computerized monitoring for adverse drug events; and tracking of abnormal test results. A number of meta-analyses now confirm that CPOE reduces medication error rates,[51–53] and most suggest that it also reduces the frequency of preventable adverse drug events. The evidence for bar coding has been less robust, but recent studies from Brigham and Women's Hospital (Boston), as described in Case Study 4-5 (beginning on this page), also suggest that it is extremely helpful for reducing dispensing- and administration-error rates. Work from LDS Hospital (Salt Lake City) first demonstrated that providers would treat critical test results more rapidly if the results were communicated directly to the responsible providers.[54] Outside the hospital, tracking important laboratory results is particularly important, and providers need tools to identify them and to ensure that they receive appropriate attention.[55]

CASE STUDY 4-5. HEALTH INFORMATION TECHNOLOGY INNOVATIONS SUPPORTING SAFETY AT BRIGHAM AND WOMEN'S HOSPITAL

Brigham and Women's Hospital has implemented a series of innovations that leverage HIT to improve safety. CPOE was implemented beginning in 1995. It initially included only a low level of clinical decision support, but nonetheless a 55% decrease in the serious medication-error rate was found post-implementa-

tion, with a more than 80% reduction in the overall medication-error rate.[1] Subsequently, a series of additions, such as dosing support for renal dosing[2] and medication dosing in the elderly,[3] have been made to the decision support. More recently, bar coding was added and was shown to reduce the potential adverse drug event rate related to dispensing errors by 63%.[4] Subsequently, bar coding reduced administration errors by 51%.[5] Furthermore, bar coding is highly cost-effective; it paid for itself in the first year.[6] An array of other technologies, including smart pumps and computerized monitoring for adverse drug events, has been implemented.

Another evaluation indicated that about 25% of the time when a patient had a critically abnormal laboratory test result, addressing it took longer than six hours. An approach was then implemented in which the responsible provider was directly paged with the test result.[7] The time that patients spent in life-threatening conditions then decreased, and there was a trend toward a lower mortality rate in the intervention group. The approach overall that the organization has taken has been to identify technologies with promise for improving safety and then to formally test the most important ones. Many, but not all, have been beneficial, and overall the technologies have had substantial impact on the safety of care, particularly for medication safety, which, as stated, has been generally true elsewhere.

References

1. Bates D.W., et al.: Effect of computerized physician order entry and a team intervention on prevention of serious medication errors. *JAMA* 280:1311–1316, Oct. 21, 1998.
2. Chertow G.M., et al.: Guided medication dosing for inpatients with renal insufficiency. *JAMA* 286:2839–2844, Dec. 12, 2001.
3. Peterson J.F., et al.: Guided prescription of psychotropic medications for geriatric inpatients. *Arch Intern Med* 165:802–807, Apr. 11, 2005.

4. Poon E.G., et al.: Medication dispensing errors and potential adverse drug events before and after implementing bar code technology in the pharmacy. *Ann Intern Med* 145:426–434, Sep. 19, 2006.
5. Poon E.G., et al.: Effect of bar-code technology on the safety of medication administration. *N Engl J Med* 362:1698–1707, May 6, 2010.
6. Maviglia S.M., et al.: Cost-benefit analysis of a hospital pharmacy bar code solution. *Arch Intern Med* 167:788–794, Apr. 23, 2007.
7. Kuperman G.J., et al.: Improving response to critical laboratory results with automation: Results of a randomized controlled trial. *J Am Med Inform Assoc* 6:512–522, Nov.–Dec. 1999.

HOW HEALTH INFORMATION TECHNOLOGY CAN BE USED TO IMPROVE QUALITY

HIT can be used in two different aspects of QI: (1) as a way to improve the measurement of quality and (2) as an intervention for the improvement of quality.

Using Health Information Technology to Improve Quality Measurement

Ancillary departmental systems, such as laboratory and pharmacy systems, in clinical settings have largely been automated for decades. However, EHRs are now making an increasing amount of clinical data, such as data related to ordering and documentation, available in automated form. The meaningful use criteria require that calculating and reporting the measures needs to be done using certified technology.[26] However, they do not mandate that the certified system capture all the data necessary for quality measure calculations; organizations are free to capture the data using noncertified systems. Provider organizations may need to go beyond the meaningful use criteria for data collection per se to have sufficient data to fulfill the clinical decision support objectives.

The certification criteria also advance the use of standard representation of medical terminology, which helps standardize the way that quality-related data are captured and reported. Notably, the meaningful use program is increasing the prevalence of EHRs and, thus, automated data in the ambulatory environment, which has heretofore been largely paper based.

The Stage 1 meaningful use criteria dictate specific quality measures, such as time from ED arrival to admit decision and ED departure, the care of stroke patients (for example, discharge on antithrombotics, anticoagulation for patients on a-fib/flutter, thrombolytics for patients arriving within two hours of symptom onset, antithrombotic therapy by end of day 2 for patients determined to have ischemic stroke), and measures related to venous thromboembolism (VTE) prophylaxis and treatment (for example, VTE prophylaxis for surgical patients within 24 hours of arrival, prophylaxis for ICU patients, adequate overlap of IV and oral therapy, platelet monitoring for patients on heparin). Subsequent phases of the meaningful use program will identify additional measures that need to be captured and reported. In many cases, however, health care provider organizations, particularly large ones, will want to capture additional data to support internal QI initiatives.[56] For example, a provider organization seeking to decrease the rate of falls among elderly patients may want to capture data on patients' mental status, while an organization wishing to track adverse drug events may want to know when the patients have experienced nausea. Although the prospect of capturing coded data elements via clinical documentation is appealing, asking clinicians to enter substantial amounts of data in coded form can be challenging—physicians and other clinicians generally recoil against such requests. Provider organizations that want clinicians to enter coded data need to limit the requests to a small number of high-leverage initiatives. Emerging capabilities, such as natural language processing, have the potential to obviate the need for capturing so much data in coded fashion.

To support robust quality measurement, data from multiple sources are aggregated onto a common platform, usually referred to as a data warehouse. Developing a data warehouse is costly, includes substantial technical challenges, and requires the involvement of persons experienced in data analysis and quality measurement. For its own data warehouse initiative, as part of a broad and multifaceted approach to QI, Denver Health (Colorado) created the position of a medical director for biostatistics to ensure that measurement, monitoring, and reporting of data were managed appropriately.[57] A QI initiative at Legacy Health (Portland, Oregon), which also entailed a data warehouse, also committed substantial resources to the display and reporting of quality metrics.[58]

In addition to having the technical capabilities to capture and report data on quality measures, organizations must focus on which quality measures are most important. Clearly, certain measures will need to be captured to support regulatory and accreditation requirements. However, other measures may be selected to support internal quality initiatives. The latter category should receive significant attention only when it is part of a QI program that includes measurement, a commitment to reengineering and education of relevant personnel, and the support of senior management. Clearly, any organization can undertake only a finite number of initiatives that require these kinds of resources, so the focus should be established before the initiative begins.

Using Health Information Technology to Improve Quality

As mentioned, EHRs have the potential to improve quality, because they fundamentally change the way that clinicians do their work. Several examples demonstrate the use of EHRs with clinical decision support in the inpatient and outpatient settings in improving clinicians' ability to track laboratory results[59]; improving compliance with guidelines[60,61]; improving response to critical laboratory results[62]; decreasing use of vancomycin in the inpatient setting[63]; decreasing adverse event rates, costs, and days of unnecessary antibiotics[64]; and improving compliance with dosing in renal insufficiency.[65] The meaningful use program, which entails the use of clinical decision support to improve quality, should increase the prevalence of EHRs in several settings.

However, as has been discussed previously, simply having electronic systems in place does not guarantee QI. Electronic systems must be implemented thoughtfully and configured to be easy to use and to support critical work-flow processes. In addition, the challenges of the modern health care environment go beyond optimizing care in a single health care environment. To get the most out of HIT, capabilities must be developed to optimize and coordinate the care of patients across settings.[66] Such capabilities include support for team-based care, the use of registries, and support for direct interaction with patients. The use of EHRs must be dovetailed with organizational commitments to improve care that include process reengineering, education of staff, communications strategies, leadership, development of the appropriate culture, alignment with reimbursement approaches, and perhaps changes to the physical clinical environment.[57] Grassroots involvement—including, for example, physicians, nurses, IT staff, laboratory staff, respiratory therapists, and rehabilitation therapists—is also a prerequisite for a successful EHR implementation.

In summary, EHRs with clinical decision support are necessary tools for the modern health care provider organization to improve quality, but they are not sufficient. HIT must be a thoughtful component of a comprehensive approach to the improvement of quality, safety, and efficiency.

Large integrated delivery systems, particularly those that serve as the health plan for some of or all the patients they track, have incentives and opportunities to reengineer care to be more effective and efficient. Two organizations that have done so are Kaiser Permanente and Geisinger Health System; both have made HIT a cornerstone of their efforts. At these organizations, HIT is used to improve the ability to measure the current state ("Improve Quality Measurement") and to improve quality and efficiency ("Improve Quality"). Case studies are provided—Case Study 4-6 (Geisinger Health System, below) and Case Study 4-7 (Kaiser Permanente, pages 104–105).

CASE STUDY 4-6. GEISINGER HEALTH SYSTEM

Geisinger is a health system in Pennsylvania with $2.5 billion of annual revenue with a fully integrated EHR that serves 37 community practice sites, 2 hospitals, and 6 work- and retail site–based clinics. Geisinger Health Plan accounts for 30% of the care delivered by Geisinger Health System (Danville, Pennsylvania). The EHR includes a personal health record that has more than 160,000 active patients. In addition, 2,600 non-Geisinger physicians use EHRs that have the ability to interact with the core Geisinger information systems.[1]

Geisinger's strategy is to achieve HIT–enabled clinical transformation through the management of data, performance measurement, and the development, implementation, and iterative improvement of best care practices.[2] Geisinger has labeled this approach "ProvenHealth."[3,4] ProvenHealth consists of five components: patient-centered primary care, integrated population management, focused systems of care (for example, referral networks), reliance on measurement of quality outcomes, and value-based reimbursement. HIT is a critical aspect of each component. For example, order sets are used to drive best practices in the primary care setting, communications tools facilitate referrals, and quality measures are obtained from EHR–derived data. Costs, admissions, patient satisfaction, and quality measures (including clinical outcomes, such as complication rates) have all improved under ProvenHealth.

Yet despite the benefits realized from ProvenHealth, it is important to realize that the role of HIT is only one facet. More important is the commitment to searching for opportunities for quality and efficiency improvement and reengineering the work flow to capture the potential improvement. The reengineering efforts are nontrivial and require vocal support from senior leaders, as well as sustained and coordinated efforts by managers at all levels.

References

1. Graf T.R.: Higher quality, lower cost: Geisinger's ability to leverage high tech and high touch solutions. Keynote address presented at the American College of Medical Informatics Annual Symposium, Bonita Springs, FL. Feb. 3–6, 2011.
2. Paulus R.A., Davis K., Steele G.D.: Continuous innovation in health care: Implications of the Geisinger experience. *Health Aff (Millwood)* 27:1235–1245, Sep.–Oct. 2008.
3. Steele G.D., et al.: How Geisinger's advanced medical home model argues the case for rapid-cycle innovation. *Health Aff (Millwood)* 29:2047–2053, Nov. 2010.
4. Gilfillan R.J., et al.: Value and the medical home: Effects of transformed primary care. *Am J Manag Care* 16:607–614, Aug. 2010.

CASE STUDY 4-7. KAISER PERMANENTE

Kaiser Permanente is an integrated delivery system and health plan, with annual revenue of $42 billion, that delivers care to 8.6 million members in nine states and in Washington, D.C. Kaiser includes 14,000 physicians and 166,000 employees (41,000 of whom are nurses). Kaiser has committed $4 billion (total 10-year operating cost) to its EHR implementation, which is known as KP HealthConnect. This EHR initiative, which is the world's largest private-sector deployment of an EHR, is targeted at the improvement of quality, service, and effectiveness. KP HealthConnect supports Kaiser's vision of an integrated and tailored care environment that supports secure and seamless transitions among multiple members of the health care team to support a patient-centric view of health care; this model explicitly includes the patient, the patient's family, and community resources as parts of the system of care.[1]

The KP HealthConnect suite interacts with other parts of the Kaiser IT infrastructure, including ancillary departmental systems, the health plan's claims processing systems, and the organization's financial systems, to provide a comprehensive information platform.[2] KP HealthConnect includes a data warehouse for analytical purposes and a personal health record, MyHealthManager, to support direct interaction of patients.[3,4] More than 50% of adult patients with Internet access make use of online features offered by Kaiser.[1] In 2010, 3.3 million Kaiser patients made 85 million online self-care visits, sent more than 10 million messages, looked up results 25 million times, and requested 8.3 million prescription refills.

Like Geisinger, Kaiser also has a vision of creating data-based, measurement-oriented, HIT–enabled, reengineered best practices that are developed iteratively over time. This approach is embodied in its primary care "Care Innovation Project," which is designed to leverage HIT to improve outcomes, increase patient satisfaction, and optimize resource use. The EHR, the personal health record, tools to support panel management (for example, registries), predictive modeling tools, and a library of automated knowledge resources (for example, calculators and access to reference materials) are all part of the approach.

Online interactions and telephone interactions, including "scheduled telephone visits," account for more than 40% of patient–provider interactions at Kaiser. The Kaiser patient panel management tools allow patients to be sorted by the extent to which a measurable gap exists between the care interventions that the patient has received and ideal care. For example, a patient who is out of compliance on two quality measures would be higher on the list than the patient who is out of compliance on one measure. Kaiser clinicians can easily toggle from a registry view to a patient-specific view to get more detail and make decisions about appropriate action. Cumulative reports can indicate the compliance of the entire cohort of patients with expected measures. Kaiser is beginning to extend this model of innovative care from the primary care setting to several specialty settings.

Kaiser contends that when compared with peer organizations, it demonstrates excellent performance in a number of quality measures in a number of its regions, demonstrating the effectiveness of these initiatives. Kaiser acknowledges that a strong sense of vision and senior-leadership support, broad management and clinical engagement, a commitment to reengineering of care delivery, and an ability to execute these activities at an operational level in a way that dovetails with other key programs are critical success factors.

References

1. Liang L.: Using the EHR to transform care delivery. Keynote address presented at the American College of Medical Informatics Annual Symposium, Bonita Springs, FL, Feb. 4, 2011.
2. Chen C., et al.: The Kaiser Permanente Electronic Health Record: Transforming and streamlining modalities of care. *Health Aff (Millwood)* 28:323–333, Mar.–Apr. 2009.
3. Zhou Y.Y., et al.: Patient access to an electronic health record with secure messaging: Impact on primary care utilization. *Am J Manag Care* 13:418–424, Jul. 2007.
4. Zhou Y.Y., et al.: Improved quality at Kaiser Permanente through e-mail between physicians and patients. *Health Aff (Millwood)* 29:1370–1375, Jul. 2010.

Kaiser and Geisinger have advantages when it comes to designing comprehensive care redesign programs. Kaiser is an integrated delivery system for almost all its members. This means that it manages the work environment of its providers and has an excellent chance to manage the work flows and the information systems. Similarly, although it is not as "closed" a system as Kaiser, Geisinger has strong administrative relationships with many of the providers in its network. For example, Kaiser serves as the health plan for its members, which allows it to directly realize the financial benefits of efficiencies it creates. Geisinger also provides a health plan for a substantial proportion of its members and is able to realize those financial benefits. Further, Geisinger extends the lessons that it learns from optimizing the care of its health plan members to all the patients that it cares for.

One of the unknowns in health system delivery reform is whether "virtual" coordinated organizations, such as accountable care organizations, will be able to manage care as tightly as such organizations as Kaiser and Geisinger, which are structurally well positioned to create efficiencies.

KEY MESSAGES TO LEADERS

In this section, we provide key messages for leaders who are working to advance innovative health system delivery reform in their organizations and their communities. Realizing the benefits of HIT that we have described in this chapter entails many challenges, and quality leaders must be bold in their willingness to disrupt the status quo and identify innovative approaches to care and QI.

Leadership Inside Organizations

From the perspective of leadership, it is imperative that the domains of safety and quality receive high priority within the organization—as reflected, for example, in the extent to which they become core concerns for boards of trustees. The attention paid to these areas by the chief executive officer is particularly important, and hospitals that have board involvement in quality and safety generally deliver higher-quality care.[67] Leaders need to recognize that HIT represents a key platform for measuring and improving safety and quality. HIT should play an increasingly important role as pressure grows to improve the integration and coordination of care, as reflected, for example, in the necessary information sharing between primary care physicians and other physicians involved in the care of the patient and hospital-based caregivers. Quality leaders, such as Geisinger and Kaiser, have already begun to make these investments.

Leadership and Dealing with the Outside World

The landscape of health information exchange is evolving rapidly. The growing imperative to make care more efficient, as reflected, for example, in the incentives implicit in planned changes in reimbursement policies in the United States, should encourage provider organizations to engage in data-sharing initiatives. Some of those initiatives may be proprietary—for example, creating an exchange only with key business partners—whereas others may be regional (or perhaps, in the United States, statewide). The meaningful use incentives are intended to advance the native data-exchange capabilities of EHRs. In other countries, national approaches have had mixed success at best. Central approaches that rely on incentives appear to have worked better than those that have used heavier-handed approaches, with more central planning. Few successes have emerged to date anywhere with respect to clinical data exchange, so this is the hardest area to predict. Leaders should follow this landscape carefully. The key driver will be the organization's business strategy and the extent to which the organization views interaction with other provider organizations as critical to its success. Whatever the nature of the organization's health information exchange strategy—and it should have one—the organization should ensure that it is sufficiently flexible and agile so it can accommodate changing conditions.

CONCLUSION

In spite of increasing incentives for adoption, the extent to which quality and safety will be improved through HIT in the near term remains unclear. Organizations that want to maximize improvement will need to ensure that their HIT includes features such as registries and population management tools for clinical decision support and care coordination. Successful organizations will recognize that HIT requires ongoing attention and continuous improvement and that, no matter how carefully it is implemented, it is likely to produce unintended consequences that will require remediation. Clinical data exchange should be highly beneficial eventually, but many hurdles will need to be surmounted in the near term. This is an exceptionally exciting time with respect to HIT, which should represent a powerful tool for improving quality and safety—and efficiency.

The authors thank Stephanie Pollard for her superb assistance with preparation of this chapter.

References

1. Health Information Technology for Economic and Clinical Health (HITECH) Act. Title XIII of Division A and Title IV of Division B of the American Recovery and Reinvestment Act (ARRA) of 2009, Pub. L No.111-5, Feb. 17, 2009.

2. U.S. Department of Health & Human Services, Centers for Medicare & Medicaid Services (CMS): *Electronic Health Record Incentive Program.* Washington, DC: CMS, 2010.

3. Blumenthal D.: Launching HITECH. *N Engl J Med* 362:382–385, Feb. 4, 2010.

4. Linder J.A., et al.: Electronic health record use and the quality of ambulatory care in the United States. *Arch Intern Med* 167:1400–1405, Jul. 9, 2007.

5. Patient Protection and Affordable Care Act (PPACA) of 2010. Pub. L. No. 111–148, Mar. 23, 2010.

6. U.S. Department of Health & Human Services: *Partnership for Patients: Better Care, Lower Costs.* Apr. 12, 2011. http://www.healthcare.gov/center/programs/partnership (accessed Sep. 23, 2011).

7. Jha A.K., et al.: The use of health information technology in seven nations. *Int J Med Inform* 77:848–854, Dec. 2008.

8. Nolte E., McKee C.M.: Measuring the health of nations: Updating an earlier analysis. *Health Aff (Millwood)* 27:58–71, Jan.–Feb. 2008.

9. U.S. Department of Health & Human Services (DHHS), Office of the Inspector General: *Adverse Events in Hospitals: National Incidence Among Medicare Beneficiaries.* Washington, DC: DHHS, 2010.

10. McGlynn E.A., et al.: The quality of health care delivered to adults in the United States. *N Engl J Med* 348:2635–2645, Jun. 26, 2003.

11. Shojania K.G., et al.: Effects of quality improvement strategies for type 2 diabetes on glycemic control: A meta-regression analysis. *JAMA* 296:427–440, Jul. 26, 2006.

12. Mangione C.M., et al.: The association between quality of care and the intensity of diabetes disease management programs. *Ann Intern Med* 145:107–116, Jul. 18, 2006.

13. Shojania K.G., et al.: Effect of point-of-care computer reminders on physician behaviour: A systematic

review. *CMAJ* 182:E216–E225, Mar. 23, 2010.

14. Zhou L., et al.: The relationship between electronic health record use and quality of care over time. *J Am Med Inform Assoc* 16:457–464, Jul.–Aug. 2009.

15. Jha A.K., et al.: Use of electronic health records in U.S. hospitals. *N Engl J Med* 360:1628–1638, Apr. 16, 2009.

16. Jha A.K., et al.: A progress report on electronic health records in U.S. hospitals. *Health Aff (Millwood)* 29:1951–1957, Oct. 2010.

17. DesRoches C.M., et al.: Electronic health records in ambulatory care—a national survey of physicians. *N Engl J Med* 359:50–60, Jul. 3, 2008.

18. Rozenblum R., et al.: A qualitative study of Canada's experience with the implementation of electronic health information technology. *CMAJ* 183:E281–E288, Mar. 22, 2011.

19. Mosquera M.: U.S., Europe will cooperate on EHR exchange standards. *Government Health IT,* Dec. 21, 2010. http://govhealthit.com/news/us-europe-will -cooperate-ehr-exchange-standards (accessed Sep. 23, 2011).

20. European Commission, Information Society: *eHealth Governance Initiative.* http://ec.europa.eu/ information_society/activities/health/policy/ehealth_ governance_initiative/index_en.htm (accessed Sep. 23, 2011).

21. Smith P.C., et al.: Missing clinical information during primary care visits. *JAMA* 293:565–571, Feb. 2, 2005.

22. Stiell A., et al.: Prevalence of information gaps in the emergency department and the effect on patient outcomes. *CMAJ* 169:1023–1028, Nov. 11, 2003.

23. World Health Organization: *International Classification for Patient Safety (ICPS).* http://www.who.int/ entity/patientsafety/taxonomy/icps_statement_of_ purpose.pdf (accessed Sep. 23, 2011).

24. eHealth Initiative: *Home Page.* http://www.ehealthinitiative.org/ (accessed Sep. 23, 2011).

25. Adler-Milstein J., Bates D.W., Jha A.K.: U.S. Regional health information organizations: Progress and challenges. *Health Aff (Millwood)* 28:483–492, Mar.–Apr. 2009.

26. Blumenthal D., Tavenner M.: The "meaningful use" regulation for electronic health records. *N Engl J Med* 363:501–504, Aug. 5, 2010.

27. U.S. Department of Health & Human Services, Office of the National Coordinator for Health Information Technology: HIT Policy Committee Meaningful Use Workgroup: Presentation. May 11, 2011. http://healthit.hhs.gov/portal/server.pt/gateway/ PTARGS_0_12811_954628_0_0_18/hitpc-mu -presentation-05-11-11.ppt.

28. U.S. Department of Health & Human Services, Office of the National Coordinator for Health Information Technology: *State Health Information Exchange Cooperative Agreement Program.* http://healthit.hhs.gov/portal/server.pt?open

=512&objID=1488&mode=2 (last accessed May 25, 2011).

29. U.S. Department of Health & Human Services, Office of the National Coordinator for Health Information Technology: *Direct Project.* http://healthit.hhs.gov/ portal/server.pt/community/healthit_hhs_ gov_direct _project/3338 (accessed Sep. 23, 2011).

30. Schiff G.D., Bates D.W.: Can electronic clinical documentation help prevent diagnostic errors? *N Engl J Med* 362:1066–1069, Mar. 25, 2010.

31. Wright A., et al.: A description and functional taxonomy of rule-based decision support content at a large integrated delivery network. *J Am Med Inform Assoc* 14:489–496, Jul.–Aug. 2007.

32. Chaudhry B., et al.: Systematic review: Impact of health information technology on quality, efficiency, and costs of medical care. *Ann Intern Med* 144:742–752, May 16, 2006.

33. Amarasingham R., et al.: Clinical information technologies and inpatient outcomes: A multiple hospital study. *Arch Intern Med* 169:108–114, Jan. 26, 2009.

34. Black A.D., et al.: The impact of eHealth on the quality and safety of health care: A systematic overview. *PLoS Med* 8:e1000387, Jan. 18, 2011.

35. Romano M.J., Stafford R.S.: Electronic health records and clinical decision support systems: Impact on national ambulatory care quality. *Arch Intern Med* 171:897–903, May 23, 2011.

36. Buntin M.B., et al.: The benefits of health information technology: A review of the recent literature shows predominantly positive results. *Health Aff (Millwood)* 30:464–471, Mar. 2011.

37. Hersh W.: Electronic health records do not impact the quality of healthcare? *Informatics Professor,* Jan. 26, 2011. http://informaticsprofessor.blogspot.com/ 2011_01_01_archive.html (accessed Sep. 23, 2011).

38. McDonald C., Abhyankar S.: Clinical decision support and rich clinical repositories: A symbiotic relationship: Comment on "Electronic health records and clinical decision support systems." *Arch Intern Med* 171:903–905, May 23, 2011.

39. Ash J.S., et al.: The unintended consequences of computerized provider order entry: Findings from a mixed methods exploration. *Int J Med Inform* 78(suppl. 1):S69–S76, Apr. 2009.

40. Sittig D.F., Singh H.: Eight rights of safe electronic health record use. *JAMA* 302:1111–1113, Sep. 9, 2009.

41. U.S. Agency for Healthcare Research and Quality: *Electronic Health Record Usability: Evaluation and Use Case Framework.* Oct. 2009. http://healthit.ahrq.gov/ portal/server.pt/community/ahrq_national_resource _center_for_health_it/650 (accessed Sep. 23, 2011).

42. U.S. Agency for Healthcare Research and Quality: *Electronic Health Record Usability: Interface Design Considerations.* Oct. 2009. http://healthit.ahrq.gov/ portal/server.pt/community/ahrq_national_resource_ center_for_health_it/650 (accessed Sep. 23, 2011).

43. Ash J.S., et al.: The extent and importance of un-intended consequences related to computerized provider order entry. *J Am Med Inform Assoc* 14:415–423, Jul.–Aug. 2007.

44. Koppel R., et al.: Role of computerized physician order entry systems in facilitating medication errors. *JAMA* 293:1197–1203, Mar. 9, 2005.

45. National Research Council: *Computational Technology for Effective Health Care: Immediate Steps and Strategic Directions.* Washington, DC: National Academies Press, 2009.

46. Karsh B.T., et al.: Health information technology: Fallacies and sober realities. *J Am Med Inform Assoc* 17:617–623, Nov.–Dec. 2010.

47. Kuperman G.J., et al.: Medication-related clinical decision support in computerized provider order entry systems: A review. *J Am Med Inform Assoc* 14:29–40, Jan.–Feb. 2007.

48. Devices: General Hospital and Personal Use Devices. Reclassification of Medical Device Data Systems. *73 Fed. Reg. 7498,* Feb. 8, 2008.

49. U.S. Department of Health & Human Services: *Press Release: Institute of Medicine Will Study Best Policies and Practices for Improving Health Care Safety with Health Information Technology.* Sep. 29, 2010. http://www.hhs.gov/news/press/2010pres/09/20100929b.html (accessed Sep. 23, 2011).

50. Bates D.W., Gawande A.A.: Improving safety with information technology. *N Engl J Med* 348:2526–2534, Jun. 19, 2003.

51. Ash J.S., Stavri P.Z., Kuperman G.J.: A consensus statement on considerations for a successful CPOE implementation. *J Am Med Inform Assoc* 10:229–234, May–Jun. 2003.

52. Ammenwerth E., et al.: The effect of electronic prescribing on medication errors and adverse drug events: A systematic review. *J Am Med Inform Assoc* 15:585–600, Sep.–Oct. 2008.

53. Eslami S., de Keizer N.F., Abu-Hanna A.: The impact of computerized physician medication order entry in hospitalized patients: A systematic review. *Int J Med Inform* 77:365–376, Jun. 2008.

54. Tate K.E., Gardner R.M.: Computers, quality, and the clinical laboratory—A look at critical value reporting. *Proc Annu Symp Comput Appl Med Care* 193–197, 1993.

55. Poon E.G., et al.: "I wish I had seen this test result earlier!": Dissatisfaction with test result management systems in primary care. *Arch Intern Med* 164:2223–2228, Nov. 8, 2004.

56. Abbett S.K., Bates D.W., Kachalia A.: The meaningful use regulations in information technology: What do they mean for quality improvement in hospitals? *Jt Comm J Qual Patient Saf* 37:333–336, Jul. 2011.

57. Gabow P.A., Mehler P.S.: A broad and structured approach to improving patient safety and quality: Lessons from Denver Health. *Health Aff (Millwood)* 30:612–618, Apr. 2011.

58. Joyce J.S., et al.: Legacy Health's "Big Aims" initiative to improve patient safety reduced rates of infection and mortality among patients. *Health Aff (Millwood)* 30:619–627, Apr. 2011.

59. Poon E.G., et al.: Design and implementation of a comprehensive outpatient Results Manager. *J Biomed Inform* 36:80–91, Feb.–Apr. 2003.

60. Overhage J.M., et al.: A randomized trial of "corollary orders" to prevent errors of omission. *J Am Med Inform Assoc* 4:364–375, Sep.–Oct. 1997.

61. Shea S., DuMouchel W., Bahamonde L.: A meta-analysis of 16 randomized controlled trials to evaluate computer-based clinical reminder systems for preventive care in the ambulatory setting. *J Am Med Inform Assoc* 3:399–409, Nov.–Dec. 1996.

62. Kuperman G.J., et al.: Improving response to critical laboratory results with automation: Results of a randomized controlled trial. *J Am Med Inform Assoc* 6:512–522, Nov.–Dec. 1999.

63. Shojania K.G., et al.: Reducing vancomycin use utilizing a computer guideline: Results of a randomized controlled trial. *J Am Med Inform Assoc* 5:554–562, Nov.–Dec. 1998.

64. Evans R.S., et al.: A computer-assisted management program for antibiotics and other antiinfective agents. *N Engl J Med* 338:232–238, Jan. 22, 1998.

65. Chertow G.M., et al.: Guided medication dosing for inpatients with renal insufficiency. *JAMA* 286:2839–2844, Dec. 12, 2001.

66. Bates D.W., Bitton A.: The future of health information technology in the patient-centered medical home. *Health Aff (Millwood)* 29:614–621, Apr. 2010.

67. Jha A., Epstein A.: Hospital governance and the quality of care. *Health Aff (Millwood)* 29:182–187, Jan.–Feb. 2010.

CHAPTER 5

Engaging Patients in Patient Safety

Saul N. Weingart, M.D., Ph.D.

Suzanne picked up this month's prescriptions from the pharmacy late Friday afternoon, right on schedule. With HIV infection, you have to be careful about taking your medicines just so. She was meticulous about taking her drugs at the right time and in the right way: one stavudine tablet twice a day, one lamivudine tablet twice a day, and two indinavir tablets three times a day on an empty stomach with lots of water. Although they caused her an upset tummy and a small "beer belly," it was a small price to pay. This was her lifeline.

What's going on here? she wondered, when she saw two unfamiliar drug names on the pill bottles. She called her physician right away, and he agreed that Stelazine (an antipsychotic medication used for schizophrenia) and ranitidine (an antihistamine medication used to treat heartburn and prevent ulcers)—although they sounded like stavudine and lamivudine—were entirely wrong.

You can't be too careful, she thought.
—Adapted from Bates[1]

Patient safety is a public health problem throughout the world. In the original Harvard study of 30,000 patients at 51 hospitals in New York State in the 1980s, researchers discovered that about 4% of hospitalized patients suffered serious injuries as a result of their medical care and that the care of about one in four of these injured patients was substandard.[2,3] In replications in the United States, Canada, Europe, Australia, and New Zealand, researchers have confirmed these findings—about 5% to 10% of hospitalized patients suffer injuries, many preventable, as a result of the well-intentioned efforts of their health care providers.[4–10]

Improving patient safety has become a priority around the world, with efforts focused on reducing infections, using surgical checklists, and introducing information technology to improve medication safety.[11–13] Patient participation in patient safety has also been identified as a potentially important improvement strategy. As in the case of Suzanne, some patients have the capacity to serve as "vigilant partners," collaborating with health care providers to protect themselves from accidental injury.[14] At least three attributes account for patients' potential ability to contribute to their own safety: immediate knowledge of their symptoms and treatments, motivation to ensure that all goes well, and close proximity to care.[15]

To promote patient engagement, prominent health care organizations have developed promotional materials to encourage patient participation in patient safety. For example, The Joint Commission and Joint Commission International (JCI) standards for hospitals and other health care organizations promote patient participation in care.[16,17]*

---

* For example, Standard RI.01.02.01: The hospital respects the patient's right to participate in decisions about his or her care, treatment, and services; Standard RI.02.01.01: The hospital informs the patient about his or her responsibilities related to his or her care, treatment, and services. (The Joint Commission: *Comprehensive Accreditation Manual for Hospitals: The Official Handbook*. Oak Brook, IL: Joint Commission Resources, 2010.) The corresponding JCI standard is as follows: Standard PFR.2: The organization support patients' and families' rights to participate in the care process. (Joint Commission International: *Joint Commission International Standards for Hospitals*, 4th ed. Oak Brook, IL: Joint Commission Resources, 2010.)

Since 2002 The Joint Commission has encouraged organizations—also including ambulatory care, long term care, behavioral health care, and home care—to conduct "Speak Up" campaigns for patients and their families to ask pertinent questions (for example, about medications, tests, and procedures) and to take precautions to avoid errors and injuries.[18] The U.S. Agency for Healthcare Research and Quality (AHRQ) has recommended that patients take five actions to ensure safer care: ask questions, make a medication list, get test results, select the right hospital, and understand what will happen if surgery is needed.[19] Parallel efforts are evident worldwide. In Denmark, for example, the Danish Society for Patient Safety disseminated tips for patients about how to participate in their own care and a handbook for staying safe during a hospitalization.[20] The World Health Organization identified patient engagement in patient safety as a component of its patient safety program.[21]

Given its widespread endorsement, does evidence suggest that patient engagement can improve patient safety? Specifically, is there a coherent theory to explain how patient participation may help ensure safer care? Do we know if patients are willing to perform safety-oriented activities, and, if so, what conditions are necessary to facilitate their involvement? Are there data to support the notion that patients' efforts can lead to safer care? Finally, what kinds of programs can health care organizations develop to promote patient engagement? I now address each issue in turn.

UNDERSTANDING PATIENT ENGAGEMENT

Patients vary in their willingness and ability to participate in their own care. We know, for example, that up to 42% of medical inpatients become confused during a hospitalization.[22] To understand the possibilities inherent in patient engagement, we have to be mindful of its limits.

Conceptual Issues

Several conditions are necessary to allow patients and their loved ones to participate in safety-oriented activities. Figure 5-1 (page 111) presents a rudimentary framework.

First, patients must be able to identify potential problems in their environment. They must be awake and alert enough to observe their surroundings and understand what is going on around them. This requires physical capabilities, such as the ability to see and to hear, as well as cognitive capabilities. Patients who are delirious, demented, or sedated are generally unable to participate without the presence of an able surrogate. One has to learn quickly about normal procedures and routines to identify unanticipated deviations.

Second, patients must be able to communicate their concerns. For example, patients with limited English-language proficiency may find it difficult to communicate with providers who speak English only. Cultural norms about expressing concerns, reporting pain, or communicating freely with medical professionals can pose additional obstacles to free and effective communication. Motivation plays a role as well. If the patient is passive, indifferent, or depressed, he or she may have insufficient "energy" to act in a self-protective way.

Third, patients and their families must be prepared to act in ways that support safe care. Participation in clinical decision making ensures that one understands the risks and benefits of a particular course of care. More intrusive or confrontational actions, such as asking a provider to wash his or her hands, explain a recommended procedure, double-check the dose of a new

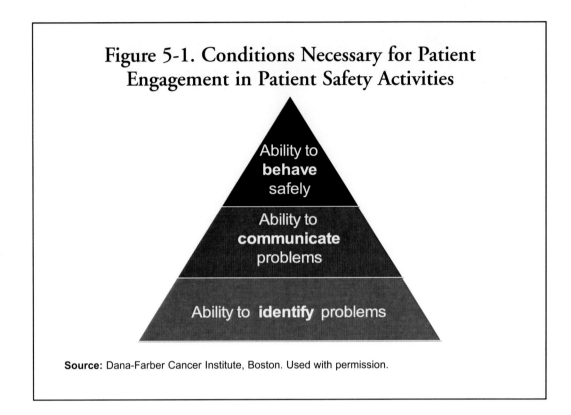

Figure 5-1. Conditions Necessary for Patient Engagement in Patient Safety Activities

Ability to **behave** safely

Ability to **communicate** problems

Ability to **identify** problems

Source: Dana-Farber Cancer Institute, Boston. Used with permission.

medication, interpret test results or side effects of treatment, or to expedite a consultation, require that patients and their families risk being perceived as difficult or "bad" patients. Active engagement requires one to believe that assertiveness will be tolerated by health care providers and effective at improving safety.

A patient's capacity to engage with practitioners is necessary but insufficient. Engagement is mediated by several factors that go beyond the attributes of the patient (*see* Figure 5-2, page 112). The patient's ability to participate in safety-oriented activities depends on the activities he or she is asked to perform, the professionals with whom he or she interacts, and the attributes of the health care organization itself. For example, some safety-oriented behaviors may require a high degree of health literacy and assertiveness, as in asking a physician to reconcile his or her recommendation with that of

another specialist. A patient's ability to communicate with staff members is dependent on the degree to which staff make themselves available, provide information, and invite questions and concerns. Patients who encounter language barriers or lack basic health care literacy may be better prepared to voice their concerns in organizations that support excellent interpreter services programs and cultural competency awareness training for staff members.

Empirical Studies

We can use empirical data to identify and understand factors that affect the willingness of a capable patient or surrogate to use safe practices. Several researchers have asked patients to assess their likelihood of using recommended patient safety practices, as well as their experiences of doing so. The results of these studies have been remarkably consistent. In a pioneering study, Hibbard et al. asked 195 subjects to

Figure 5-2. Factors Mediating Between Patients' Capacity for Engagement and Engagement Activities

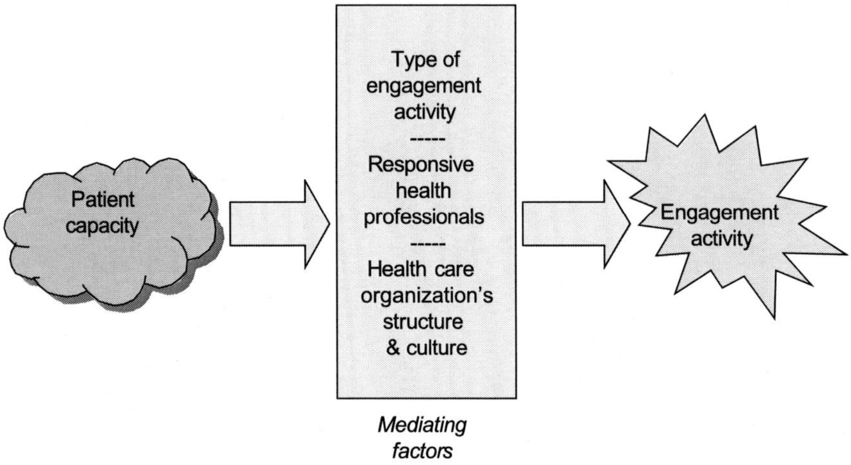

Patient capacity

Type of engagement activity

Responsive health professionals

Health care organization's structure & culture

Mediating factors

Engagement activity

Source: Dana-Farber Cancer Institute, Boston. Used with permission.

assess the perceived effectiveness of 14 recommended actions for preventing medical errors, such as making sure physicians are aware of the patient's medications and choosing a hospital with computerized order entry.[23] Subjects viewed most actions as likely to be effective in preventing medical errors. Respondents also indicated, however, that they were unlikely to perform certain activities, particularly those that required confrontation with a physician. Patients' perceived self-efficacy was an important predictor of the use of safety-oriented behaviors in the study.

Using a similar approach, Waterman and colleagues interviewed 2,078 patients discharged from 11 hospitals in the United States in 2003 about their comfort with and performance of error-prevention activities during a recent hospitalization.[24] Patients reported that they were very comfortable with the idea of performing

many activities, such as asking questions about medications and medical care, having family or friends watch for errors, reporting errors to the medical staff, helping mark surgical sites, and asking whether a medical staff member had washed his or her hands. Yet only a minority of the patients had actually taken these actions when hospitalized. For example, whereas 84% of patients reported that they were comfortable asking a nurse to confirm his or her identity, only 38% had done so. Similarly, 72% were comfortable helping mark surgical sites, but only 17% had done so.

Subsequent studies have shown similar results.[25] Summarizing this literature in a systematic review, Schwappach examined 12 studies published from 1995 to 2008.[26] He concluded that patient self-efficacy, perceived preventability of incidents, and the perceived effectiveness of actions affected patients' intention to use error prevention–oriented behaviors. Schwappach and Wernli's subsequent study of 479 oncology patients in Switzerland corroborated these findings.[27] Although patients endorsed the value of safety-oriented behaviors, they also reported that they were less likely to use behaviors, such as asking a physician if he or she had washed his or her hands, that required confrontation with providers. Patients' intentions to engage in safety-oriented behaviors again exceeded their actual use of such behaviors. As in the Waterman et al. study, this may have been due in part to a tendency to overestimate their ability and willingness to execute such behaviors. It may also have reflected limited opportunities to do so. For example, patients would not need to ask providers to wash their hands if providers did so routinely.

The social environment in which patients find themselves has a particularly important impact on patient engagement. In 71 interviews and 12 focus groups of patients in the United Kingdom, Entwistle and colleagues asked patients and family members about their experiences with speaking up about safety concerns. They found that speaking up was directly related to patients' assessments about the gravity of the threat, its seriousness compared to other patient needs and demands facing clinical staff members, patients' confidence about the grounds for the concern, their acceptance of this role, and the likely consequences of speaking up.[28] Patients' willingness to speak up was profoundly influenced by the way that health care staff interacted with them, including staff members' expectations of engagement and their instructions to patients.

"Activated" patients (that is, who actively participate in their care) in an unreceptive environment may be less inclined to act than less-activated patients in an environment that encourages patient participation. Indeed, Davis and colleagues' survey of 80 surgical patients at a London teaching hospital found that patients were much more willing to ask clinicians factual than challenging questions.[29] Willingness to ask questions was also more likely among women, educated patients, and those who were employed, and *when physicians encouraged patients to ask.*

In sum, engagement is a complex and nuanced phenomenon that relies in part on patient attributes, including patients' health literacy, knowledge of safety-oriented behaviors, experience in using such behaviors, judgment as to their likely efficacy, and propensity or willingness to act. The degree of self-protective behaviors relies also on such factors as the task itself (in particular, whether it requires active actions that may challenge providers).[30–32] Finally, engagement depends on the specific activities and organization climate that tolerate or encourage patient engagement.

This research is instructive but limited because it reflects patients' perceptions of their willingness to behave in certain prescribed ways. To what extent do we know what patients and their families actually do?

Acting Safely

Large surveys confirm that many patients and their families perform the kinds of activities that safety experts think may make for safer care. In a 2008 survey of 1,517 adults in the United States by the Kaiser Family Foundation, many respondents described things that they did to ensure the safety of their care.[33] Patients checked the medications that a pharmacist gave them against the prescriptions that their physicians wrote (70%); called to check on the results of a medical test (64%); brought a list of the prescription and nonprescription medications that they were taking to physicians' appointments (59%); brought friends or relatives to physician appointments so they could help ask questions and understand what the physician said (47%); or told a physician, nurse, or surgeon about drug allergies even when the clinician did not ask for this information (40%). These findings suggest that some patients use some of these behaviors at least some of the time.

The problem with interpreting this type of research is that we do not know whether the safety-oriented behavior was used once or often, when it was used last, and whether it was used consistently. The results tell us how often respondents recall performing certain behaviors during the course of their lifetimes (the prevalence of the behavior) but not whether they used them during recent medical encounters (the incidence). Simply knowing the prevalence of a behavior does not help us understand whether and under what circumstances the action took place.

To better understand the incidence of patients' use of safety-oriented behaviors, Weissman and colleagues, in the largest study of its kind to date, interviewed 2,582 recently discharged patients from 16 Massachusetts hospitals and reviewed the medical records for 998 of them.[34] In this methodologically rigorous study, the investigators compared medical records reviews with patient interviews to understand the incidence and risk factors for adverse events in this population and to understand whether patients know something about adverse events that hospitals do not. The investigators also sought to understand the types of participation behaviors that sick patients use in the hospital and the impact of participation on perceptions of quality and on patient safety.[35] The forms of participation included a spectrum of activities. Some

activities were relatively passive, such as talking with providers, obtaining information, and participating in care decisions. "Active" participation included checking one's medications and having a proxy who advocated on one's behalf. The results were striking (see Table 5-1, page 115). Of the 2,025 patients who answered all seven participation-related questions, the majority (83%) reported that they were sufficiently awake, alert, and aware to understand why they were admitted. They usually felt well enough to communicate with their caregivers (86%), obtain information from physicians and nurses (87%), discuss the pros and cons of treatment (80%), and participate in care decisions (99%).[35]

Consistent with Hibbard et al.[23] and Schwappach,[26] fewer patients performed the more active behaviors, such as having a family member or friend advocate for the patient with the hospital staff (79%) or check one's medications (39%). Of note, 81% of patients used five or more participation activities during the admission. These highly participatory patients were five times more likely to judge the quality of care as "good" or "excellent" compared to less participatory patients. Moreover, in multivariable regression models that adjusted for potential confounders, patients with high levels of participation were half as likely to experience an adverse event during the hospitalizations (adjusted odds ratio 0.5, 95%, confidence interval 0.3–0.8). In this observational study, participation protected patients against adverse events in the hospital.

STRATEGIES FOR PROMOTING PATIENT ENGAGEMENT

Patients endorse the value of many safety-oriented behaviors; many indicate their willingness to use these behaviors, although the confrontational activities are less popular than

Table 5-1. Patient-Reported Participation Activities (*N* = 2,025)

Survey Question	%
How much did you know about the medical problem for which you were admitted? (A lot or some)	82.7
How often did you feel well enough to be able to talk with your doctors and nurses? (Usually or always)	86.0
When you wanted information about your care and treatment, how easy or difficult was it to find a doctor or nurse to tell you what you wanted to know? (Somewhat or very easy)	86.7
When decisions had to be made, how often did your doctors and nurses describe the good and bad things about your treatment options? (Usually or always)	80.3
Did you participate in the decisions your doctors made about your care? (About the right amount or more than wanted)	98.7
If you had a friend or family member visit you, did that person help you make sure your health care wishes were being followed by the hospital staff? (Always or usually)	79.1
When you were given medicines, how often did you check to make sure they were the correct ones? (Usually or always)	39.4

Source: Adapted from Weingart S.N., et al.: Hospitalized patients' participation and its impact on quality of care and patient safety. *Int J Qual Health Care* 23:269–277, Jun. 2011.

activities that do not involve challenging the providers. It is clear from anecdotal evidence and research that many patients and their companions behave in safety-oriented ways at least some of the time. And tantalizing evidence suggests that safety-oriented behaviors are associated with safer care.

At the same time, we must recognize that patient engagement does not exist in a vacuum. Organizations may create conditions that enable participation by facilitating access to providers, by discussing treatment options and alternatives, and by encouraging interaction. Regrettably, there are few rigorous experimental studies of the effectiveness of interventions to promote patient involvement in patient safety.[36] In a 2010 systematic review, Hall and colleagues identified only 14 experimental and quasi-experimental studies, all of which sought to ensure safe medication delivery through patient participation.[37] Unfortunately, the investigators were unable to draw conclusions about the effectiveness of most interventions because of concerns about the methodological quality of the studies. Studies of efforts to bolster patient engagement by targeting the attitudes and actions of staff members are almost entirely lacking.

Several health care organizations have developed programs that invite patient participation in patient safety activities. The next section highlights several of these initiatives, including pilot projects and research studies that illustrate the potential value of patient engagement in five areas: (1) patient education, (2) adverse event reporting, (3) teamwork training, (4) information technology, and (5) patient advocacy.

Educating Patients on Engagement

Many organizations have developed and distributed educational materials that are intended to raise patients' awareness of safety risks, motivate and empower them to get involved in their care, and educate them about how to assess or to mitigate risk. Materials have been prepared for paper and electronic distribution as leaflets, posters, pamphlets, and Web pages. Several videos have also been produced and released,[38] including an entertaining clip prepared by the Advertising Council and the AHRQ that advises patients to ask questions.[39] Few methodologically rigorous assessments have been made regarding the impact of patient-education interventions on patient safety outcomes.[40]

Materials for patients focus on several areas, including general safety in the community, safe use of medications, preparation for surgery, and safe care in the hospital. General safety measures include advice about infection control, vigilance, communication, and care coordination. Medication safety materials commonly encourage patients to keep and to update lists of their current prescription and nonprescription medications, vitamins, and supplements and to bring the lists to medical appointments.[41] Materials that advise patients to prepare for hospitalization or surgery include sets of questions about the surgeons' and hospitals' experiences with that type of surgery, how to

prepare for the surgery, and what to expect during the hospitalization and recovery periods.

Patient safety educational materials address several of the conditions required for participation, including the ability to recognize deviations from expected care (by understanding what is to be expected) and motivating patients to play a role (by encouraging patients to speak up and to participate in medical decision making) and to identify actions that patients and families might take to ensure safe care (by checking their medications in the hospital and at home, encouraging hand hygiene, and knowing whom to call in an emergency).

All recommendations are not created equal. In a study of 160 distinct safety-oriented recommendations for patients offered by eight health care organizations in the United States, researchers found that the value of such recommendations was quite variable.[42] An expert panel judged that few of the recommendations were based on scientific evidence or were likely to have a significant impact on patient safety or to be used by patients. The experts' mothers, a plausibly sensible comparison group, concurred with this assessment. The highest-rated recommendations are listed in Sidebar 5-1 (page 117).

Encouraging Reporting

Building on the concept of the vigilant partner, several groups have examined the possibility that patients may have important information to relay to providers about problematic episodes of care.

In an early study, Weingart and colleagues interviewed 228 patients on a general medical ward, asking them about problems, injuries, and errors that affected them. The research team found that 8% of patients experienced an

---

Sidebar 5-1. Expert Panel's Highest-Rated Patient Safety Recommendations for Consumers

- If you think you have taken an overdose or a child has taken medication by accident, call your local poison control center or your health care provider at once.
- If you develop itching or swelling or have trouble breathing after taking a new medicine, get medical help immediately.
- Make sure care providers identify you before they initiate any procedure or medication.
- Ask about risks and potential complications of surgery, expected outcomes, and alternatives to surgery.
- Review your medications with your doctor, nurse, or pharmacist before going home. Change your medication list accordingly.
- Report unexpected symptoms or reactions to your doctor or pharmacist.
- Wear a medical-alert bracelet if you have severe drug or food allergies.
- Use child-resistant caps.
- Make sure the surgical site is correctly marked.
- Make a list of all medications you are taking. Include dosage and over-the-counter drugs, herbal supplements, and vitamins.
- List your medication and food allergies.
- Keep medicine out of children's reach.
- Ask if you can take your regular medications before hospitalization or surgery, and what to eat and drink.

Source: Adapted from Weingart S.N, et al.: Rating recommendations for consumers about patient safety: Sense, common sense, or nonsense? *Jt Comm J Qual Patient Saf* 35:206–215, Apr. 2009.

---

adverse event and that an additional 4% experienced near misses ("close calls").[43] Examples of events included problems with medication allergies, delayed antibiotic infusions, and deep vein thrombosis at a venous catheter. Some 40% of the patients reported events that could be corroborated on retrospective review of the medical record, but none of the events were documented in the hospital's incident-reporting systems. Other groups reported similar adverse event rates using this method to elicit patient adverse event reports in the emergency department and in other inpatient settings.[44,45]

How good are patient reports? In the Weissman et al. study of recently discharged patients from 16 Massachusetts hospitals,[34] investigators compared medical-record reviews with patient interviews to understand the incidence and risk factors for adverse events in this population. Physician reviewers judged whether patient reports represented adverse events and classified the type and severity of the events. Physician reviewers classified the majority of these reports as adverse events, with positive predictive values of 60% to 94%.[46] Among 998 study patients, 23% had at least one adverse event detected by an interview, and 11% had at least one adverse event identified by record review. The results were striking. Not only was the incidence of adverse events higher than reported in previous studies, but two thirds of the incidents were detected by patient interview alone. Patient-reported events were enriched in adverse drug events compared to events identified by medical record alone. This research demonstrated the extent to which patients identified adverse events of which the hospital was unaware.

This general principle applies in ambulatory settings as well as in the acute care hospital. In a study of 661 primary care patients, Weingart and colleagues identified adverse drug events through medical-record reviews and patient interviews.[47] As in the Weissman et al. inpatient study, Weingart et al. found that patient reports were complementary to events identified on medical-record reviews. Of 181 adverse drug events, 73% were identified by patient reports only, 9% on chart reviews only, and 19% by both. In the same study, patients reported 286 symptoms that they attributed to their medications. Patients' own primary care physicians agreed with the patients' attribution in 86% of cases.

In another study, Weingart and colleagues asked patient volunteers to elicit incident reports from ambulatory oncology patients during office and treatment visits.[48] This study illustrated a novel role for patient volunteers in eliciting patient safety events. In this study, the volunteers elicited reports from 193 patients and found that staff members consistently performed safety practices such as hand hygiene and patient-identity checking. Nevertheless, one in five patients expressed a concern about patient safety. Most of the "safety" events involved waits and delays or difficult interactions with staff rather than medical errors or iatrogenic injuries. The investigators theorized that such experiences and interactions might lead patients to worry about the safety of the care environment.[49]

Patient reporting is a promising method,

although it has not yet been widely adopted or integrated into routine health care operations. Patient reports may offer a perspective on problems in care that is not otherwise available to health care leaders.[50] Although patient incident reports are accepted by state health departments, boards of medicine, and other regulatory and accreditation bodies, health care delivery organizations in the United States are just beginning to solicit such reports.[51,52] A Danish Cancer Society patient reporting system that was introduced in 2008 (*see* Sidebar 5-2, page 119) demonstrates the value of this approach. In its first year of operation, the reporting system uncovered problems involving patient-provider communication and coordination of care. It also elicited information about the psychological and social impact of these events and informed the development of a national consumer reporting system.[53]

Promoting Teamwork

High-performance teamwork training has become an area of intense interest in health care. Hospitals have adapted the crew resource management model developed in aviation[54,55] to labor and delivery suites, emergency departments, intensive care units, and operating rooms. It uses briefings, closed-loop communication techniques, appropriate assertiveness, and monitoring of the environment to ensure communication and coordination of care.[56,57] Although these programs have been oriented toward professional staff members, explicit engagement of patients as members of high-performance teams has potential benefits.

At Dana-Farber Cancer Institute (Boston), patients and staff members together developed an initiative that was intended to translate the concepts of high-performance teamwork training into actions that could help patients keep themselves safe.[58] In this fast-paced ambulatory

---

Sidebar 5-2. The Danish Cancer Society's Patient Reporting System

Background: The Danish Cancer Society developed a patient and family member reporting system in 2008, using an electronic reporting form that was available through the society's Web site. It contained a combination of fixed response items as well as fields for free-text narrative. The system was announced on the Society's Web site, in pamphlets that were distributed to hospitals, in newsletters and magazines, and by word of mouth.

Results: During the December 2008–October 2009 pilot, patients and family members reported 151 events. Although some of the safety hazards were known from other data sources, patient reports uncovered newly discovered problems related to patient–provider communication and coordination of care. Furthermore, the reports demonstrated the importance of psychological and social consequences of these events.

Impact: As a result of the reporting system, which remains in operation, the Cancer Society has done the following:
• Established a national working group on safety issues in cancer care
• Published patient safety information for cancer patients on the Society's Web site
• Contributed questions about safety issues to a national survey of cancer patients' experiences completed by the Cancer Society
• Provided information that has been used to further develop the national Danish Patient Safety Database and a national patient reporting system

Next Steps: After the pilot, the reporting system was revised to include additional questions about communication with staff members. In addition, patients are now offered the opportunity to report "good stories" that describe positive experiences that can be used to improve cancer care. Finally, the Danish Cancer Society's system led to the development of a national patient reporting system scheduled to be launched in Denmark in 2011.

Source: The sidebar was kindly contributed by Henriette Lipzack, M.D., and Janne Lehmann Knudsen, M.D., Danish Cancer Society, Copenhagen.

---

treatment environment, high-risk hazards include medication errors and infections. The "You CAN" program offered one-on-one training to patients and families in checking their medications (environmental monitoring), asking providers to disinfect their hands (appropriate assertiveness), and notifying clinicians of last-minute changes in therapy (briefing, communication). The intervention reached more than 1,000 patients in its initial three-month launch, and 39% of the patients said that it changed their behavior. Elements of success required building support among staff in advance, patient participation in creating the project, and a supportive culture.

In other initiatives, family members and friends are engaged in identifying conditions that require urgent medical attention. Such organizations as North Carolina Children's Hospital (Chapel Hill) and Minnesota Children's Hospital (Minneapolis) developed "Code H" (for Help) or "Family Alert" systems that allow anyone to call for an emergency medical-team assessment.[59] These programs acknowledge that the patient and his or her visitors are astute observers of changes in the patient's condition and should be encouraged to mobilize the care teams in the event of a perceived emergency.

Using Technology

Information technology offers promising new opportunities to engage patients in their care by providing ready access to personal health information. In theory, the ability to review medical information and to correct inaccurate medication lists or allergies may help ensure safer care. Internet-based surveys allow for patient reporting of adverse events.[60] Newer applications permit even more sophisticated interactions with care providers, including access to secure messaging.[61] Portals and other Web-based tools can be used to collect and to relay information to providers about the accuracy of medication lists,[62] chemotherapy toxicities,[63] health maintenance,[64] and the management of cancer[65] and chronic conditions, such as heart failure[66] and diabetes.[61,67,68]

In one study, researchers used an electronic patient portal to send adult primary care patients electronic messages 10 days after receiving a new or changed prescription. The messages asked whether the patients had filled the prescription or had problems with it.[69] The system generated more than 5,000 messages during this 15-month project. In an evaluation involving 267 users of the patient portal, 79% had opened the message and 12% had responded. Half the respondents reported problems filling their prescriptions, 12% noted problems with drug effectiveness, and 10% described medication-related symptoms. Clinicians responded to most messages within a week. Although the experience of nonrespondents could not be assessed, the study suggested that electronic portals could be used to assess medication adherence and elicit information about adverse events. The patient portal also provided a new vehicle for patients and their primary care physicians to communicate outside the physician office about medications and medication-related symptoms.[69]

Demonstrating measurable improvements in patient safety based on patient engagement interventions can be challenging. However, information in the hands of patients can be lifesaving, as illustrated in the following case:

Dr. Webster's pager went off at 9:00 o'clock on a Friday night. Here we go again, he thought. He kissed his 9-year-old daughter good night and then returned the call. "This is Dr. Webster. How may I help you?"

The man on the telephone was a patient of Dr. Arnold, another internist in Dr. Webster's practice. The patient was a 50-year-old man who had developed new-onset headaches about a month earlier. Symptoms of meningitis were absent: There was no fever, stiff neck, or rash. He denied pounding or throbbing that would suggest late-onset migraines. No sinus pressure. No tightness or squeezing that improved with ibuprofen, characteristics of a tension headache. "It's probably nothing," said Dr. Arnold, "But let's check an MRI [magnetic resonance image] to be sure. I don't often see persistent new headaches in an adult."

The patient told Dr. Webster that he had completed his brain MRI scan a day earlier and had just now reviewed the report on the hospital's patient Internet portal. He was concerned to learn that he had a brain tumor called a meningioma. He wondered whether the "cerebral edema" described in the report might be related to his worsening headaches and new nausea and vomiting.

Indeed they were. Dr. Webster thanked the patient for paging him and explained that this was an urgent situation. He called an ambulance and met the patient at the hospital, where the patient received corticosteroid medications and ultimately had a successful resection of the tumor.

Although this case was a patient engagement success, it illustrated multiple system failures. For example, the radiologist was a new, part-time clinician who was unfamiliar with standard notification protocols for critical test results. In addition, Dr. Arnold's practice had no robust results-tracking or sign-out systems. This case led to a variety of practice improvements.

Advocating for Change

This chapter has emphasized self-defense at the bedside and conditions that facilitate effective patient participation in patient safety. Patients and family members can also play a variety of collaborative and advocacy roles that promote safe care and that can help patients and providers cope with the aftermath of medical accidents.

- Medically Induced Trauma Survivor Service (http://www.mitss.org/) is a Massachusetts-based, survivor-led group that provides emotional support for providers and patients who have been harmed as a result of medical care.
- Medical College of Georgia has been recognized for its work involving patients in a family advisory council and the organization's patient safety committee. Patients serve as faculty members, helping train medical students in patient-centered care.[70]
- Dana-Farber Cancer Institute created patient/family advisory councils in the 1990s. Council members participate in about 100 committees, including the board-level quality committee.[71] They help select senior leaders and participate in initiatives related to quality improvement and patient safety. On the strength of this and related programs, the Massachusetts legislature required health care organizations to establish patient/family advisory councils begin-

ning in 2010.[72]
- The World Health Organization has supported an international collaboration of patients and family members affected by medical errors.[73] This Patients for Patient Safety group has organized workshops and events and is working on a reproductive health checklist for mothers and their babies.

SUMMARY, CHALLENGES, AND NEXT STEPS

Patients and their families are powerful resources for supporting safe medical care—sources of resilience in the health care system. Many serve as vigilant partners, identifying and reporting potential problems before they result in injuries. Many are prepared to speak up on behalf of themselves or their loved ones, asking providers to provide reassurance that care is seamless and coordinated, that medications are correct, and that the risk of the spread of infection is minimal.

Patient engagement as a care improvement strategy does have limitations. Patients' willingness and ability to participate may vary dramatically from one person to another, from one setting to another, and over the course of an illness or lifetime. Similarly, it is unreasonable to expect that acutely ill patients will be able to use safety-oriented behaviors consistently or reliably or without significant amounts of coaching.[73] Timing is important in that a patient's most vulnerable period may be early in the illness or hospital admission—precisely when he or she is least able to process new information and for "safety" interventions to occur. The tasks that we request of patients bear scrutiny as well. For example, when 100 orthopedic patients were asked to mark "No" on the non-surgical limbs, 59 marked the limbs correctly, 37 made no mark, and 4 made marks other than "No."[74] In short, we have to be careful about the activities that we ask patients to perform; certain observations or actions may be beyond their current capabilities. Patients may also worry about offending the caregivers on whom they depend and may interact in ways that are well intentioned but ineffective.

Patients' contributions to medical errors require further investigation. The extent of poor medication adherence in ambulatory care, even among patients with a serious or life-threatening illness, is sobering.[75,76] A team of New Zealand investigators offered a taxonomy of 70 potential types of patient errors.[77] The investigators described problematic patient actions, such as attendance errors (for example, failure to make or show up for an appointment), nonadherence with tests or treatments, and defensive or confrontational communication with providers. They distinguished these problematic patient behaviors from "mental" errors, which include problems with memory, knowledge deficits, poor judgment, and unconstructive or uncooperative attitudes toward medical care.

Given the potential contributions of patients and their families, health care organizations need to create opportunities for patients and families to partner with health care providers (*see* Table 5-2, page 123).

Peat and the U.K. Patient Involvement in Patient Safety (P.I.P.S.) Group have proposed three major categories of patient-engagement interventions.[78] Patients, they argue, can help do the following:

1. Inform the management plan (by sharing information with health professionals and ensuring that the proposed plan is appropriate)
2. Monitor and ensure safe treatment (by checking that planned treatments are delivered on time, adhering to self-treatment or monitoring recommendations, and following instructions after treatment)
3. Inform systems improvement (by providing feedback to providers or acting as patient representatives)

We have seen examples of promising projects and programs in each of these domains.

Yet, as stated earlier, patients' ability to participate in the safety of their own care is highly dependent on the receptiveness of health care providers and their organizations to embrace this possibility. Health care practitioners must enable patients to participate in their care by educating them about their care, by inviting them to communicate concerns, and by making themselves available. In creating environments that facilitate engagement, health care organizations must recognize that some patients are more capable partners than others due to their health literacy, experience, temperament, or health status. Patients find certain behaviors more challenging or frightening than other behaviors. We have seen that patients can and do participate in their care quite frequently, even in acute care hospitals where patients are most severely ill and at risk. Opportunities for partnership exist in this setting as well as in the ambulatory environment. However, the opportunity will be realized only if health care professionals and institutions take responsibility for enabling patients and families to participate.

As we create a menu of opportunities for patients to participate in safer care, we have to be careful about attempts to shift responsibility for care to patients and their loved ones.[79] The willingness and ability to participate in their care varies among patients and over time. Health care organizations must create and support participation opportunities while acknowl-

Table 5-2. Strategies and Action Items for Promoting Patient Engagement in Patient Safety

Strategy	Action Items
Educating Engagement	• Distribute paper brochures and pamphlets with patient safety tips. • Develop Web-based resources with commonly asked questions and patient advice prior to hospitalization or surgery. • Distribute medication safety information sheets to help patients maintain updated medication lists. • Show videos that identify specific actions that patients and families can undertake to support safe care (for example, hand hygiene).
Encouraging Reporting	• Develop easy-to-implement methods of patient reporting. • Promote patient awareness, using posters and brochures, of risk factors for adverse events.
Promoting Teamwork	• Develop training programs to encourage patients and families to become active members of the care team. • Implement emergency alert systems that patients and families can use to mobilize emergency medical teams in such situations. • Build and maintain hospital staff support for patient engagement by describing and rewarding patient-centered behaviors.
Using Technology	• Provide patients access to personal health information, such as test results, problem summaries, and medication lists, through Web-based patient portals. • Use electronic messaging systems that allow patients to communicate with their medical practices.
Advocating for Change	• Form and support patient/family advisory groups within your health care organization that empower patients and families to make meaningful contributions to health care quality and safety. • Support organization-based as well as state (U.S.), regional, and international programs that collaborate with patient/family groups in promoting safety. • Organize workshops for patients that teach patient safety participation methods. • Invite patients to support medical school faculties' training of medical students in patient-centered care.

Source: Dana-Farber Cancer Institute, Boston. Used with permission.

edging their own ultimate responsibility for ensuring patient safety.

The author gratefully acknowledges Laurinda Morway for her invaluable assistance in performing and organizing a literature search and bibliographic annotations as well as Ian Watt for his insightful and constructive comments on an earlier draft of this chapter.

References

1. Bates D.W.: A 40-year-old woman who noticed a medication error. *JAMA* 285:3134–3140, Jun. 27, 2001.

2. Brennan T.A., et al.: Incidence of adverse events and negligence in hospitalized patients. Results of the Harvard Medical Practice Study I. *N Engl J Med* 324:370–376, Feb. 7, 1991.

3. Leape L.L., et al.: The nature of adverse events in hospitalized patients. Results of the Harvard Medical Practice Study II. *N Engl J Med* 324:377–384, Feb. 7, 1991.

4. Vincent C., Neale G., Woloshynowych M.: Adverse events in British hospitals: Preliminary retrospective record review. *BMJ* (7285)322:517–519, Mar. 3, 2001.

5. Baker G.R., et al.: The Canadian Adverse Events Study: The incidence of adverse events among hospital patients in Canada. *CMAJ* 170:1678–1686, May 25, 2004.

6. Wilson R.M., et al.: The Quality in Australian Health Care Study. *Med J Aust* 163:458–471, Nov. 6, 1995.

7. Thomas E.J., et al.: Incidence and types of adverse events and negligent care in Utah and Colorado. *Med Care* 38:261–271, Mar. 2000.

8. Michel P., et al.: French national survey of inpatient adverse events prospectively assessed with ward staff. *Qual Saf Health Care* 16:369–377, Oct. 2007.

9. Davis P., et al.: Adverse events in New Zealand public hospitals I: Occurrence and impact. *N Z Med J* 115:U271, Dec. 13, 2002.

10. Aranaz-Andrés J.M., et al.: Impact and preventability of adverse events in Spanish public hospitals: Results of the Spanish National Study of Adverse Events (ENEAS). *Int J Qual Health Care* 21:408–414, Dec. 2009.

11. Institute for Healthcare Improvement: *Patient Safety.* http://www.ihi.org/explore/PatientSafety/Pages/default.aspx (accessed Sep. 23, 2011).

12. The Health Foundation: *Safer Patients Initiative.* http://www.health.org.uk/areas-of-work/improvement-programmes/safer-patients-initiative/ (accessed Sep. 23, 2011).

13. World Health Organization: *WHO Patient Safety.* http://www.who.int/patientsafety/en/ (accessed Sep. 23, 2011).

14. Hibbard J.H., et al.: Can patients be part of the solution? Views on their role in preventing medical errors. *Med Care Res Rev* 62:601–616, Oct. 2005.

15. Lyons M.: Should patients have a role in patient safety? A safety engineering view. *Qual Saf Health Care* 16:140–142, Apr. 2007.

16. The Joint Commission: *Comprehensive Accreditation Manual for Hospitals: The Official Handbook.* Oak Brook, IL: Joint Commission Resources, 2010.

17. Joint Commission International: *Joint Commission International Standards for Hospitals,* 4th ed. Oak Brook, IL: Joint Commission Resources, 2010.

18. The Joint Commission: *Speak Up Initiatives.* http://www.jointcommission.org/speakup.aspx (accessed Sep. 23, 2011).

19. U.S. Agency for Healthcare Research and Quality: *Five Steps to Safer Health Care: Patient Fact Sheet.* http://www.ahrq.gov/consumer/5steps.htm (accessed Sep. 23, 2011).

20. Danish Society for Patient Safety: *Activities.* http://patientsikkerhed.dk/en/about_the_danish_society_for_patient_safety/activities/ (accessed Sep. 23, 2011).

21. World Health Organization: *Patients for Patient Safety.* http://www.who.int/patientsafety/patients_for_patient/en/ (accessed Sep. 23, 2011).

22. Siddiqi N., House A.O., Holmes J.D.: Occurrence and outcome of delirium in medical in-patients: A systematic literature review. *Age Ageing* 35:350–364, Jul. 2006.

23. Hibbard J.H., et al.: Development and testing of a short form of the patient activation measure. *Health Serv Res* 40:1918–1930, Dec. 2005.

24. Waterman A.D., et al.: Brief report: Hospitalized patients' attitudes about and participation in error prevention. *J Gen Intern Med* 21:367–370, Apr. 2006.

25. Marella W.M., et al.: Health care consumers' inclination to engage in selected patient safety practices: A survey of adults in Pennsylvania. *J Patient Saf* 3:184–189, Dec. 2007.

26. Schwappach D.L.: Review: Engaging patients as vigilant partners in safety: A systematic review. *Med Care Res Rev* 67:119–148, Apr. 2010.

27. Schwappach D.L., Wernli M.: Predictors of chemotherapy patients' intentions to engage in medical error prevention. *Oncologist* 15:903–912, Aug. 2010.

28. Entwistle V.A., et al.: Speaking up about safety concerns: Multi-setting qualitative study of patients' views and experiences. *Qual Saf Health Care* 19:e33, Dec. 2010.

29. Davis R.E., Koutantji M., Vincent C.A.: How willing are patients to question healthcare staff on issues related to the quality and safety of their healthcare? An exploratory study. *Qual Saf Health Care* 17:90–96, Apr. 2008.

30. Entwistle V.A., Watt I.S.: Patient involvement in treatment decision-making: The case for a broader conceptual framework. *Patient Educ Couns* 63:268–278, Nov. 2006.

31. Davis R.E., et al.: Patient involvement in patient safety: What factors influence patient participation and engagement? *Health Expect* 10:259–267, Sep. 2007.

32. Schwappach D.L., Wernli M.: Barriers and facilitators to chemotherapy patients' engagement in medical error prevention. *Ann Oncol* 22:424–430, Feb. 2011.

33. The Kaiser Family Foundation/U.S. Agency for Healthcare Research and Quality: *2008 Update on Consumers' Views of Patient Safety and Quality Information.* Menlo Park, CA: Kaiser Family Foundation, 2008.

34. Weissman J.S., et al.: Comparing patient-reported hospital adverse events with medical record review: Do patients know something that hospitals do not? *Ann Intern Med* 149:100–108, Jul. 15, 2008.

35. Weingart S.N., et al.: Hospitalized patients' participation and its impact on quality of care and patient safety. *Int J Qual Health Care* 23:269–277, Jun. 2011.

36. Longtin Y., et al.: Patient participation: Current knowledge and applicability to patient safety. *Mayo Clin Proc* 85:53–62, Jan. 2010.

37. Hall J., et al.: Effectiveness of interventions designed to promote patient involvement to enhance safety: A systematic review. *Qual Saf Health Care* 19:e10, Oct. 2010.

38. The Joint Commission: *Speak Up.* http://www.youtube.com/user/TheJointCommission#g/c/96EE3EE3F1C6B859 (accessed Sep. 23, 2011).

39. U.S. Agency for Healthcare Research and Quality: *Questions Are the Answer.* http://www.ahrq.gov/questions (accessed Sep. 23, 2011).

40. See L.C., et al.: Animation program used to encourage patients or family members to take an active role for eliminating wrong-site, wrong-person, wrong-procedure surgeries: Preliminary evaluation. *Int J Surg* 9(3):241–247, 2011.

41. Weingart S.N., et al.: Medication reconciliation in ambulatory oncology. *Jt Comm J Qual Patient Saf* 33:750–757, Dec. 2007.

42. Weingart S.N., et al.: Rating recommendations for consumers about patient safety: Sense, common sense, or nonsense? *Jt Comm J Qual Patient Saf* 35:206–215, Apr. 2009.

43. Weingart S.N., et al.: What can hospitalized patients tell us about adverse events? Learning from patient-reported incidents. *J Gen Intern Med* 20:830–836, Sep. 2005.

44. Friedman S.M., et al.: Errors, near misses and adverse events in the emergency department: What can patients tell us? *CJEM* 10:421–427, Sep. 2008.

45. Agoritsas T., Bovier P.A., Perneger T.V.: Patient reports of undesirable events during hospitalization. *J Gen Intern Med* 20:922–928, Oct. 2005.

46. Zhu J., et al.: Can we rely on patients' reports of adverse events? *Med Care* Epub Jun. 2, 2011.

47. Weingart S.N., et al.: Patient-reported medication symptoms in primary care. *Arch Intern Med* 165:234–240, Jan. 24, 2005.

48. Weingart S.N., et al.: Patient-reported safety and quality of care in outpatient oncology. *Jt Comm J Qual Patient Saf* 33:83–94, Feb. 2007.

49. Wolosin R.J., Vercler L., Matthews J.L.: Am I safe here? Improving patients' perceptions of safety in hospitals. *J Nurs Care Qual* 21:30–38, Jan.–Mar. 2006.

50. Kuzel A.J., et al.: Patient reports of preventable problems and harms in primary health care. *Ann Fam Med* 2:333–340, Jul.–Aug. 2004.

51. Blenkinsopp A., et al.: Patient reporting of suspected adverse drug reactions: A review of published literature and international experience. *Br J Clin Pharmacol* 63:148–156, Feb. 2007.

52. Dana-Farber Cancer Institute: *Patient Safety Reporting Form.* http://www.dana-farber.org/Apps/patient-safety-form.aspx (accessed Sep. 23, 2011).

53. The Danish Cancer Society: Fortæl om dine erfaringer med kræftbehandling [Tell us about your experience with cancer treatment]. http://www.cancer.dk/patientrapportering (accessed Sep. 23, 2011).

54. U.S. Agency for Healthcare Research and Quality: *TeamSTEPPS®: National Implementation.* http://teamstepps.ahrq.gov/ (accessed Sep. 23, 2011).

55. Morey J.C., et al.: Error reduction and performance improvement in the emergency department through formal teamwork training: Evaluation results of the MedTeams project. *Health Serv Res* 37:1553–1581, Dec. 2002.

56. Pratt S.D., et al.: John M. Eisenberg Patient Safety and Quality Awards. Impact of CRM-based training on obstetric outcomes and clinicians' patient safety attitudes. *Jt Comm J Qual Patient Saf* 33:720–725, Dec. 2007.

57. Neily J., et al.: Association between implementation of a medical team training program and surgical mortality. *JAMA* 304:1693–1700, Oct. 20, 2010.

58. Weingart S.N., et al.: The You CAN campaign: Teamwork training for patients and families in ambulatory oncology. *Jt Comm J Qual Patient Saf* 35:63–71, Feb. 2009.

59. National Patient Safety Foundation: *Media Advisory: Socius Award Winner Announced at Annual Patient Safety Congress.* May 4, 2007. http://www.npsf.org/pr/pressrel/2007-05-4_2.php (accessed Sep. 23, 2011).

60. Wasson J.H., MacKenzie T.A., Hall M.: Patients use an Internet technology to report when things go wrong. *Qual Saf Health Care* 16:213–215, Jun. 2007.

61. Beckjord E.B., et al.: Use of the Internet to communicate with health care providers in the United States: Estimates from the 2003 and 2005 Health Information National Trends Surveys (HINTS). *J Med Internet Res* 9:e20, Jul. 12, 2007.

62. Staroselsky M., et al.: An effort to improve electronic health record medication list accuracy between visits: Patients' and physicians' response. *Int J Med Inform* 77:153–160, Mar. 2008.

63. Basch E., et al.: Patient online self-reporting of toxicity symptoms during chemotherapy. *J Clin Oncol* 23:3552–3561, May 20, 2005.

64. Wright A., et al.: Effectiveness of health maintenance reminders provided directly to patients. *AMIA Annu Symp Proc* p. 1183, Nov. 6, 2008.

65. Berry D.L., et al.: Enhancing patient-provider communication with the electronic self-report assessment for cancer: A randomized trial. *J Clin Oncol* 29:1029–1035, Mar. 10, 2011.

66. Wu R.C., et al.: Pilot study of an Internet patient-physician communication tool for heart failure disease management. *J Med Internet Res* 7:e8, Mar. 26, 2005.

67. Grant R.W., et al.: Practice-linked online personal health records for type 2 diabetes mellitus: A randomized controlled trial. *Arch Intern Med* 168:1776–1782, Sep. 8, 2008.

68. Leveille S.G., et al.: Health coaching via an Internet portal for primary care patients with chronic conditions: A randomized controlled trial. *Med Care* 47:41–47, Jan. 2009.

69. Weingart S.N., et al.: Medication safety messages for patients via the Web portal: The MedCheck intervention. *Int J Med Inform* 77:161–168, Mar. 2008.

70. Institute for Patient- and Family-Centered Care: *Profiles of Change.* http://www.ipfcc.org/profiles/prof-mcg.html (accessed Sep. 23, 2011).

71. Dana-Farber Cancer Institute: *Establishing Patient- and Family-Centered Care.* http://www.dana-farber.org/Adult-Care/New-Patient-Guide/Adult-Patient-and-Family-Advisory-Council/Establishing-Patient-and-Family-Centered-Care.aspx (accessed Sep. 23, 2011).

72. Massachusetts Department of Public Health 105 CMR 130.1800.

73. Weingart S.N., et al.: Lessons from a patient partnership intervention to prevent adverse drug events. *Int J Qual Health Care* 16:499–507, Dec. 2004.

74. DiGiovanni C.W., Kang L., Manuel J.: Patient compliance in avoiding wrong-site surgery. *J Bone Joint Surg Am* 85-A:815–819, May 2003.

75. DiMatteo M.R.: Variations in patients' adherence to medical recommendations: A quantitative review of 50 years of research. *Med Care* 42:200–209, Mar. 2004.

76. Partridge A.H., et al.: Adherence to therapy with oral antineoplastic agents. *J Natl Cancer Inst* 94:652–661, May 1, 2002.

77. Buetow S., et al.: Patient error: A preliminary taxonomy. *Ann Fam Med* 7:223–231, May–Jun. 2009.

78. Peat M., et al.: Scoping review and approach to appraisal of interventions intended to involve patients in patient safety. *J Health Serv Res Policy* 15(suppl. 1):17–25, Jan. 2010.

79. Entwistle V.A., Mello M.M., Brennan T.A.: Advising patients about patient safety: Current initiatives risk shifting responsibility. *Jt Comm J Qual Patient Saf* 31:483–494, Sep. 2005.

CHAPTER 6

Improving Management of Chronic Disease

William G. Weppner, M.D., M.P.H., F.A.C.P.; Katie Coleman, M.S.P.H.; Robert J. Reid, M.D., Ph.D.; Eric B. Larson, M.D., M.P.H., M.A.C.P.

In the past several decades, treatment of people with chronic disease and its complications have emerged as the predominant task of health care. Chronic diseases constitute the largest cause of death worldwide and continue to increase in prevalence.[1,2] In September 2011 the United Nations General Assembly was slated to hold a summit on the threat posed by four noncommunicable diseases—cardiovascular disease, diabetes, cancer, and chronic respiratory diseases—that are responsible for 35 million annual deaths globally.[3]

Chronic illnesses are conditions that typically last a year or more and have ongoing symptoms or potential for progression that require unremitting care.[4] The most common chronic conditions in the United States, where almost half the population is estimated to have at least one chronic condition,[5] include hypertension, diabetes, arthritis, vascular disease, and certain types of cancers. For example, 25.8 million people (8.3% of the population) in the United States have diabetes,[6] as do more than an estimated 220 million people around the world.[7]

Chronic conditions range from asymptomatic diagnoses that are risk factors for further disease to severe and debilitating illnesses with associated morbidity. Either way, they typically require sustained care and management to help limit existing symptoms and prevent future debilitating complications. Chronic infectious diseases, such as HIV and hepatitis C, present slightly different challenges, with complex and intense treatment regimens important to preventing progression as well as transmission to uninfected persons.[8,9] Chronic behavioral health issues, such as depression or substance abuse, also can seriously affect a patient's well-being. Although advances in treatments can help manage symptoms and complications of chronic diseases, such treatments are typically not curative. Accordingly, the number of people with chronic diseases (and associated costs) is expected to continue to increase.[4]

However *chronic disease* is defined, providing high-quality care for persons with chronic disease is an important goal for any health care system. The need for better management of chronic diseases demands better coordination of care across ambulatory care settings, hospitals and other health care organizations, and the community. Ongoing policy efforts attempt to address the inefficiencies and fragmentation in care in the United States and other countries around the world.[10–12] Some of these approaches focus on arranging delivery of chronic disease care (for example, the Chronic Care Model [CCM][13]), and some also focus on payment structures (for example, accountable care organizations [ACOs] in the United States[12]), whereas other approaches offer a combination of the two (for example, the Patient-Centered Medical Home [PCMH] in the United States, which uses provider reimbursement to incentivize coordination activities[11] [see pages 148–152]). Yet creating systems that lead to high-quality care can be challenging to implement in specific practice settings and across different systems. Traditional approaches to patient care have focused on episodic care in a specific setting, particularly treatment of acute illnesses and conditions. In this chapter, we discuss how traditional approaches need to be reconsidered to better address the specific needs of patients with chronic diseases.

MULTIPLYING CHRONIC ILLNESSES

Many patients are faced with not one chronic disease but multiple, interrelated conditions. In the United States, it is estimated that a quarter of the population has two or more chronic conditions.[14] Persons with chronic diseases tend to have predisposing "risk factors" that make them more susceptible to developing these diseases. A single risk factor is often associated with multiple chronic conditions. For example, obesity is a strong risk factor for hypertension, diabetes, and arthritis. Furthermore, the diagnosis of some diseases, such as diabetes or cardiovascular disease, can also lower what is considered "ideal" levels of blood pressure or cholesterol, creating additional needs for treatment and monitoring for a patient. When a patient is given a new diagnosis of diabetes, he or she may also face a new diagnosis of relatively high blood pressure and cholesterol (even though the same values were considered "normal" before the diagnosis). Chronic conditions tend to feed into one another, so that a patient with one

chronic condition is more likely to develop multiple chronic conditions as well as acute complications from the underlying condition. Finally, increased age also adds to the probability of developing multiple chronic illnesses; approximately two thirds of persons older than 65 years of age in the United States have multiple chronic conditions.[15]

As patients age and develop multiple chronic diseases—which necessitate increasingly complex medical treatment regimens—they are at greater risk for other health problems, such as adverse drug events, unnecessary hospitalizations, duplicative tests, conflicting medical advice, worsened functional status, and death.[4] In addition, chronic mental health issues are interwoven with other conditions, which can create a vicious cycle in which behavioral issues, such as depression, can erode patients' confidence and competence in managing their illnesses, thereby aggravating disability with worsened outcomes. Patients with multiple chronic conditions require considerable support and health care resources; as 28% of the population, they account for an estimated two thirds of total health care spending in the United States.[15]

INAPPROPRIATE TARGETING OF RESOURCES

As patients scramble to adapt to living with one or more chronic diseases, it is becoming more and more apparent that existing methods of medical care and allocations of resources are inadequate to address the problem. In many countries, primary care physicians are tasked with meeting the needs of patients with common chronic problems, such as diabetes, hypertension, stroke, asthma, coronary artery disease, and chronic obstructive lung disease.[16] In other countries, primary care physicians must deal with these chronic diseases as well as chronic infectious diseases, such as HIV or tuberculosis.[17,18] In general, it appears that the availability of primary care physicians has been associated with improved health outcomes in the United States and elsewhere.[19,20] Yet it is difficult for one primary care provider to address all the chronic care needs of his or her patients. As is often cited, it would take an estimated 18.0 hours *per day* for one physician to provide all the recommended evidence-based preventive care (7.6 hours)[21] and chronic disease care (10.4 hours) for an average-size (2,500-patient) primary care panel.[22] To make matters worse, the United States already has an inadequate primary care workforce (including associated staff), and increasingly smaller numbers of physicians are choosing to go into primary care.[23]

However, simply increasing resources for primary care is unlikely to be sufficient in addressing the complex problem of managing chronic diseases. Primary care providers work in a health system that relies on sporadic face-to-face visits to treat patients with chronic diseases who require long-term and proactive management and support. This system is well-suited for caring for patients with acute needs. For example, the 20-minute face-to-face visit may be sufficient to treat an uncomplicated infection or rash. Moreover, patients with chronic conditions are likely to have symptomatic complaints related to their underlying illnesses. Take, for example, the patient with diabetes who comes to the physician for a regularly scheduled visit. He complains that his foot neuropathy is worse and is interfering with sleep, preventing him from being as active as he would like. His physician can see that the patient's weight has increased, that his cholesterol and triglycerides levels are worse, and that his blood sugars are no longer in control. During a short visit, it is impossible to address all the concerns of the patient and provider,

both of whom often leave such meetings feeling like the main issues have not been appropriately addressed. We need a system of care that affords patients and their care providers the framework to deal with acute needs while still providing the resources to manage patient conditions over the long term to help reduce disability and painful complications.

The disconnect between the system of *episodic* encounters and the need for *ongoing* chronic care would suggest that most patients with chronic disease are not receiving recommended evidence-based care. Indeed, much evidence shows that for a majority of patients, such conditions as hypertension, diabetes, high cholesterol, congestive heart failure, atrial fibrillation, asthma, and depression are not being adequately treated.[24] To make advances in truly improving health outcomes for patients, we need to develop a new model of care for the patients who have illnesses that they will be living with for years, or even decades. This model of care should (1) be proactive and supportive of the patient and his or her team of care providers; (2) ensure that planned, preventive care needs are met so avoidable complications do not occur; and (3) recognize that patients are essential partners in caring for themselves.

HEALTH CARE DELIVERY AND THE CHRONIC CARE MODEL
The Primacy of Primary Care

Chronic care most optimally takes place in primary care practice settings, which are best positioned to help manage and coordinate care. This is due to the integral and comprehensive role that primary care plays for an individual patient as the first point of access, the source of long-term care relationships, and the provider of comprehensive services and coordinator of care with specialists, hospitalists, and other care providers.[19] In addition to these essential pillars of primary care, increasing evidence shows that it is most important for a spectrum of types of care—preventive, acute, chronic, and end-of-life care. This is likely one explanation why high-performing health systems around the world are noted to have strong primary care structures.[25] PCMHs combine measures to strengthen access to and reimbursement for primary care providers with the principles of chronic care management found in the CCM.

The Chronic Care Model

The CCM is a guiding theory that suggests how chronic care should be provided in a clinical setting. Developed by Ed Wagner and colleagues at the MacColl Institute more than 20 years ago, it is based on research and experience with improving chronic disease delivery in clinical settings.[13] The CCM identifies the essential elements of a health care system that encourage high-quality chronic disease care as follows:

• The community (resources and policies)
• Health systems (organization of health care)
• Self-management support
• Delivery system design
• Decision support
• Clinical information systems

As described in the model, evidence-based change concepts under each element, in combination, foster productive interactions between informed, "activated patients" (that is, who actively participate in their care) and a prepared, proactive practice team.

We will review the model in more detail, but its key implications are as follows:

1. Productive interactions depend on *collaborative work* by a patient and his or her team of health care workers.
2. The health care system (organization of health care) should be designed to support

the team and the patient so they are *better prepared* for all types of health care interactions.
3. The system is designed specifically to encourage *proactive, planned, and coordinated* care for ongoing health conditions.

These key elements help prevent what Bodenheimer et al. describe as the "tyranny of the urgent,"[24(p. 1775)] in which symptomatic or acute problems dominate the health care interaction.

The CCM helps provide a blueprint for practice redesign by which health care organizations can systematize evidence-based support for patient care while encouraging patient-centeredness, self-management, and collaboration. At the most basic level, this model helps us define who is on the team, what they do, and how they will interact to accomplish the goal of chronic disease management in an ordered and logical way. In this model, the patient is both an individual and a member of a larger population of persons with a shared condition. As an individual, the patient is acknowledged as a partner in his or her health decisions and self-management. The patient, as a member of a particular population, such as people with diabetes, is also recognized as someone who needs particular care (for example, periodic visits for screening for complications related to eyes, kidneys, and feet) and proactive support (for example, ongoing monitoring of glycemic control and self-management support to encourage compliance and healthy lifestyle) that can be tailored to a patient's individual needs. Thus, goals of chronic care are to develop a team and strategy to address different conditions and also to individualize a plan for each patient. This helps balance evidence-based, guideline-driven efforts with personalized and patient-centered care to optimize results.

The CCM has been used to make changes in a variety of care settings around the world, including the United Kingdom (*see* Case Study 6-1, below), France, Denmark, Italy, Germany, and the Netherlands.[10]

CASE STUDY 6-1. THE NATIONAL HEALTH SERVICE AND THE SOCIAL CARE MODEL FOR PEOPLE WITH LONG-TERM CONDITIONS

Setting: In 2005 the United Kingdom National Health Service (NHS) introduced the Social Care Model for people with long-term conditions.

Theoretical Approach: On the basis of the Chronic Care Model, as well as examples by Kaiser Permanente in the United States, they established a generic model that "provides a structured and consistent approach to the management of long term conditions—matching care to need."

Application: NHS officials use risk prediction to identify patients who are frequently hospitalized, and thus at higher risk of readmission. They then stratify them according to their level of need, and coordinate services to meet those needs.

- Tier 1: Patients with complex needs, whether single or multiple chronic conditions (estimated to be approximately 5% of patients)
- Tier 2: Patients with medium level of needs (estimated to be approximately 25% of patients)
- Tier 3: Patients with low level of needs, with conditions under relatively good control (approximately 70% of patients)

Services Delivered: Based on each level of need, they provide case management, personalized care planning, self-management support (including an Experts Patients Program), and assistive technology.

Source: Adapted from U.K. Department of Health: *Supporting People with Long Term Conditions. Feb. 9, 2007.* http://www.dh.gov.uk/en/Publicationsand statistics/Publications/PublicationsPolicyAndGuidance/Browsable/DH_4100317 (accessed Sep. 23, 2011).

WHAT NEEDS TO BE DONE

So what does a prepared, proactive primary care practice look like? What characteristics ensure that high-quality care is delivered and patients' health is optimized? The CCM and the medical literature provide a guide to how we might recognize excellent care (*see* Table 6-1, page 132).

On the basis of these characteristics, we present a "checklist," which constitutes most of the rest of the chapter, of important concepts that each practice or health care system should embrace.

☑ Patients' Relationships with Their Physicians and Care Teams Are the Core of Good Care.

Today, health care is fragmented, as patients receive care from a wide variety of physicians and other medical professionals, who often work in different places. Yet the major building block of any health care system—and the source of much care and healing—is the interaction between patients and their personal caregivers (in the United States, usually a physician), working as part of a team.[26] Effective primary care practices support and build on this relationship by valuing and promoting continuity between patients and providers over time.[27] These strong patient–provider relationships, which focus on people rather than just individual diseases, foster improved communication, trust, and knowledge of patient contexts and preferences, which all lead to improved patient

Table 6-1. Elements, Goals, and Specific Actions Representing the Chronic Care Model

Element	Goal	Action
The health system	Create a culture, organization, and mechanisms that promote safe, high-quality care.	From senior leadership down to frontline staff, the system must encourage care improvement with strategies, incentives, quality improvement, and care-coordination agreements.
Delivery system design	Ensure the delivery of effective, efficient clinical care and self-management support.	Define roles, distribute tasks, use planned interactions based on evidence and guidelines, provide clinical care management services that are appropriate for cultural background, and provide needed follow-up.
Self-manage-ment support	Empower and prepare patients to manage their health and health care.	Recognizing that the patient is the most important person in managing his or her health, the system reorganizes to best support long-term self-management strategies.
Decision support	Promote clinical care that is consistent with scientific evidence and patient preferences.	Integrate evidence-based guidelines as well as specialist expertise into daily clinical practice and share this information with patients to encourage participation.
Clinical information systems	Organize patient and popula-tion data to facilitate efficient and effective care.	Seek or develop information systems that ensure ready access to key clinical data on individual patients as well as populations of patients with shared conditions. Identify important populations for proactive care, provide timely reminders, and monitor performance by team and system.
The community	Mobilize community resources to meet the needs of patients.	Facilitate patients' participation in effective community programs. Partner with organizations to provide resources that the system cannot by itself. Advocate for policies to improve care.

Source: Adapted from Improving Chronic Illness Care: *Home Page.* Group Health Research Institute. http://www.improvingchroniccare.org/ (accessed Sep. 23, 2011).

and provider satisfaction.[28,29] Continuity of care has also been associated with better health behaviors,[30,31] health outcomes,[32] and reduction of emergency department and hospital visits.[33–35]

However, it is important to balance continuity between an individual patient and his or her physician with the ability to use the entire health care team to care for the patient.[36] One technique to improve continuity may include "team branding," in which a member of the team introduces him- or herself in relation to the patient's identified primary care physician or provider. In recommending a specific team member to the patient, the physician is reinforcing the team-based nature of care—which must include clear communication and coordination among different members of the team, as we discuss later in the chapter.

Supporting continuity of care means linking the patient and his or her providers in such a way that all recognizes one another as *partners* in care.[37] One way that practices unintentionally disrupt continuity of care is by using rigid scheduling protocols to maximize immediate access for patients at the expense of seeing patients' established providers. Appointments are offered on the basis of the assumption that, if given the choice, a patient would prefer to obtain an appointment on the same day that he or she telephones rather than waiting to see his or her own health care teams at later dates. Anecdotal evidence suggests, however, that this may not be the case. For example, in one study, patients more often chose to see their own care teams, even when that meant waiting a few days.[38]

One approach to try to balance continuity with timely appointments is known as "advanced access" (also called *open access* or *same-day sched-*

uling). Implementing advanced access helps free up a given provider's schedule to allow flexibility to see his or her patients in a more timely manner.[39] In a well-implemented advanced-access model, physicians and providers start their days with a substantial number of their scheduled slots open, allowing for patients to be seen in a same-day fashion. This runs contrary to traditional models of access, which depend on scheduled appointments for follow-ups and double-booking or protected "carve-out" slots for urgent issues.[16] Instead, advanced access is intended to reduce the backlog of scheduled patients, balance supply and demand, provide alternatives to face-to-face visits, and identify resources that need to be augmented to make it happen. In the process, the providers and their practices have a menu of different communication options, which include secure electronic messaging, scheduled telephone visits, planned care with team members, and Internet-based disease management. This allows for a variety of different "touches" between patients and their physicians, which improves the continuity of their relationships.

- *How You Recognize It:* When asked, a patient tells you who members of his or her team are and who his or her physician is, and physicians know their patients. Patients and physicians are given every opportunity to connect directly with one another through a variety of means.

- For more tools and resources on understanding and implementing advanced access scheduling, see *Improve Primary Care Access* on the Institute for Healthcare Improvement Web site: http://www.ihi.org/explore/Primary CareAccess/Pages/default.aspx (accessed Sep. 23, 2011).

- For more information about alternatives to

the face-to-face visit, including e-visits, group visits, and team-based care, visit the TransforMED℠ Web site: http://www.trans formed.com/whoweare.cfm.

☑ Patients Are Supported to Care for Themselves.

Even in the context of a long-term relationship with a physician, a patient will spend more than 99% of his or her life outside the medical office, self-managing an illness. The patient will choose how and when to take medications, which foods to eat, how often to exercise, whether to smoke, when to get rest, and hundreds of other decisions that will affect the course of his or her health and chronic illness care. Helping the patient to recognize that it takes practice to manage the behaviors, thoughts, and feelings that accompany a chronic disease is a key role for primary care. Traditionally, primary care practices offered patient education in the form of printed brochures or posters. Although patients certainly needs a basic level of knowledge to manage their illness well, what is far more important to patients' long-term success is the *confidence* that they can make changes that will matter for their health and their ability to problem-solve when barriers arise.[40] The idea of self-management support must be incorporated into multiple aspects of a patient's care before, during, and after the visit (*see* Figure 6-1, page 135).

Practices can support patients in self-managing their illnesses in several specific ways, such as referring patients to chronic disease self-management programs in the local community or to online support groups.[41] Practices might also train medical assistants or other team members in motivational interviewing, goal setting, and action planning. Using these skills, team members work with patients to set health goals together. For example, a patient newly diag-

nosed with diabetes typically will have many behavior changes to consider. If exercise, weight control, or the ability to stay mobile is important, the patient may work with the team and establish a goal of walking three times a week. To build confidence, starting slowly with obtainable goals is important. After collaboratively setting goals, team members follow up with patients, build motivation, discuss progress, and brainstorm ways to overcome any obstacles that may have emerged. Building in the capacity to support patient self-management is essential if health outcomes are to improve.

Other ways that practices and hospital systems can facilitate self-management support include providing physician-led group visits for general chronic conditions, facilitated peer groups for support related to specific diseases, and/or patient-triggered action plans for diseases marked by acute exacerbations.[42] When done correctly, group visits can generate income while facilitating peer interaction and shared learning. Emerging evidence shows that linking patients to peers with the same medical conditions can be a low-cost but highly effective method of providing self-management support and improving outcomes. Key elements and specific examples of chronic disease self-management support practices are listed in Table 6-2 (pages 136–137).

Patients can be empowered to make decisions using the best evidence available. Providing information about guidelines to patients can help them clarify goals and share treatment decisions with clinicians. When guidelines fail to identify a recommended course of action for a patient, he or she may need help to understand the options available and the associated risks and benefits, which should involve the patient's clarification of his or her values related

Figure 6-1. Integrating Self-Management Support to Improve Collaborative Care of Chronic Diseases

Source: Excerpted from Schaefer J., et al.: *Partnering in Self-Management Support: A Toolkit for Clinicians*. Cambridge, MA: Institute for Healthcare Improvement, 2009. Available at http://www.improvingchroniccare.org. Used with permission.

to those risks and benefits.[43] Shared decision making between patients and their providers can help improve this process; the use of specific techniques or specific tools (such as videos, Internet-based aids, or booklets) has been shown to improve patients' knowledge and satisfaction related to these choices.[44] These techniques and tools can be provided by the caregiver or staff members during a primary care visit or can be linked to primary care visits (for

example, for prostate cancer screening[45]) and to specialty referrals (for example, for consideration of back surgery[46] or bariatric surgery[47]).

Case Study 6-2 (pages 138–139) illustrates how a small primary health care service in a disadvantaged rural community in the central part of the state of Victoria, Australia, mobilized its efforts across the community to enhance patients' self-management of chronic conditions.

Table 6-2. Twelve Elements of Self-Management Support and Examples of Use

Element	Description	Implementation Example
1. Brief Targeted Assessment	Assessing clinical severity, functional status, patient's problems and goals, behaviors, and barriers related to self-management	Use of an automatic reminder, as per Public Health Service Tobacco Treatment Guideline,* which increased rates of clinician interventions and doubled smoking cessation rates
2. Tailored Educational Interventions	Information alone is insufficient; patients and providers need to use educational interventions that promote skill development.	In adult smokers, self-help materials do not provide additional benefit over advice from a health care professional, except for pregnant women, in which self-help interventions doubled the quit rate; this represents a group for which this intervention may be appropriate.
3. Nonjudgmental Approach	Clinicians more effectively support patient self-management when they provide evidence-based information in a non-judgmental manner.	"Motivational interviewing" is a form of directive counseling that avoids confrontation or judgment; its use is associated with improvements in substance abuse care, weight management, cholesterol, and blood pressure.
4. Collaborative Priority and Goal-Setting	Patients and providers working together to identify priorities, goals, and specific plans.	Collaborative problem definition, followed by realistic goal-setting and a personalized plan, improves outcomes related to health maintenance, clinic attendance, and medical adherence in such diseases as chronic obstructive pulmonary disease (COPD) and diabetes.
5. Collaborative Problem Solving	Providers facilitating patients to develop solutions to ongoing problems	"Problem-solving therapy" improved pain control in arthritis and outcomes in depression.
6. Self-Management by Diverse Providers	Different members of the health care team, as well as laypersons, can effectively deliver support with appropriate role definition and training.	Nurses can provide important guidance regarding lifestyle, medication adherence, and problem solving, with improved outcomes in hypertension, back pain, hyperlipidemia, and other chronic diseases.

(continued on page 137)

Table 6-2. Twelve Elements of Self-Management Support and Examples of Use (continued)

Element	Description	Implementation Example
7. Self-Management Interventions in Diverse Formats	Self-management interventions can be effectively delivered by means of individual face-to-face, group visit, telephone, and self-instruction formats.	Group visits for self-management of persons with Type 2 diabetes improved fasting blood glucose, glycolated hemoglobin (A1C), and knowledge regarding the need for diabetes medication.
8. Patient Self-Efficacy	Enhancing patient self-efficacy regarding chronic illness management improves the process and outcomes of care.	In patients with COPD, a program to improve patient "self-sufficiency" in managing their medications for COPD was associated with reductions in hospitalizations.
9. Active Follow-up	Ongoing follow-up, supported by feedback and reminders for clinicians and patients, helps sustain behaviors and improve outcomes.	Computerized systems to support the primary care provider in completing reminders related to diabetes outpatient care were as good as specialist-coordinated care.
10. Guideline-Based Case Management for Selected Patients	Case management can improve self-management and patient outcomes if (and only if) it is goal directed and guideline based.	Mixed evidence exists for case management; overall, interventions targeting specific diseases are more successful than general conditions supervised by generalists.
11. Evidence-Based Community Programs	Self-management should include evidence-based community-based programs, if possible.	The six-week, peer-led "Arthritis Self-Management Program" developed by Lorig and colleagues[†] led to improved pain and fatigue management for up to four years following the course; this approach has been expanded to other chronic conditions.
12. Multifaceted Interventions	Combinations of different components rather than individual items lead to more effective interventions.	A multifaceted approach to smoking cessation using teams of providers, group visits, and individual sessions were more successful than either alone.

* U.S. Department of Health & Human Services, Public Health Service: *Clinical Practice Guideline: Treating Tobacco Use and Dependence: 2008 Update.* May 2008. http://www.surgeongeneral.gov/tobacco/treating_tobacco_use08.pdf (accessed Sep. 23, 2011).

† Lorig K.R., Mazonson P.D., Holman H.R.: Evidence suggesting that health education for self-management in patients with chronic arthritis has sustained health benefits while reducing health care costs. *Arthritis Rheum* 36:439–446, Apr. 1993.

Source: Adapted from Battersby M., et al.: Twelve evidence-based principles for implementing self-management support in primary care. *Jt Comm J Qual Patient Saf* 36:561–570, Dec. 2010.

CASE STUDY 6-2. COMMUNITYWIDE MOBILIZATION FOR SELF-MANAGEMENT OF CHRONIC CONDITIONS

Setting: At Maryborough District Health Service, a primary care health service, care across the inpatient and community services was traditionally focused on an acute model. When older patients with chronic conditions were offered the possibility of support for chronic condition self-management, the health workers' responses were usually along the lines of, "Don't bother wasting your time" and "It's not relevant, they are acute."

Intervention: The new approach, the Hospital Admission Risk Program (HARP), which began in 2008, was intended to prevent avoidable hospital presentations and admissions by providing community-based self-management support for persons with chronic conditions and/or complex needs who frequently used urgent care centers and hospitals and who could benefit from coordinated care.[1] The increasing demands on this primary care health service—in particular, high caseloads with insufficient staff and physical resources to meet patient needs—prompted the need for change. The Chronic Care Model domains,[2] the Assessment of Chronic Illness Care (ACIC), and the Patient Assessment of Care for Chronic Conditions (PCIC) tools[3,4] informed a range of systematic change steps. The Flinders Program, a self-management care-planning tool,[5] was also implemented with patients enrolled in HARP as part of a broader communitywide effort to engage and to mobilize support. HARP included diverse and creative partnerships with services and programs not usually thought of when considering health partnerships, such as the local YMCA, library, local service clubs, local council, supermarkets, schools, and others that connected to where people lived in their community. A common chronic condition self-management language was also embedded into workforce development across the services, including training, communities of practice, performance appraisals, position descriptions, and team meetings, to promote a whole service culture to support the changes. This prepared the various support systems to be more proactive in working with people with chronic conditions by building capacity for health promotion, relapse prevention, and chronic condition self-management to prevent and reduce unnecessary hospital admissions.

Results: Hospital admission rates and lengths of stay have significantly declined, particularly for inpatients who need high levels of care. For example, admissions, which totaled more than 150 bed-days per month (August–October) in 2008, decreased to 30, 10, and 0, respectively, for these months in 2009. These results have been maintained into 2010 and 2011.

Impact: The most important lesson learned from this experience has been that if you are going to implement effective health care, you need community participation and engagement; health is not just about health services. These lessons have been taken up by further translation work by Flinders Human Behaviour & Health Research Unit, Flinders University, as reflected, in particular, by two large initiatives now in progress (2011–2014): (1) a National Flinders Closing the Gaps program, in which the Aboriginal Health Workforce is being trained and supported to embed chronic condition self-management support into its practice; and (2) a National Department of Veterans Affairs program, which entails capacity building for general practitioners, practice nurses, and community nurses to apply chronic condition–management approaches to veterans at high risk of hospitalization.

References

1. Austin Health: *Hospital Admissions Risk Program (HARP).* http://www.austin.org.au/Page.aspx?ID=580 (accessed Sep. 23, 2011).
2. Wagner E.H., Austin B.T., Von Korff M.: Organizing care for patients with chronic illness. *Milbank Q* 74(4):511–544, 1996.
3. Improving Chronic Illness Care: *ACIC Survey.* Group Health Research Institute. http://www.improving chroniccare.org/index.php?p=ACIC_Survey&s=35 (accessed Sep. 23, 2011).
4. Improving Chronic Illness Care: *PACIC Survey.* Group Health Research Institute. http://www.improving chroniccare.org/index.php?p=PACIC_survey&s=36 (accessed Sep. 23, 2011).
5. Flinders University: *The Flinders Program™.* http://www.flinders.edu.au/medicine/sites/fhbhru/ self-management.cfm (accessed Sep. 23, 2011).

Source: Provided by Sharon Lawn, Ph.D., M.S.W., Associate Professor, Flinders Human Behaviour & Health Research Unit, Flinders University, Adelaide, Australia, with acknowledgment of Raelene Liddicoat, HARP Registered Nurse, Victoria, Australia.

- *How You Recognize It:* Patients set goals for themselves in partnership with their care teams. Care team members or peer supports follow up via phone or e-mail to provide help.

- For more tools and resources about building self-management support into clinical practice, see *New Health Partnerships: Improving Care by Engaging Patients* at http://www.newhealthpartnerships.org.

- For more information on tools for shared decision making with patients, visit the Web site of the Foundation for Informed Medical Decision Making: http://www.informed medicaldecisions.org.

☑ **Clinical Interactions Are Informed by the Most Up-to-Date Evidence on Effectiveness.**
Much has been written about the importance of using clinical practice guidelines to improve health outcomes for patients with chronic dis-eases. New research is constantly emerging that aims to clarify which treatments, tests, and pharmacological interventions are most effective at controlling symptoms and improving health. But none of those guidelines are effective if they are not integrated into the everyday practice of clinical care. Many practices rely on the physician to remember to order all the laboratory tests for each illness, but we know that this method is not successful at ensuring that high-quality care is delivered. McGlynn and colleagues showed that patients receiving care in this manner received the recommended treatment less than half the time.[48]

Clinical decision support is a term that describes the practice of "hardwiring" evidence-based recommendations and best practices into a practice's work flow. State-of-the-art tools now go beyond "pop-up" boxes or flagged reminders that appear in charts or electronic medical records for physicians alone. Although memory aids, such as computer-based reminders, may be helpful, far more successful are activities that transform clinical guidelines into standard work processes, delegate tasks, and empower more members of the team. For example, nurses, pharmacists, and medical assistants can use standing physician orders to order appropriate monitoring tests, provide vaccinations, make medication adjustments, perform screenings, or make referrals for recommended preventive health appointments. Clinical protocols can be built into electronic medical records that flag hazardous drug interactions, link to order sets for appropriate laboratory testing, and prompt nurses to conduct reminder phone calls.

With increasingly potent pharmaceutical options and a growing number of patients with multiple chronic diseases, nurses and pharmacists can play an important role in helping adjust medications on the basis of standing protocols.[49,50] Team members can use agreed-on protocols and algorithms that have the goal of treating to target for clinical diseases, such as diabetes.[51] Clinical pharmacists can be particularly helpful to patients and providers in adjusting medications to ensure that treatment goals are realized, checking for drug interactions, and ensuring that patients know how to take their medications as prescribed.[52–54] Although smaller clinics may not have access to clinical pharmacists, clinics that do can develop chronic disease management referrals for ongoing or intensive management of medication-intensive conditions, such as hypertension, diabetes, or coronary artery disease. Nurses can train to use guideline-based algorithms to adjust medications for such problems as hypertension or hyperlipidemia and serve as important points of contact to review compliance and lifestyle changes related to chronic diseases.[55,56] Case Study 6-3 (below) explores the program used by Group Health, an integrated group practice and health plan in Washington State (United States), in which primary care practice–based nurse care managers help facilitate evidence-based care of chronic diseases.

CASE STUDY 6-3. THE TEAMCARE APPROACH FOR MULTIPLE CHRONIC DISEASES

Background: TEAMcare is an integrated program that improves disease control and quality of life for patients with diabetes and/or cardiovascular disease and depression. In a two-year study ending in 2010, this collaborative care program was tested as part of a randomized trial at 14 Group Health Cooperative clinics. TEAMcare involves using a nurse care manager, embedded in the patient's primary care home, to systematically monitor patient progress, empower the patient to change health behaviors, and work closely with the patient's primary care physician to adjust medications.

Intervention: The TEAMcare intervention was guided by evidence-based clinical guidelines for the management of depression and cardiovascular disease and/or diabetes. Care was staged to improve patient confidence and quality of life by addressing depression first.

Specifically, the TEAMcare nurses did the following:
- Worked with patients to identify specific, measureable goals for disease control (blood pressure, glycolated hemoglobin [A1C] values)
- Systematically and proactively monitored progress
- Collaborated with the primary care physicians to persistently tailor pharmacotherapy to boost patient response
- Supported patient self-care
- Conducted regular clinical case reviews with the supervising psychiatrist, nurses, and primary care provider

Results: Testing in these clinics showed that the TEAMcare program is significantly more effective than usual primary care in improving patients' glucose, blood pressure, and cholesterol and depression control.

Impact: On the basis of these results, the Group Health Foundation funded piloting of the intervention in several sites, where they are testing operational and implementation adjustments.

- *How You Recognize It:* Nurses, medical assistants, pharmacists, or other team members share in the clinical care of patients by ordering tests or conducting screenings on the basis of standing orders.

- For more information on the TEAMcare approach, visit the organization's Web site: http://www.teamcarehealth.org/ (accessed Sep. 23, 2011).

☑ **Timely, High-Quality Data Are Available.** To provide proactive planned care, a practice must know who its patients are and what they need. A "registry" is a method of collecting timely, accurate clinical data that are easily aggregated and sorted to make this work much easier. Some practices do chart reviews or manually enter clinical data into spreadsheets for certain patient subpopulations. Practices with electronic health records (EHRs) can sometimes use special programs to aggregate patient data in this way. Generally, clinical data, as compared with claims data, provide much more accurate and timely views into the planned care needs of patients. Finding a low-cost, relatively efficient way of collecting data is worth undertaking because accurate data are essential for determining the extent of improvement in care.

Disease-specific registries provide information on plans of care and whether measurable goals are being met.[57] Registries can also be used to track ordering and completion of recommended screenings—for example, for colorectal, breast, or cervical cancer—to help the physician or practice provide better care for the entire population in a patient-centered manner. For example, a designated member of the practice can "query" the registry via an intranet site (*see* Figure 6-2, page 143) to determine which patients have not had recommended screenings, narrow the list to those patients who have upcoming visits, and then call or send letters to ask those patients to stop by the laboratory to complete the necessary tests. Evidence related to diabetes, for example, suggests that this communication can be associated with improved outcomes.[58] Case Study 6-4 (beginning below) describes a registry for diabetes.

One note of caution about EHRs: Many practices that are adopting EHRs with the hopes of getting quick access to population-based data such as registries are disappointed to find that many vendors do not offer registry reporting as part of their platform. In fact, a recent article by Romano and colleagues found that EHRs *alone* do nothing to improve quality.[59] EHRs are typically designed to improve billing, documentation, and compliance. EHRs may improve reporting of chronic disease measures as part of a larger quality improvement (QI) effort.[60] The registry functionality—and using that functionality—is also linked to improved care.[61] Just because you've implemented an EHR does not mean that you have easy access to clinically important population data. During this time of expanding EHR incentives and options, decision makers need to be aware that implementing an EHR is an opportunity to have a new tool to improve care, not just a better way to store information.

CASE STUDY 6-4. USING A REGISTRY TO IMPROVE CHRONIC DISEASE CARE: THE GREEN MEADOWS CLINIC IN AUSTRALIA

Setting: Green Meadows Clinic, East Melbourne (Victoria, Australia); in conjunction with the Whitehorse Division of General Practice "Navigating Self-Management" Program

Intervention: At the start of the project, in June 2006, Green Meadows Clinic had approximately 100 patients with diabetes on its books. Staff from the local division believed that this figure could be much higher. With the assistance of the Divisions of General Practices (http://www.gpv.org.au/), which are spread throughout Australia and help general practices improve their business operations, the clinic established a registry, which indicated that the practice had an actual population of 537 patients with diabetes. The clinic then started to complete an annual cycle of care (ACC) for most of those patients. An ACC outlines the steps in best-practice care for diabetes management, as described in evidence-based guidelines for diabetes care. Associated costs can be claimed through the Australian government's Service Incentive Payments if the practice is registered with the Practice Incentive Program. The registry provided information indicating that an ACC was being completed on only 5% of people with diabetes.

Results: By establishing a registry and improving its recall system, Green Meadows Clinic increased its completion of ACC to 30% within an eight-month period. Not only did this have benefits for the people receiving chronic disease care, but the clinic was rewarded financially. Through the Australian government's Medicare Benefits Scheme, the clinic boosted its income by $35,000.

Lessons Learned: Lessons learned included the need to (1) start with "data cleaning" for most general practices, (2) train general practitioners in change management, and (3) alert practices to the benefits of self-management support work, in terms of improvements in efficiency or outcomes for patients returning for the same problem.

Source: Kubina N., Kelly J.: *Navigating Self-Management . . . A Practical Approach to Implementation for Australian Health Agencies.* Melbourne East GP Network, 2007. http://www.megpn.com.au/Docs/ChronicIllness/GoodLife Club/NavigatingSelfManagement.pdf (accessed Sep. 23, 2011). Used with permission of Naomi Kubina and Jill Kelly, with additional information provided by Kubina, consultant, Healthy Active Partners, Jun. 27, 2011.

- *How You Recognize It:* The practice can easily and repeatedly identify which patients need improved preventive or chronic care.

- For more information on Web-based disease registries, see http://www.ipipprogram.org/.

- For more information on meaningful use criteria for EHRs in the United States, see *Being a Meaningful User of Electronic Health Records* from the U.S. Department of Health & Human Services, Office of the National Coordinator for Health Information Technology: http://healthit.hhs.gov/portal/ server.pt/community/healthit_hhs_gov__ meaningful_use_-_providers/2998.

☑ **Care Is Proactive and Population-Based.**
To live full and healthy lives, patients with chronic illnesses cannot wait until medical emergencies drive them to seek care. Rather, they benefit from ongoing, proactive support and partnerships that help them care for themselves and avoid health problems before they start. That means that a primary care practice is responsible not just to those patients who come into the office for a visit but to those who do not come in as well. When physicians take accountability for a population, or panel, of patients, they can begin to ensure that everyone is receiving the care they need. As stated earlier, registries and similar panel-management applications can help physicians and their teams identify and reach out to patients who are in need of recommended care. Registry functions can allow clinics to contact patients with upcoming appointments to improve care in a patient-centered manner. Case Study 6-5 (pages 143-144) demonstrates how chronic disease registries can be appropriately incorporated into clinical work flows as part of a successful PCMH transformation.

Figure 6-2. Diabetes Registry Intranet Page for Cleveland Department of Veterans Affairs Medical Center

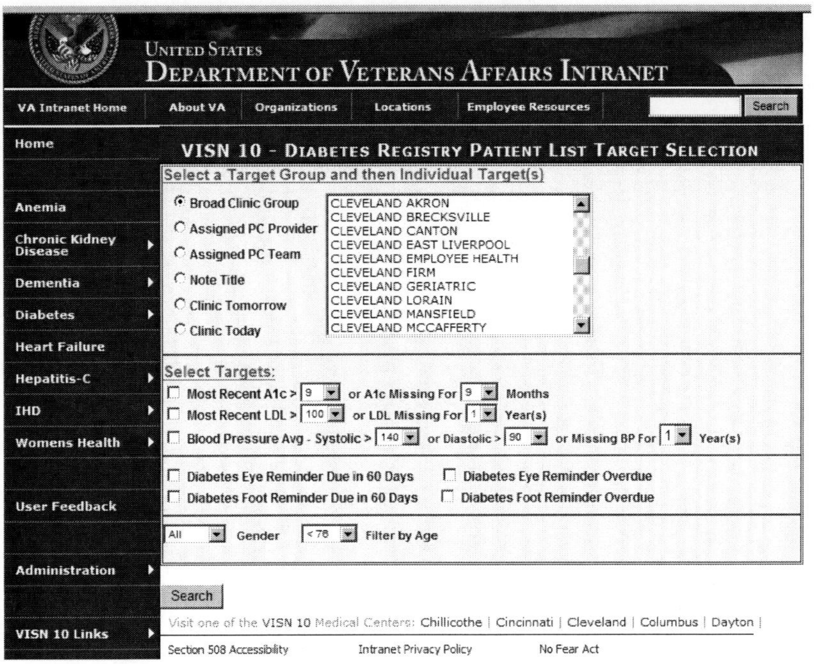

Source: Provided courtesy of Veteran's Integrated Service Network 10, personal communication between author [W.G.W.] and Brook Watts, M.D., M.P.H., director, Medical Quality Improvement, Cleveland Department of Veterans Affairs Medical Center.

CASE STUDY 6-5. USING DATA FOR PROACTIVE CARE SETTING

Setting: In 2006 Group Health (Seattle) initiated a redesign of its Factoria Medical Center clinic (Bellevue, Washington) as part of a PCMH pilot. Multiple simultaneous changes were made by the administration and clinic staff, including ensuring that each provider had a reasonable panel of patients (which entailed a reduction from an average of 2,300 to 1,800 patients per full-time provider). Physicians were then asked to work with their care teams to improve the care for their assigned panels of patients.

Intervention: Clinic staff gathered data from electronic health records and developed patient care exception reports. Each of these reports listed a patient who was missing a guideline-based screening, test, or laboratory value for a chronic condition. Each morning, the team would review the list of patients coming in for visits and discuss who would be responsible for ensuring that the planned care needs were met, even if the patients were coming in for other reasons. The care team called patients who did not have scheduled visits and invited them to come in for planned care visits. They also sent birthday cards to each patient with recommended preventive screenings relevant for their ages and sexes.

Results: An evaluation of Group Health's PCMH showed that the quality of patient care improved, that providers and patients felt more satisfied with their care experiences, and that the cost savings in the first two years offset the initial investment.

Source: Adapted from Reid R.J., et al.: The Group Health medical home at year two: Cost savings, higher patient satisfaction, and less burnout for providers. *Health Aff (Millwood)* 29:835–843, May 2010.

Private-practice physicians may view the idea of patient panels as only relevant to large, capitated provider groups. However, many efforts across the United States are helping fee-for-service practices shift from a practice perspective focused on the care of individual patients to one that systematically assesses and cares for the needs of a population, or panel, of patients.[62,63]

- *How You Recognize It:* Patients receive reminders for preventive care screenings and chronic illness care. Providers actively reach out to patients whose planned care needs have not been met and invite them to come in for visits.

- For more resources and tools to help practices redesign their care to be proactive, planned, and population based, see the "Integrating Chronic Care and Business Strategies in the Safety Net" toolkit at http://www.improvingchroniccare.org.

☑ **Care Is Coordinated.**

No matter how good the primary care system, patients with chronic diseases often need specialist consultants to support their care. Visits to podiatrists, ophthalmologists, nutritionists, exercise programs, laboratories, and/or pharmacies are likely to be regular features of the lives of patients with complex chronic illness. Coordinating this care, providing referrals, and following up with patients to ensure that their questions are answered are part of the work of the primary care practice. Coordinating care can dramatically improve patients' experiences and has the potential to result in cost savings by reducing duplicate tests and by helping patients access appropriate care (for example, heading to a primary care provider rather than the emergency department for a complication related to known congestive heart failure).

Some patients need minimal levels of support, such as facilitating a referral to a specialist, providing the consulting physician with relevant clinical data, and ensuring that follow-up information is received. However, for other patients with many chronic diseases or social needs, increasingly intensive care management may be needed. This clinical and logistical care support is often provided by a registered nurse ("navigator") who is trained in intensive self-management support and medication adjustment aimed at treating patients to target. Care managers can also offer robust logistic support to patients by helping them navigate the health system and access community resources. The relationship between higher-level clinical care management and less-intensive clinical care follow-up and care coordination is depicted in Figure 6-3 (page 145).

Many organizations have experimented with how best to deliver this high-intensity care management.[64] Should the nurse work in the

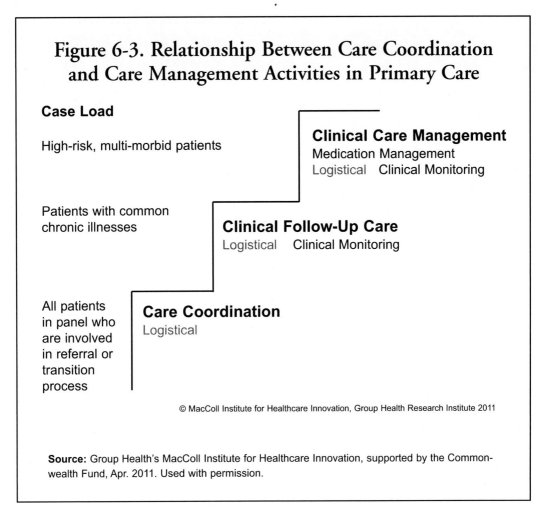

Figure 6-3. Relationship Between Care Coordination and Care Management Activities in Primary Care

Case Load

High-risk, multi-morbid patients

Clinical Care Management
Medication Management
Logistical   Clinical Monitoring

Patients with common chronic illnesses

Clinical Follow-Up Care
Logistical   Clinical Monitoring

All patients in panel who are involved in referral or transition process

Care Coordination
Logistical

© MaccColl Institute for Healthcare Innovation, Group Health Research Institute 2011

Source: Group Health's MacColl Institute for Healthcare Innovation, supported by the Commonwealth Fund, Apr. 2011. Used with permission.

practice with the physician, or can she contact the patient via telephone from a remote location? How do you identify which patients need intensive care management? How do you know when they are "done"? Who should do the care management—a nurse, a social worker, or someone else? Evidence suggests that care managers do best when linked closely with the patients' regular source of care. In fact, the more integrated they are into the regular care team, the more effective they seem to be.[65] Coordinators colocated with physicians can make it easier to collaborate and to decide which patients may need more help or when a patient's problems have become sufficiently sta-

ble so the patient no longer requires intensive care management.

• *How You Recognize It:* Patients with the most complex needs receive extra support from a care manager embedded in the primary care practice.

• For more tools and resources about creating a care management program in your practice, see Johns Hopkins University's Guided Care® Web site: http://www.guidedcare.org.

☑ **Care Is Provided by a Team.**

For a practice to improve chronic disease care, it must weave together multiple different functions into its day's work flow. However, how does a practice ensure that the following conditions are met?

- Patients and providers are linked, have continuous relationships, and recognize one another as partners in care. Patients receive self-management support and are activated to manage their diseases.
- The clinical practice is guided by evidence and timely data to deliver a planned, proactive, population-based approach to caring for patients.
- Care is coordinated.

The estimated 18 hours per day for a physician to provide all the recommended preventive and chronic disease care for an average-size primary care panel,[21] as cited previously, does not include caring for acute needs. Clearly, one person cannot do this work alone—it takes a team of medical assistants, nurses, pharmacists, and others to take on various roles. For team members' skills to be fully optimized, team members must be given responsibility and accountability for meaningful processes—having the physician delegate tasks is not enough. For example, the front-desk staff might be responsible for ensuring that patients see their chosen teams, reaching out to them when follow-up care is needed, and reminding patients with planned care visits to bring in their medications. We know that highly functional teams are one of the most powerful tools to improve care and can have a greater impact on improving patients' health than almost any other factor.[62] However, this requires that teams develop work flows that are based on what patients need. Case Study 6-6 (beginning on this page) provides insight into important components for successfully implementing case management related to diabetes.

CASE STUDY 6-6. THE INGREDIENTS FOR AN INTEGRATED TEAM APPROACH TO DIABETES CARE: PARTNERSHIPS FOR HEALTH IN ONTARIO, CANADA

Setting: In 2008 Partnerships for Health was introduced as a quality improvement initiative that employed the Chronic Disease Prevention and Management Framework in Ontario, Canada.

Intervention: The program brought together key primary health care providers—family physicians, internal and external administrative staff, and allied providers, including Community Care Access Centre (CCAC) case managers—in an integrated approach to improve the management of diabetes in primary care sites in the region. The program put an emphasis on (1) enhancing the sharing of information across the continuum of care for improved collaboration, (2) engaging and supporting patient self-management, (3) using evidence-based guidelines to deliver planned and proactive care, and (4) making better use of technology to track and to monitor patient data and to inform quality improvement efforts. One of the main objectives was to develop a partnership between the practice team and the CCAC case manager, who would assist persons with diabetes in navigating the health care system, accessing community resources, and linking to specialist services and tertiary care, when appropriate.

Key Ingredients: (1) Canadian Diabetes Association evidence-based guidelines for care; (2) Chronic Disease Prevention and Management Framework (a system redesign strategy); (3) the Model for Improvement, a quality-improvement approach[1]; (4) the Breakthrough Series Learning Collaborative, an action-oriented adult-learning methodology[2]; and (5) timely and ongoing information technology support.

Results: Overall, team functioning improved, and multiple factors that influence the establishment of partnerships were identified. Beyond team functioning, the results showed improvement in the knowledge of and adherence to best-practice guidelines, understanding of data and technology, and the use of data for quality improvement. All these improvements were described by health care participants as contributing to the significant improvement observed in clinical outcomes, particularly for patients who were out of target at baseline, and to improved professional job satisfaction as well as patient satisfaction. Patients' perceptions of many aspects of the new approach to care were mixed.

Updates: The Partnerships for Health Project ended in March 2011, but the work of the teams continues in their local practices and through the South West Local Health Integration Network's Quality and Process Improvement Program (http://www.partnershipsforhealth.ca/). Furthermore, some teams have joined the Learning Communities Program implemented provincewide by the Quality Improvement and Innovation Partnership (http://learningcomm unity.qiip.ca/).

References

1. Institute for Healthcare Improvement: *How to Improve.* http://www.ihi.org/IHI/Topics/Improvement/ ImprovementMethods/HowToImprove/ (accessed Sep. 23, 2011).
2. Institute for Healthcare Improvement (IHI): *The Breakthrough Series: IHI's Collaborative Model for Achieving Breakthrough Improvement.* IHI Innovation Series white paper. 2003. http://www.ihi.org (accessed Sep. 23, 2011).

Source: Adapted from *Final Report of the Three Year CDPM Initiative: Partnerships for Health: Improving Diabetes Care in the South West LHIN.* Mar. 22, 2011. http://www.partnershipsforhealth.ca/Partnership_docs/ PartnershipsForHealthFinalReport.pdf (accessed Sep. 23, 2011); and *Partnerships for Health Evaluation—Brief Overview of Results and Findings.* Jan. 31, 2011. http://www.partnershipsforhealth.ca/Partnership_docs/ PFHEvaluationSummaryReport.pdf (accessed Sep. 23, 2011). Additional information was provided by Dr. Stewart Harris and Jann Paquette-Warren, who led the external evaluation of the project from the Centre for Studies in Family Medicine at the University of Western Ontario (London, Ontario, Canada).

However, creating functioning clinical teams can be a challenge in practice. Colocating a group of professionals is only the beginning. For teams to be truly functional, they need the elements shown in Sidebar 6-1 (page 148).

- *How You Recognize It:* Instead of starting when the provider walks into the examination room, the value-added, clinically important part of a patient's visit begins when he or she walks in the door and talks to the receptionist.

- Team functioning is something that can always be improved. For more resources and tools for creating and developing clinical teams, see Qualis Health's *Implementation Guide: Continuous and Team-Based Healing Relationships,* available at http://www.qhmedicalhome.org/ safety-net/upload/TBC-12_20_V1.pdf.

☑ **Care Is Constantly Being Improved.**
As stated elsewhere, "Organizations that improve quality outcomes are organizations that have a culture of quality improvement and see quality improvement as directly related to patient outcomes."[66] Practices that excel at caring for chronically ill patients almost always have a relentless focus on data and improvement. Such practices refer to population-based data to better ensure that everyone is getting the guideline-based care they need; they look at individual data to ensure that blood sugars and hypertension, for example, are under control. They look at the percentage of time patients see

---

Sidebar 6-1. Critical Elements for Functional Teams

- Senior leadership support for reorganizing staff, investing in training, and colocating team members

- A composition that enables them to address the common needs of the community. Patient populations, and the communities from which they come, vary substantially in demographics, disease prevalence, and social circumstances. To respond to those unique needs, the composition of primary care teams must also vary.

- Time to meet regularly to plan and improve care

- A shared recognition of and respect for other care providers and family members whom patients consider essential parts of the care team, even those outside the practice

- A shared commitment to supporting the panel of patients and other team members

---

their own care teams and how long it takes patients to get an appointment. However, such practices do not just refer to data; they act on them. Just as a clinician adjusts medications when a patient is not meeting a clinical target, teams adjust their approach when quality goals are not being met.[67] Having an organized and standard approach to QI that involves team members, physicians, and patients is essential to improving the processes of care and the health of patients. We briefly discuss approaches to QI methods later in this chapter.

- *How You Recognize It:* Data are visible throughout the practice. Plans for improvement involve patients.

- For more tools and resources about quality improvement, search Joint Commission Resources, http://www.jcrinc.com/Search/; the Institute for Healthcare Improvement, http://www.ihi.org; and *The Joint Commission Journal on Quality and Patient Safety*™, among other resources.

IMPLEMENTING CHANGE: THE PATIENT-CENTERED MEDICAL HOME

The PCMH is one model that has been advanced in the United States for the redesign of primary care practices to be better able to provide chronic care in a team-based manner. It is defined by seven basic principles, as shown in Sidebar 6-2 (page 149), many of which are also present in the CCM. Outside the United States, some health care systems have adopted principles of the CCM and then continued to address issues of access, continuity, and quality improvement that are in keeping with the PCMH. For example, in Sweden, collaboration between the Jönköping County health system and an innovation and learning center within the health system facilitated an effective combination of "top down" (health care leadership–initiated) and "bottom up" (frontline caregiver–enacted) actions, with excellent results.[68] Initial evidence from the United States suggests that improvements are possible in care outcomes, staff burnout, patient satisfaction, and costs.[69,70] Case Study 6-7 (pages 149–150) illustrates how larger-scale efforts to introduce the PCMH

Sidebar 6-2. Principles of the Patient-Centered Medical Home

- Each patient has a personal physician.

- Care is provided in terms of a whole-person orientation.

- The patient's personal physician leads a team of individuals at the practice level who collectively take responsibility for his or her ongoing care.

- Care is coordinated and integrated, facilitated by the use of patient registries and health information technology, such as electronic health records, across all elements of the health care system and the community.

- The medical practice focuses on quality and safety.

- Access to care is promoted.

- Changes in health care financing and physician payment systems support the other components of the model.

Source: Adapted from Rittenhouse D.R., et al.: Small and medium-size physician practices use few patient-centered medical home processes. *Health Aff (Millwood)* 30:1575–1584, Aug. 2011.

---

with CCM principles can be successful in improving chronic disease care in a variety of sites.

CASE STUDY 6-7. PATIENT-CENTERED MEDICAL HOME IMPLEMENTATION GUIDED BY THE CHRONIC CARE MODEL: A STATEWIDE MULTIPAYER INITIATIVE IN PENNSYLVANIA

Background: A unique statewide multipayer initiative in Pennsylvania was undertaken to implement the PCMH guided by the Chronic Care Model (CCM), with diabetes as an initial target disease. This project represented the first broad-scale CCM implementation with payment reform across a diverse range of practice organizations and one of the largest PCMH multipayer initiatives.

Methods: Practices implemented the CCM and PCMH through regional Breakthrough Series learning collaboratives, supported by Improv-ing Performance in Practice (IPIP) practice coaches, with required monthly quality reporting enhanced by multipayer infrastructure payments. Some 105 practices, representing 382 primary care providers, were engaged in the four regional collaboratives. The practices from the Southeast region of Pennsylvania (SEPA) focused on diabetes patients ($n = 10,016$).

Results: During the first intervention year (May 2008–May 2009), all practices achieved at least Level 1 National Committee for Quality Assurance Physician Practice Connections Patient-Centered Medical Home recognition. The percentage of patients who had evidence-based complications screening and who were on therapies to reduce morbidity and mortality (statins, angiotensin-converting enzyme inhibitors) improved significantly. In addition, small but statistically significant improvements were made in key clinical parameters for blood pressure and cholesterol levels, with the greatest absolute improvement in the highest-risk patients.

Impact: The intervention in SEPA was the first step of a statewide multipayer effort. Rollouts followed in the remaining six regions (Southcentral, Southwest, Northeast, Northwest, Northcentral, and Southeast-2), three with payer involvement and three under a small state grant program. Statewide, 152 practices and 644 providers have been involved in similar regional learning collaboratives supported by practice coaching. Over time, it will be important to continue to monitor the intervention to fully assess the impact of these improvements in clinical care on costs. Subsequent years of the rollout are focusing on better identifying the highest-cost individuals, engaging community resources more effectively, and uniformly incorporating care management into routine clinical flow.

Source: Adapted from Gabbay R.A., et al.: Multipayer patient-centered medical home implementation guided by the Chronic Care Model. *Jt Comm J Qual Patient Saf* 37:265–273, Jun. 2011.

Sidebar 6-3 (page 151) presents the specific changes that the 105 Southeast region of Pennsylvania (SEPA) practices described as their single best improvement at the end of Year 1 (May 2009).

The PCMH model is promising, but it is too early to know whether its success in certain settings can be easily reproduced in different practice settings.[71] In the United States, PCMH projects are under way in many states, with more and more being implemented.*

These projects are taking place in smaller clinics, as well as in large integrated health care systems. The U.S. Department of Veterans Affairs is undertaking one of the largest efforts to implement principles of the PCMH as part of its Patient Aligned Care Teams transformation.[72] This initiative, in combination with evaluations of PCMH pilot sites, can offer useful information and examples of what works and what does not.

Although each experience is specific to a particular site, some commonalities are apparent. In an evaluation of 36 practice sites involved in the TransforMED PCMH pilot, Nutting and colleagues suggested that for the medical home to be successful, practice settings needed to move beyond incremental reforms (such as same-day appointments, chronic disease registries, or designated care management nurses) to truly transform the relationships among team members, improving communication and collaboration around a patient's needs.[73] Nutting et al. suggested that such a transformation required time (likely, three to five years), coordination of technology (often across multiple different settings), and sufficient "adaptive reserve"—"an internal capability for organizational learning and development"[73(p. 442)]—to deal with the complex process of ongoing changes in the practice. In terms of the improvement of chronic care, some of the most difficult challenges related to changing established routines and traditional roles, as well as incorporating proactive population management and team-based care.[73]

- For more tools and resources about PCMH, see the Patient-Centered Primary Care Collaborative's *Who We Are* page at http://www.pcpcc.net/who-we-are.

- For more information about standards and accreditation for the Patient-Centered

---

* For an interactive display of demonstrations by state, see *Pilots & Demonstrations* on the Patient-Centered Primary Care Collaborative Web site: http://www.pcpcc.net/pcpcc-pilot-projects (accessed Sep. 23, 2011).

Sidebar 6-3. One "Best-Practice Change," Reported by Individual Southeastern Pennsylvania Region Practices at Year 1 by Key Components of the Chronic Care Model and Patient-Centered Medical Home

Access and Communication
- Patient reminder systems for primary care and specialist visits
- Open-access scheduling
- Learning to meld planned visits with open-access scheduling

Patient Tracking and Registry Functions
- Using a disease registry to track patients individually and as a population
- Implementing an electronic health record (EHR) system
- Standardized data collection/input into an EHR system
- Using a standardized visit template to address all needed care
- Risk stratification of patients
- Embedding clinical guidelines into work flow

Care Management/Delivery System Design
- Previsit planning and outreach to address gaps in care
- Daily care team huddle to plan care for patients scheduled that day
- Involving medical assistants more in the care of patients (completing flow sheets, doing monofilament tests, medication reconciliation)
- Introduction of care management for high-risk patients
- On-site ophthalmology clinic

Patient Self-Management Support
- Change in attitude to recognize patient as team member
- Asking patients how to help them better manage their conditions
- New health educator to provide enhanced self-management support
- New diabetes self-management tool geared toward low-literacy patients
- Group visits
- Patient progress reports to help patients track their conditions
- More-intensive patient education

Change Management
- Adopting Plan-Do-Study-Act process as change agent to help focus weekly meetings
- Hiring advanced practice nurses to manage improvement processes and train staff

Source: Gabbay R.A., et al.: Multipayer patient-centered medical home implementation guided by the Chronic Care Model. *Jt Comm J Qual Patient Saf* 37:265–273, Jun. 2011.

Medical Home, see *Primary Care Medical Home* on the Joint Commission's Web site: http://www.jointcommission.org/accreditation/pchi.aspx.

- Tools and resources about PCMH, including *Patient-Centered Medical Home Guidelines: A Tool to Compare National Programs,* can also be found at the Medical Group Management Association Web site: http://www.mgma.com/PCMH.

- For more information on assessment tools for recognition of PCMH, see the Urban Institute's *Patient-Centered Medical Home Recognition Tools: A Comparison of Ten Surveys' Content and Operational Details.* http://www.urban.org/publications/412338.html.

MEASURING CHANGE AND EVALUATING IMPROVEMENT: FRAMEWORKS FOR EVALUATING CHANGE

To help guide any efforts at improving chronic disease care, it is imperative that practice sites choose and use organized QI strategies, which provide a structure to conduct ongoing evaluation of the success or failure of individual interventions. Although an in-depth discussion of evaluating change is beyond the scope of this chapter, we discuss a few approaches in brief, with a relevant case study.

One QI approach developed at Dartmouth identifies each "clinical microsystem"—"a small group of people who work together on a regular basis to provide care to discrete subpopulations of patients"[74(p. 7)]—as a specific area that may be evaluated and changed. The first step in this approach is to make an assessment of the current practice setting using the "5 Ps"—purpose, patients, professionals, processes, and patterns. This approach helps clarify the goals of a practice setting and determine how important processes related to that goal occur. More importantly, it can serve as the framework of a group exercise to communicate about the goals and actions of a practice and to provide a visual product that can serve as a "map" of the clinic for all the members of the system to view and to comment upon. Case Study 6-8 (below) shows how an individual clinic used a systematic approach to gain an understanding of how it was spending clinical time.

CASE STUDY 6-8. APPLYING THE "5 Ps" TO A PRIMARY CARE PRACTICE: THE GREENHOUSE INTERNISTS EXAMPLE

Background: Greenhouse Internists, a five-physician community-based internal medicine practice in Philadelphia, wanted to evaluate how much work was done outside "regular" reimbursable visits through the year to better determine how its time was being spent. The practice had 8,440 patients between 15 and 99 years of age. The practice had four full-time-equivalent physician positions—that is, five physicians providing 15 to 31 visit-hours per week. Support staff included four medical assistants, five front-desk staff, one business manager, one billing manager, one health educator, two full-time clerical staff (or approximately 3.5 support staff per 1 full-time physician).

Methods: The electronic health record was used to identify 1 of 24 different "document types" to track activity for each physician during the 2008 calendar year; one week's worth of documents was reviewed for associated content and actions.

Impact: As a result of this review of activity, the author and colleagues hired a registered nurse

Results:

Volume and Type of Services for an Active Case Load of 8,440 Patients at Greenhouse Internists in 2008*

Type of Service (Total No.)*	No. per Visit	No. per Physician per Day[†]	No. per Patient per Year
Patient visits (16,640)	n/a	18.1	2.0
Telephone call (21,796)	1.31	23.7	2.6
Prescription refills (11,145)	0.67	12.1	1.3
E-mail messages (15,499)	0.93	16.8	1.8
Laboratory reports (17,974)	1.08	19.5	2.1
Imaging reports (10,229)	0.61	11.1	1.2
Consultation reports (12,822)	0.77	13.9	1.5

* Patients were included in the active case load if they had any interaction with the practice in the listed categories of activities during calendar year 2008. N/a denotes not applicable.

† The values are based on the work of four full-time-equivalent physicians who each worked 50 to 60 hours per week for 230 workdays per year.

to perform "information triage" of incoming laboratory reports, consultation notes, and telephone calls. Additional front-desk staff and medical assistants were hired to help with chronic disease tracking and management. Finally, they redefined a "full-time physician" to be one that offered 24 hours of face-to-face time for visits and have included telephone calls and e-mails as part of their productivity metric.

Source: Baron R.J.: What's keeping us so busy in primary care? A snapshot from one practice. *N Engl J Med* 362:1632–1636, Apr. 29, 2010. Used with permission.

After a specific intervention or potential improvement is identified, practices can use small, rapid-cycle changes to test whether the changes they are making are resulting in improvements. The Model for Improvement method can help a team guide the goal of the intervention as well as the assessment of how it is implemented.[75] Based on a long-standing methodology—the Plan-Do-Study-Act (PDSA; also known as the "Deming" or "Shewhart" Cycle)—it is meant to facilitate rapid and continuous evaluations of different individual components of a larger improvement process.[73] In the "Plan" step, the team identifies what is to be done, who will do it, and how it will be measured related to a specific practice or intervention. Following these preparations, the "Do" phase is when the pilot actually begins. At the same time, a member of the team is tasked with evaluating the impact of the pilot, using qualitative and quantitative data. After the intervention is instituted and associated data are collected for a period of time, the "Study" phase can begin. This is when the data are analyzed, disseminated, and discussed. The team must decide whether the expected positive results and/or any negative outcomes occurred. Finally, the "Act" phase is when the team must decide whether the intervention should be refined, expanded, or abandoned based on the results of the pilot. The PDSA cycle for a given intervention can occur again and again until the desired outcome is obtained. At that point, the intervention evolves from an experimental state and is "standardized" and embedded into the daily work flow.[74] As such, evaluation does not cease, but a new PDSA cycle emerges, as the evaluation continues to ensure continued success.

ISSUES IN IMPROVING MANAGEMENT OF CHRONIC DISEASES

Making the Business Case

In any organization, the cost implications for any suggested changes or improvements are important. In the United States, expenditures on persons with chronic diseases represent an enormous amount of spending—85% of all health care dollars spent.[15] However, this amount of spending is for *persons with chronic illness,* not on *chronic illness management,* specifically. Given the burden of preventable acute illness that results from poorly controlled chronic conditions, there is an opportunity to significantly reduce costs and improve care for patients. Improved chronic disease care can be cost-effective within a short period,[76,77] and disease management programs can yield a favorable return on investment,[78] particularly when they, as well as clinical management and self-management training programs, are consistent with the CCM.[79–81]

In addition, emerging evidence shows that redeploying health care resources toward staffing and other support for coordination of chronic care may improve patient satisfaction.[82] Although physicians and other health care providers can be frustrated with the difficulties in coordinating care for patients with chronic diseases,[83] investments in staffing and coordinated approaches to care may reduce staff and primary care provider burnout.[70] Improving chronic disease care, then, has the potential to improve patient satisfaction, patient outcomes, and return on investment.

Although spending on patients with chronic illnesses accounts for the majority of public and private health care costs in the United States, improving outcomes and coordination of care over time does not represent a large part of traditional reimbursement for organizations and practices. However, as stated earlier in this chapter, considerable activity—as represented, for example, by ACOs and PCMHs—is attempting to better coordinate and manage care of chronic diseases. The number of initiatives to adopt the CCM throughout the United States and many other countries is also growing.[10,84] Enhanced fees for service, bundled payments, population-based payments, and robust performance payments are all being used to promote coordination of care and to reign in exploding health care costs.

Understanding the Change Process

When considering transformational changes to improve delivery of health care, we have to remember that unintended consequences may result. Systematic interviews with physicians suggest what most practice administrators know—that additional work requirements without additional support can jeopardize physicians' efforts in other areas of care.[85] Providers and staff can often feel that recommendations for change are burdens to be added to the usual required duties. Even in motivated practices that self-selected to engage in medical home pilots, "change fatigue" may creep in.[73] Successful practices do not just take on additional duties but rethink how they deliver care and let go of some tasks and systems that are not working. For change to be successful, front-office and administrative staff must acknowledge the additional work necessary for such change and must truly empower patients, staff, and providers by seeking their input prior to and feedback during this process. Finally, although improvement often requires a series of steps, each individual change may not be enough; an integrated system of improvements is needed for optimal results. It takes a comprehensive strategy to address all the components for truly proactive planned care, including high-functioning teams, accessible evidence and guidelines, useful data and registries, self-management support, and care coordination.

Besides the tension between change and stability, many other competing forces must be balanced. Although systematizing evidence-based medicine into daily work flow and care requires standardization, we must be careful not to lose track of the fact that care must be individualized for each patient; for example, some patients may have difficulty in following care recommendations. The relationship between a patient and his or her physician needs to be balanced with the team approach necessary for improved support, as do concerns regarding improving access and maintaining continuity. Attention to these issues can help practices and their administrative leaders anticipate problems accordingly.

Innovations in Information Technology

Information technology innovations to help manage chronic disease are constantly evolving. The principles behind disease-based registries are being expanded and refined into "panel management" software, which will allow more global assessment of the health of the patients in a particular primary care physician panel or practice. The expansion of integrated health information exchanges brings increasing opportunities to share information between previously separated EHRs,[86] as well as the opportunity to compile this information to improve health care services for the chronically ill on a larger scale. "Patient-facing" technologies (that is, technologies used by patients), such as personal health records, disease self-management applications, secure electronic messaging, patient kiosks, and shared decision-making tools, further empower patients with the information, tools, and communication services to allow them to better manage their conditions.

Improved health care applications that use the data in the EHR will enable innovative approaches to connect patients and their care teams and to empower local clinics and practice settings to tailor clinical care applications for the patients' specific needs.

CONCLUSION

It is safe to say that the business of caring for patients with chronic conditions will continue to grow. Given the increasing burden and associated social costs of chronic disease, pressure to improve the efficiency of care while continuing to produce good outcomes and high satisfaction for patients with chronic illnesses will be ongoing. In addition, the future of health care systems will no longer simply be a matter of offering services and collecting reimbursements. Providers, clinics, and hospitals will be held accountable for the overall outcomes in their patient populations, and payments will be adjusted accordingly. It is up to the leaders in these systems to find ways to ensure that patients with potentially debilitating chronic illnesses have access to appropriate evidence-based care. We will need to maximize the benefit that a patient realizes from each and every interaction with his or her care team, which means moving from a physician-centric, hierarchical model of care to a model in which care is distributed and shared by a collaborative team supported by a highly functional system. We must find methods of reimbursement or workload credit for care provided outside the traditional face-to-face encounter. We must support training and education to help providers and their teams transform their methods of communicating, evaluating care processes, and implementing changes to improve care.

Today, we have insightful theories and an ever-growing body of evidence on how to improve care of patients with chronic diseases. Health care leaders will need not only the knowledge of what works in different places but the wisdom to know how to make it work in a specific practice setting—and if it does not, how to alter it. It is only with these skills and the vision to make it happen that management of chronic diseases will continue to improve, one practice at a time.

References

1. Yach D., et al.: The global burden of chronic diseases: Overcoming impediments to prevention and control. *JAMA* 291:2616–2622, Jun. 2, 2004.

2. World Health Organization: *2008–2013 Action Plan for the Global Strategy for the Prevention and Control of Noncommunicable Diseases.* 2009. http://www.who.int/nmh/publications/9789241597418/en/index.html (accessed Sep. 23, 2011).

3. World Health Organization: Chronic diseases and health promotion: World on cusp of radical shift in prevention and control of NCDs. *NMH Newsletter* Issue 1, Jan. 2011. http://www.who.int/nmh/newsletters/2011_1/en/index1.html (accessed Sep.23, 2011).

4. U.S. Department of Health & Human Services: *Multiple Chronic Conditions: A Strategic Framework: Optimum Health and Quality of Life for Individuals with Multiple Chronic Conditions.* Dec. 2010. http://www.hhs.gov/ash/initiatives/mcc/mcc_framework.pdf (accessed Sep. 23, 2011).

5. DeVol R.: *An Unhealthy America: The Economic Burden of Chronic Disease: Charting a New Course to Save Lives and Increase Productivity and Economic Growth.* Presentation for Stakeholder Forum, Santa Monica, CA, Oct. 11, 2007. Milken Institute, 2007. http://www.milkeninstitute.org/pdf/econ_burden_rdv.pdf (accessed Sep. 23, 2011).

6. American Diabetes Association: *Diabetes Statistics.* http://www.diabetes.org/diabetes-basics/diabetes-statistics (accessed Sep. 23, 2011).

7. World Health Organization: *Diabetes.* Aug. 2011. http://www.who.int/mediacentre/factsheets/fs312/en/index.html (accessed Sep. 23, 2011).

8. Severe P., et al.: Early versus standard antiretroviral therapy for HIV-infected adults in Haiti. *N Engl J Med* 363:257–265, Jul. 15, 2010.

9. Shepard C.W., Finelli L., Alter M.J.: Global epidemiology of hepatitis C virus infection. *Lancet Infect Dis* 5:558–567, Sep. 2005.

10. Singh D., Ham C.: *Improving Care for People with Long-Term Conditions: A Review of UK and International Frameworks.* NHS Institute for Innovation and Improvement, University of Birmingham, 2006. http://www.improvingchroniccare.org/downloads/review_of_international_frameworks__chris_hamm.pdf (accessed Sep. 23, 2011).

11. Crabtree B.F., et al.: Summary of the National Demonstration Project and recommendations for the patient-centered medical home. *Ann Fam Med* 8(suppl. 1):S80–S90, S92, 2010.

12. Lowell K.H., Bertko J.: The Accountable Care Organization (ACO) model: Building blocks for success. *J Ambul Care Manage* 33:81–88, Jan.–Mar. 2010.

13. Improving Chronic Illness Care: *The Chronic Care Model.* Group Health Research Institute. http://improvingchroniccare.org/index.php?p=The_Chronic_Care_Model&s=2 (accessed Sep. 23, 2011).

14. Wu S.Y., Green A.: *Projection of Chronic Illness Prevalence and Cost Inflation.* Santa Monica, CA: RAND Health, Oct. 2000.

15. Wolff J.L., Starfield B., Anderson G.: Prevalence, expenditures, and complications of multiple chronic conditions in the elderly. *Arch Intern Med* 162:2269–2276, Nov. 11, 2002.

16. Bodenheimer T., Grumbach K.: *Improving Primary Care: Strategies and Tools for a Better Practice.* New York City: Lange Medical Books/McGraw-Hill: 2007.

17. Zwarenstein M., et al.: Outreach education for integration of HIV/AIDS care, antiretroviral treatment, and tuberculosis care in primary care clinics in South Africa: PALSA PLUS pragmatic cluster randomised trial. *BMJ* 342:d2022, Apr. 21, 2011.

18. Metrikin A.S., et al.: Is HIV/AIDS a primary-care disease? Appropriate levels of outpatient care for patients with HIV/AIDS. *AIDS* 9:619–623, Jun. 1995.

19. Starfield B., Shi L., Macinko J.: Contribution of primary care to health systems and health. *Milbank Q* 83(3):457–502, 2005.

20. Macinko J., Starfield B., Shi L.: The contribution of primary care systems to health outcomes within Organization for Economic Cooperation and Development (OECD) countries, 1970–1998. *Health Serv Res* 38:831–865, Jun. 2003.

21. Yarnall K.S., et al.: Primary care: Is there enough time for prevention? *Am J Public Health* 93:635–641, Apr. 2003.

22. Østbye T., et al.: Is there time for management of patients with chronic diseases in primary care? *Ann Fam Med* 3:209–214, May–Jun. 2005.

23. Bodenheimer T., Chen E., Bennett H.D.: Confronting the growing burden of chronic disease: Can the U.S. health care workforce do the job? *Health Aff (Millwood)* 28:64–74, Jan.–Feb. 2009.

24. Bodenheimer T., Wagner E.H., Grumbach K.: Improving primary care for patients with chronic illness. *JAMA* 288:1775–1779, Oct. 9, 2002.

25. Phillips R.L. Jr., Starfield B.: Why does a U.S. primary care physician workforce crisis matter? *Am Fam Physician* 70:440, 442, 445–446, Aug. 2004.

26. Dartmouth College: *Clinical Microsystems.*

http://www.clinicalmicrosystem.org/ (accessed Sep. 23, 2011).

27. Haggerty J.L., et al.: Continuity of care: A multi-disciplinary review. *BMJ* 327(7425):1219–1221, Nov. 22, 2003.

28. Hjortdahl P., Laerum E.: Continuity of care in general practice: Effect on patient satisfaction. *BMJ*(6837) 304:1287–1290, May 16, 1992.

29. Stokes T., et al.: Continuity of care: Is the personal doctor still important? A survey of general practitioners and family physicians in England and Wales, the United States, and the Netherlands. *Ann Fam Med* 3:353–359, Jul.–Aug. 2005.

30. Berry L.L., et al.: Patients' commitment to their primary physician and why it matters. *Ann Fam Med* 6:6–13, Jan.–Feb. 2008.

31. Wasson J.H., et al.: Continuity of outpatient medical care in elderly men. A randomized trial. *JAMA* 252:2413–2417, Nov. 2, 1984.

32. Saultz J.W., Lochner J.: Interpersonal continuity of care and care outcomes: A critical review. *Ann Fam Med* 3:159–166, Mar.–Apr. 2005.

33. Weiss L.J., Blustein J.: Faithful patients: The effect of long-term physician-patient relationships on the costs and use of health care by older Americans. *Am J Public Health* 86:1742–1747, Dec. 1996.

34. Gill J.M., Mainous A.G. III: The role of provider continuity in preventing hospitalizations. *Arch Fam Med* 7:352–357, Jul.–Aug. 1998.

35. Cabana M.D., Jee S.H.: Does continuity of care improve patient outcomes? *J Fam Pract* 53:974–980, Dec. 2004.

36. Wagner E.H., Reid R.J.: Are continuity of care and teamwork incompatible? *Med Care* 45:6–7, Jan. 2007.

37. Qualis Health: *The Patient-Centered Medical Home.* http://www.qhmedicalhome.org (accessed Sep. 23, 2011).

38. Clinica Campesina Presentation: *Safety Net Medical Home Initiative Summit,* Boston, 2011.

39. Murray M., Berwick D.M.: Advanced access: Reducing waiting and delays in primary care. *JAMA* 289:1035–1040, Feb. 26, 2003.

40. Bodenheimer T., Abramowitz S.: *Helping Patients Help Themselves: How to Implement Self Management Support.* Oakland, CA: California HealthCare Foundation, Dec. 2010. http://www.chcf.org/publications/2010/12/helping-patients-help-themselves (accessed Sep. 23, 2011).

41. Brady T.J., et al. (ASMP/CDSMP Meta-Analysis Project Team): *Sorting Through the Evidence for the Arthritis Self-Management Program and the Chronic Disease Self-Management Program.* May 2011. Atlanta: Centers for Disease Control and Prevention. May 2011. http://www.cdc.gov/arthritis/docs/ASMP-executive-summary.pdf (accessed Sep. 23, 2011).

42. Battersby M., et al.: Twelve evidence-based principles for implementing self-management support in primary care. *Jt Comm J Qual Patient Saf* 36:561–570, Dec. 2010.

43. O'Connor A.M., et al.: Toward the "tipping point": Decision aids and informed patient choice. *Health Aff (Millwood)* 26:716–725, May–Jun. 2007.

44. O'Connor A.M., et al.: Decision aids for people facing health treatment or screening decisions. *Cochrane Database Syst Rev* (3):CD001431, Jul. 8, 2009.

45. Volk R.J., et al.: Patient education for informed decision making about prostate cancer screening: Randomized controlled trial with 1-year follow-up. *Ann Fam Med* 1:22–28, May–Jun. 2003.

46. Deyo R.A., et al.: Involving patients in clinical decisions: Impact of an interactive video program on use of back surgery. *Med Care* 38:959–969, Sep. 2000.

47. Arterburn D.E., et al.: Randomized trial of a video-based decision aid for bariatric surgery. *Obesity (Silver Spring)* 19:1669–1675, Aug. 2001.

48. McGlynn E.A., et al.: The quality of health care delivered to adults in the United States. *N Engl J Med* 348:2635–2645, Jun. 26, 2003.

49. Schedlbauer A., Schroeder K., Fahey T.: How can adherence to lipid-lowering medication be improved? A systematic review of randomized controlled trials. *Fam Pract* 24:380–387, Sep. 2007.

50. Glynn L.G., et al.: Interventions used to improve control of blood pressure in patients with hypertension. *Cochrane Database Syst Rev* CD005182, Mar. 17, 2010.

51. Katon W.J., et al.: Collaborative care for patients with depression and chronic illnesses. *N Engl J Med* 363:2611–2620, Dec. 30, 2010.

52. Carter B.L., Zillich A.J., Elliott W.J.: How pharmacists can assist physicians with controlling blood pressure. *J Clin Hypertens (Greenwich)* 5:31–37, Jan.–Feb. 2003.

53. Carter B.L., et al.: Physician and pharmacist collaboration to improve blood pressure control. *Arch Intern Med* 169:1996–2002, Nov. 23, 2009.

54. Green B.B., et al.: Effectiveness of home blood pressure monitoring, Web communication, and pharmacist care on hypertension control: A randomized controlled trial. *JAMA* 299:2857–2867, Jun. 25, 2008. Erratum in *JAMA* 302:1972, Jun. 25, 2008.

55. Fahey T., Schroeder K., Ebrahim S.: Interventions used to improve control of blood pressure in patients with hypertension. *Cochrane Database Syst Rev* CD005182, Oct. 18, 2006.

56. Andersen U.O., et al.: Treating the hypertensive patient in a nurse-led hypertension clinic. *Blood Press* 19:182–187, Jun. 2010.

57. Kern E.F.O., et al.: Building a diabetes registry from the Veterans Health Administration's computerized patient record system. *J Diabetes Sci Technol* 2:7–14, Jan. 2008.

58. Stroebel R.J., et al.: A randomized trial of three diabetes registry implementation strategies in a community internal medicine practice. *Jt Comm J Qual*

Improv 28:441–450, Aug. 2002.

59. Romano M.J., Stafford R.S.: Electronic health records and clinical decision support systems: Impact on national ambulatory care quality. *Arch Intern Med* 171:897–903, May 23, 2011.

60. Cebul R.D., et al.: Electronic health records and quality of diabetes care. *N Engl J Med* 365:825–833, Sep. 1, 2011.

61. Shojania K.G., et al.: Effects of quality improvement strategies for type 2 diabetes on glycemic control: A meta-regression analysis. *JAMA* 296:427–440, Jul. 26, 2006.

62. Coleman K., et al.: Evidence on the Chronic Care Model in the new millennium. *Health Aff (Millwood)* 28:75–85, Jan.–Feb. 2009.

63. Marx R., et al.: Creating a medical home in the San Francisco Department of Public Health: Establishing patient panels. *J Public Health Manag Pract* 15:337–344, Jul.–Aug. 2009.

64. Gilfillan R.J., et al.: Value and the medical home: Effects of transformed primary care. *Am J Manag Care* 16:607–614, Aug. 2010.

65. Coleman K., et al.: Untangling practice redesign from disease management: How do we best care for the chronically ill? *Annu Rev Public Health* 30:385–408, Apr. 2009.

66. *Final Report of the Three Year CDPM Initiative: Partnerships for Health: Improving Diabetes Care in the South West LHIN.* Mar. 22, 2011. http://www.partnershipsforhealth.ca/Partnership_docs/PartnershipsForHealthFinalReport.pdf (accessed Sep. 23, 2011).

67. O'Connor P.J., et al.: Primary care clinic-based chronic disease care: Features of successful programs. *Disease Management & Health Outcomes* 9:691–698, Dec. 2001.

68. Bodenheimer T., Bojestig M., Henriks G.: Making systemwide improvements in health care: Lessons from Jönköping County, Sweden. *Qual Manag Health Care* 16:10–15, Jan.–Mar. 2007.

69. Reid R.J., et al.: Patient-centered medical home demonstration: A prospective, quasi-experimental, before and after evaluation. *Am J Manag Care* 15:e71–e87, Sep. 1, 2009.

70. Reid R.J., et al.: The group health medical home at year two: Cost savings, higher patient satisfaction, and less burnout for providers. *Health Aff (Millwood)* 29:835–843, May 2010.

71. Friedberg M.W., et al.: A guide to the medical home as a practice-level intervention. *Am J Manag Care* 15(10 suppl.):S291–S299, Dec. 2009.

72. U.S. Department of Veterans Affairs: *Patient Aligned Care Team (PACT): Overview.* http://www.va.gov/PRIMARYCARE/PACT/index.asp (accessed Sep. 23, 2011).

73. Nutting P.A., et al.: Transforming physician practices to patient-centered medical homes: Lessons from the National Demonstration Project. *Health Aff (Millwood)* 30:439–445, Mar. 2011.

74. Nelson E.C., Batalden P.B., Godfrey M.M. (eds): *Quality by Design: A Clinical Microsystems Approach.* San Francisco: Jossey-Bass, 2007.

75. Langley GL, et al.: *The Improvement Guide: A Practical Approach to Enhancing Organizational Performance,* 2nd ed. San Francisco: Jossey-Bass, 2009.

76. Wagner E.H., et al.: Effect of improved glycemic control on health care costs and utilization. *JAMA* 285:182–189, Jan. 10, 2001.

77. Huang E.S., et al.: The cost-effectiveness of improving diabetes care in U.S. federally qualified community health centers. *Health Serv Rev* 42:2174–2193, Dec. 2007.

78. Goetzel R.Z., et al.: Return on investment in disease management: A review. *Health Care Financ Rev* 26:1–19, Summer 2005.

79. Gilmer T.P., et al.: The cost to health plans of poor glycemic control. *Diabetes Care* 20:1847–1853, Dec. 1997.

80. Gilmer T.P., et al.: Impact of office systems and improvement strategies on costs of care for adults with diabetes. *Diabetes Care* 29:1242–1248, Jun. 2006.

81. Gilmer T., O'Connor P.J.: Cost effectiveness of diabetes mellitus management programs: A health plan perspective. *Disease Management & Health Outcomes* 11:439–453, Jul. 2003.

82. Wagner E.H.: The role of patient care teams in chronic disease management. *BMJ* (7234)320:569–572, Feb. 26, 2000.

83. Mathematica Policy Research, Inc. (MPR): *National Public Engagement Campaign on Chronic Illness—Physician Survey.* Princeton, NJ: MPR, 2001.

84. Patient-Centered Primary Care Collaborative: *Pilots & Demonstrations.* http://www.pcpcc.net/pcpcc-pilot-projects (accessed Sep. 23, 2011)

85. Tufano J.T., Ralston J.D., Martin D.P.: Providers' experience with an organizational redesign initiative to promote patient-centered access: A qualitative study. *J Gen Intern Med* 23:1778–1783, Nov. 2008.

86. Bates D.W., Kuperman G.J.: The role of health information technology in quality and safety. In The Joint Commission: *Front Office to Front Line: Essential Issues for Health Care Leaders,* 2nd ed. Oak Brook, IL: Joint Commission Resources, 2011, pp. 87–126.

CHAPTER 7

Implementing, Sustaining, and Spreading Quality Improvement

John Øvretveit, Ph.D., C.Psychol., C.Sci.

The need for fast and widespread improvement has been demonstrated in many studies. Research ranging from the 2001 Institute of Medicine (IOM) report *Crossing the Quality Chasm*[1] to evidence of the costs and savings associated with improvement[2,3] indicates the high cost of underperformance in health care in terms of patient and financial outcomes. Patients and purchasers are becoming more informed about quality and are able to compare health systems' performances. We know that great variation exists in the extent to which evidenced-based treatments and best practices are provided to similar patient populations.[3,4] Put more positively, all but the very best health care organizations have considerable potential for improvement. High-achieving organizations are distinguished by their ability to implement and sustain best practices.

In one improvement approach, identified best practices are broken down into critical elements,[2–4] which the frontline providers then implement using "spread" structures and strategies. In another approach—"diffusion"—best practices are naturally adopted in the absence of efforts to "push" them into practice.[5]

This chapter is intended to help improvement leaders consider the actions that they can take to carry out improvement changes in their services, hospitals, or other health care organizations. There are no simple prescriptions because those actions depend on the types of change, the situations, and the leaders' positions and responsibilities. However, principles, findings, and lessons from research can guide leaders' improvement activities.

The importance of leadership for achieving widespread improvements was clearly shown in a collection of case studies from 14 health care organizations; Schilling concluded that "an improvement infrastructure, leadership and accountability, and a clear understanding of the relation of the improvement to the desired outcome" are all essential. The "secret" to success in performance improvement is "leadership, leadership, leadership."[6(pp. 219–220).]

This chapter draws on research into implementation and spread (or "scale up") of proven or promising improvements to show how leaders can make their improvement programs more effective. Sidebar 7-1 (page 160) explains what is meant by *implementation, sustainability,* and *spread.*

159

Sidebar 7-1. Implementation, Sustainability, and Spread

Implementation is the work of enabling organizations to make more use of proven treatments, practices, or service delivery models to improve patient experiences and outcomes and to reduce waste. The *sustainability* of a change refers to whether the change is maintained in routine practice or to how the service is organized.

Spread or "scale up" is an intentional strategy to enable many different units and organizations to adopt a defined change. For example, in the World Health Organization (WHO) High 5s program—coordinated by the WHO Collaborating Centre for Patient Safety, which is led by The Joint Commission and Joint Commission International (JCI)—Australia, Canada, France, Germany, the Netherlands, Saudi Arabia, Singapore, the United Kingdom, and the United States are implementing five patient safety solutions that address the following issues:

- Concentrated injectable medicines
- Medication accuracy at transitions in care
- Correct procedure at the correct body site
- Communication failures during patient handovers
- Health care–associated infections

Source: Adapted from World Health Organization: *Action on Patient Safety—High 5s.* http://www.who.int/patientsafety/implementation/solutions/high5s/en/index.html (accessed Sep. 23, 2011).

CHALLENGES FOR IMPROVEMENT LEADERS

Even after health care leaders have determined which improvements need to be made, implementing, sustaining, and spreading improvement entails five key challenges.

1. Measuring Performance

The first challenge is measuring performance and determining the gap between your organization and the best in the field. It is necessary to identify the most-important performance measures, which may reflect the organization's strategic financial performance measures, or external requirements, such as Joint Commission and Joint Commission International standards and performance measures[7–10] and Joint Commission National Patient Safety Goals.[11] Many leaders use a balanced scorecard approach, which entails choosing a few carefully selected measures that provide a rounded picture of clinical process and patient outcomes to define and to track the overall performance of the organization.[12] A leader could ask, for example, about the performance of the service on the Healthcare Effectiveness Data and Information Set (HEDIS)[13] measures or Joint Commission core measures[14] and how it compares to the performance of the best in the field.

2. Determining Which Change Is Most Likely to Bring Improvement

Finding a proven or promising change to close the performance gap presents the second challenge—that is, finding which change is most likely to bring improvement. For example, research may show that use of an early warning score to identify deteriorating patients could save lives.[15] But how do we know whether the change will work on our own local units?

3. Planning and Testing a Local Version of the Change

A third challenge lies in carrying out an initial change locally and observing the results. Research-informed quality improvement (QI) usually requires that a change proven elsewhere be adapted and tested locally. One theory is that it is more effective and efficient to copy improvements that have worked elsewhere. This is the idea behind "evidence-based improvement," which says, "take a proven improvement and implement it locally." Experience shows, however, that it is sometimes easier and more effective to implement a change that is "home grown"—that is, developed by local personnel, leaders, and staff—with political insight about how to "sell" the change. Which is better, the exact copy or the locally developed approach—or does it depend on the type of change and the situational context?

Evidence of effectiveness elsewhere helps leaders persuade their colleagues to try the change. However, leaders need to have the skills to appropriately adapt the change to the local environment and measure the outcomes in such a way as to be reasonably certain that the implemented changes improved them.

4. Maintaining the Improvement and/or Enabling Continuing Improvement

Even if the change is implemented and achieves a measurable improvement, the challenges for improvement leaders are not over. The subsequent challenge is to maintain the improvement and to enable continuing or sustained improvement. Initial changes are often made in the course of participation in a project, which may entail, in the case of a QI collaborative, for example, a series of interventions, improvement support, and learning sessions, often with external financial support or budgeted resources. The transition to routine operations after the collaborative is over can be difficult; perhaps the energy and focus of the original project has waned, the change now must be carried out by the entire organization rather than the original group, or financial resources for sustaining and spreading the project are not available. In a follow-up study conducted one year after completion of a QI collaborative on reducing falls and fall-related injuries, Neily et al. found that sustained change depended on leadership support, experience with QI and teamwork, teamwork skills, and continual application of skills gained from the improvement project.[16]

In addition, the often frequent changes in financing, staffing, and support systems can undermine the continuation of the established improvements. How can leaders make the change and the goal of improvement part of routine work if health care workers do not see them as part of their everyday responsibilities?

5. Spreading the Change to Other Patient Populations, Units, Organizations, or Systems

The fifth challenge consists of spreading a proven change outside the original target group or setting. If there is evidence of effectiveness and experience about how to make the change, then it should be easier for others in your organization to adopt the change and to do so more quickly. Yet special strategies are still needed to spread improvements to other systems, such as Internet and intranet sites for providing information and allowing communication among implementers and leaders across sites.[1]

Sidebar 7-2. Barriers to Implementation

Practice Environment—Organizational Context
- Financial disincentives (lack of reimbursement)
- Organizational constraints (lack of time)
- Perception of liability (risk of formal complaint)
- Patient's expectations (expressed wishes related to prescription)

Prevailing Opinion—Social Context
- Standards of practice (usual routines)
- Opinion leaders (key persons not agreeing with evidence)
- Medical training (obsolete knowledge)
- Advocacy (pharmaceutical companies)

Knowledge and Attitudes—Professional Context
- Clinical uncertainty (unnecessary test for vague symptoms)
- Sense of competence (self-confidence in skills)
- Compulsion to act (need to do something)
- Information overload (inability to appraise evidence)

Sources: Adapted from Oxman A.D., Flottorp S.: An overview of strategies to promote implementation of evidence-based health care. In Silagy C., Haines A. (eds.): *Evidence-Based Practice in Primary Care,* 2nd ed. London: BMJ Books, 2001, pp. 101–119; and Grol R., Grimshaw J.: From best evidence to best practice: Effective implementation of change in patients' care. *Lancet* 362:1225–1230, Oct. 11, 2003.

FACING THE IMPLEMENTATION CHALLENGES

Implementation science is the systematic and replicable research of how to put knowledge into practice to improve health or health care. Such research considers how changes that are proven effective or thought to be promising are then put into practice—or how they fail to be established despite efforts to do so. Investigators describe and seek to explain why some changes are taken up by some providers and not by others as well as the actions or strategies used to encourage "take up" adoption and adaptation. Implementation science can help leaders learn how others have addressed the challenges of implementing, sustaining, and spreading improvements. For example, implementation leaders can benefit from research-based knowledge about the barriers to implementing effective interventions, as summarized in Sidebar 7-2 (above).

In considering how to best implement change, leaders can find studies of interventions similar to those that they are attempting to implement; those studies should provide information about the barriers encountered and how the improvement leaders attempted to address them. Alternatively, they can carry out their own "barrier analysis," using available resources, such as a toolkit (for example, *Understanding Barriers to Implementation*[17]) or "readiness-for-change" surveys.[18]

DECIDING WHETHER TO IMPLEMENT AN "EXACT COPY": THE ROLE OF FIDELITY

Using a change that has been proven elsewhere is often a faster and more effective way to make an improvement than inventing an intervention. However, improvement leaders need to be aware of which proven changes have to be exactly copied and which can be modified to fit the local environment. It is here that some of the limitations of the research in this new science become apparent: It is not always clear whether or how modification of a change is possible or necessary. Such details of implementation methods are often excluded from published reports because of space limitations. In addition, the causes of a local problem may be different from those in another organization or even in another unit in the same organization and may thus require a different set of changes. The Joint Commission Center for Transforming Healthcare, which has been conducting a series of patient safety projects, found that the initial group of eight hospitals in the hand hygiene project noted differing sets of causes for the failure to clean hands. For example, five of the hospitals identified ineffective placement of dispensers or sinks, and another combination of six noted a lack of accountability and just-in-time coaching.[19] As Chassin observed, the first important innovation represented by the Center "is to discard the notion of a one-size-fits-all best practice and instead to develop a portfolio of interventions that are targeted to the specific causes of the problem in different locations."[20(p. 476)]

The following sections address some of the issues involved in assessing whether to copy exactly or to modify a change locally.

"Fidelity" and "Adaptation Latitude"

In implementation science, *fidelity* refers to how good a copy is—that is, how closely an improvement change "intervention" (for example, a treatment, service delivery model, training, program) follows either an original intervention or a plan for an intervention. Implementation is often carried out after an intervention has been tested or piloted and found to be effective in one setting—for example, in a controlled evaluation of a change, typically in a university teaching hospital.

A key issue is whether the original change that was tested has to be copied exactly elsewhere to be effective or whether and how much parts of it can be changed ("adaptation latitude"). To date, much of implementation science has assumed that fidelity is necessary for effectiveness. Implementation science has only begun to ask, "Do some interventions have to be copied exactly?" and "Do some need to be adapted to be effective, and, if so, which, when, and how?" Therefore, definitive guidance cannot be provided about how to proceed in a particular situation.

Strategy 1. When Fidelity Is Effective. If every 100 patients who are likely to experience a stroke took aspirin, then 23 strokes could be prevented.[21] Yet many providers do not assess and treat stroke effectively. "Fidelity of aspirin delivery," as it is called by some researchers, refers to ensuring that those patients most likely to benefit do in fact take the aspirin. This requires that providers and patients carefully follow effective methods for assessing the risk of stroke and for enabling treatment compliance.

Fidelity has also been found to be important for the effectiveness of more complicated interventions. For example, some services that implemented with high fidelity a parent-training program found significantly better parenting practices than those services implementing with less fidelity.[22] Similarly, outcomes in employment programs for people with behavioral problems were found to depend on how well the programs followed the proposed model.[23] Higher-implementation fidelity was also associated with higher performance for substance abuse and smoking prevention programs.[24,25] For "high-fidelity-dependent" improvements, a leader would need to use various methods, such as audits and feedback, to ensure implementation compliance among the implementers.

Strategy 2. When Infidelity Is Necessary. For some interventions and situations, it is necessary to modify an intervention to make it possible to be implemented in part or in whole. For example, some health care organizations may have fewer resources than the organization(s) where the original and proven improvement was implemented; leaders may lack staff, equipment, or certain expertise, such as information technology specialists. In these situations, the content of the change may have to be altered even for any change to be implemented, and implementation may have to be conducted in phases. Implementation science is only beginning to examine which interventions can or must be modified, by how much, and how best to do so. The best methods for adaptation may vary, depending on the type of improvement change being attempted. For interventions that need to be adapted, successful modification before and during implementation is best achieved through systematic methods, such as the following examples:

- Methods for analysis of change barriers to assess and address likely obstacles to change before and during implementation[26,27]
- QI methods that provide the implementers with feedback on outcomes so they can determine whether their modifications are effective[28]

Summary. Whereas some proven interventions are best implemented by exactly copying the original intervention, others are best implemented by appropriately adapting it. If in doubt as to whether to copy or to adapt—and how to do so—consider others' experiences and whether your organization has the skills and capacity to adapt the change successfully. In addition, one strategy for improvement does not require that the change has been proven through research but rather focuses on the process of enabling professionals to choose improvements and then to steer the implementation of the changes in the "bottom-up implementation" approach.

Strategy 3. Bottom-up Implementation. In a *bottom-up implementation approach,* leaders and frontline providers agree on what to change and how to do it. This approach may be well suited to changes in clinical coordination and integration,[3] as represented, for example, in a study by Vedel et al. of an intervention aimed at improving care for the elderly in an area of Paris.[29] Instead of implementing a specific proven intervention, the researchers steered the participants through a process whereby the managers and health care professionals collectively defined areas for improvement, formulated solutions, and then made the changes themselves.

This study systematically gathered data about the current practices, issues, and expectations of health care professionals and managers so as to sketch the defining features of a successful intervention. The researchers carried out interviews and focus groups to summarize the challenges facing the health care professionals in their different settings and types of practice in caring for older people with chronic conditions in health and social services, hospitals, and community-based organizations. The research-

---

Sidebar 7-3. Questions to Ask When Planning Spread

- Type of improvement to be spread ("What" is spread?)
- Receiving person, organization, or system ("To whom" is it spread?)
- The method, structure, and system ("How" is it spread?)
- Responsible spread implementer ("By whom?")
- Results ("What" are the outcomes?)

---

ers and health care professionals then drew on the data to develop the intervention. In this case, the work could have been carried out by a project team from another organization.

The changes decided on—and then carried out by the health care professionals—included strengthening primary care, with the primary care physician (PCP) as the main medical practitioner. In addition, a multidisciplinary team was created, including case managers and the PCPs; and actions for improving coordination and communication between primary care, secondary care, and a community-based geriatrician were all instituted. The results from the evaluation showed that more appropriate care was provided, with a reduction in unnecessary health care service utilization; PCPs and nurses actively participated in the intervention and were satisfied with its design and implementation.

It was possible that, in defining the changes to make, the professionals were influenced by reports of effective interventions elsewhere, but this was not an explicit part of the implementation. Not only was implementation easier as a result of the local ownership of the problems and solutions, but the solutions were then found by the researchers to be effective in improving care for patients.

As shown by Videl et al.,[29] if an improvement

process is followed, the intervention can be effective, even if its effectiveness had not previously been demonstrated. However, it took more than two years to work through this process as a result of the many types of health care settings and professionals involved—for example, just arranging meetings took considerable advanced planning. Videl et al. suggested the following:

> In situations where the intervention is less complex . . . a pre-intervention study would not need to be as long. . . . When proven interventions are available, even if the barriers to their implementation need to be identified, it may not be necessary to develop all the key features of the intervention, and a shorter pre-intervention study will probably suffice.[29]

FROM PILOT TO SPREAD

Regardless of whether a given change is proven elsewhere first or home-grown and tested locally, it could also benefit additional patient populations, units, or organizations. Improvement leaders can spread, or scale up, interventions quickly and at low cost if they follow some of the guidance and experience of other leaders who have been successful with rapid spread of similar interventions. Leaders can ask the questions listed in Sidebar 7-3 (above) in planning the spread strategy.

Spread is depicted in Case Study 7-1 (pages 166–167), regarding an improved service delivery model for depression care (the "TIDES" program); and in Case Study 7-2 (pages 167–168), which concerns an intervention for preventing bloodstream infections. The case studies involve two stages of implementation: (1) the formulation of an effective improvement, pilot testing, and revision at the pilot or demonstration sites; and (2) the development of wider structures and strategies to enable the change to be spread.

In Case Study 7-1 the improvement was developed by researchers and practitioners and implemented through line management.

CASE STUDY 7-1. THE TIDES DEPRESSION CARE IMPROVEMENT, VETERANS HEALTH ADMINISTRATION SERVICES

The U.S. Veterans Health Administration (VHA), which provides health care for armed forces veterans and their dependents, is organized through 21 regional Veterans Integrated Service Networks (VISNs), which are overseen by a national central office. The intervention in this example originated in the Chronic Care Model for providing community-based and coordinated service for patients with chronic health problems.[1]

The intervention—the TIDES (Translating Initiatives for Depression into Effective Solutions) model—was developed through a collaboration between researchers and providers. The researchers provided practitioners with evidence about effective changes and frameworks for using QI methods to implement and test these changes. The changes, using case managers and other interventions in the TIDES model, were intended to improve depression treatment and support in primary care.[2,3]

The model was tested and further refined in seven "first-generation" clinics in three VHA regions between 2002 and 2004. The model was spread to additional sites in these regions by line managers and through using directives through the line-management operations structure of regional and local management. In 2008 the VHA made adoption of the model a national policy and provided funding for it. The spread involved a national dissemination plan, with goals addressing (1) guidelines and quality indicators, (2) training in clinical processes and evidence-based QI, (3) marketing, and (4) informatics and logistics support. The spread program enabled providers to use social marketing methods, which "emphasize social responsibility and the benefits of adopting change."[4]

The approach to spread in this case study was conventional in the sense that it was implemented through a management hierarchy in the VHA system, with funding allocated for it through this system. It was unconventional in that the model's development, testing, and refinement were conducted through a researcher–service collaboration and through the use of QI methods to obtain and to act on feedback for the results of implementation in each site.

In the second implementation stage, in which the model was spread to the other regions, less development was needed, but the implementation leaders still required support. This support was provided by a more "routine" VHA support service rather than by the researchers. The critical success factors—which may be relevant to other implementation programs—included the following[5]:

- Engagement of stakeholders at various levels in ways that make best use of their expertise
- Access to scientists who know or can interpret the evidence base for the chronic care and TIDES model
- Identification and securing of help from

many different experts, including informatics specialists

- Accurate measurement of performance for data to use in Plan-Do-Study-Act (PDSA) cycles and to help sustain the change over time
- Development of training, tools, and protocols about how to operate the new approach

References

1. Wagner E.H., et al.: Improving chronic illness care: Translating evidence into action. *Health Aff (Millwood)* 20:64–78, Nov.–Dec. 2001.
2. Rubenstein L.V., et al.: Understanding team-based quality improvement for depression in primary care. *Health Serv Res* 37:1009–1029, Aug. 2002.
3. Rubenstein L.V., et al.: Using evidence-based quality improvement methods for translating depression collaborative care research into practice. *Fam Syst Health* 28:91–113, Jun. 2010.
4. Luck J., et al.: A social marketing approach to implementing evidence-based practice in VHA QUERI: The TIDES depression collaborative care model. *Implement Sci* 4:64, Sep. 28, 2009.

In Case Study 7-2 (below), the move from the Stage 1 pilot demonstrations and the Stage 2 spread was not planned, and the spread method differed accordingly—proceeding from pilot testing to specification and the campaign.

CASE STUDY 7-2. AN INTERVENTION FOR PREVENTING CENTRAL LINE–ASSOCIATED BLOODSTREAM INFECTION (CLABSI)

In a famous case, which occurred at Johns Hopkins Hospital (Baltimore), an 18-month-old child, Josie King, died of cardiac arrest; staff had missed warning signs of dehydration. The child's mother, Sorrel King, resolved to prevent such an error happening again. Together with Peter Pronovost, an anesthesiologist and critical care specialist, and other leaders, they started a safety program that involved creating a culture of safety.[1]

In Stage 1 of implementation, Pronovost and colleagues established an eight-step program to improve safety in two ICUs.[2] The first step was to find out staff's safety concerns, one of which, as generated from discussions and data analysis, was the number of central line–associated bloodstream infections (CLABSIs). Further analysis revealed that safe and effective practices for inserting central lines were not being followed. An improvement team developed a set of procedures based on the U.S. Centers for Disease Control and Prevention (CDC) evidence-based guidelines[3] and used a checklist method as part of the implementation process to ensure that the procedures were followed.

The infection rates decreased by 96%, with no infections occurring during a nine-month period. Pronovost et al. highlighted clinical leaders' commitment to the change, authorization for nurses to speak out if the procedures were not followed, and timely feedback of infection measures to the teams as key to the implementation's success.[2]

In Stage 2 of implementation (starting in 2003), Johns Hopkins partnered with the Michigan Health & Hospital Association's Keystone Center for Patient Safety & Quality to implement evidence-based interventions to prevent CLABSI. All Michigan ICUs were invited to take part voluntarily in the program, which used a QI collaborative Breakthrough Series method.[4] QI project teams from each ICU were trained on the changes to be made, how to make the changes, and how to measure and to evaluate results. For 103 ICUs, the baseline median CLABSI rate was 2.7; after 3 months, the rate was 0.0, which was maintained through 18 months of the project.[5] The program was interrupted by U.S. federal authorities concerned about patient privacy, which prevented further data collection and reporting. This reminds us that changes in the environment surrounding an improvement implementation can help or hinder implementation. However, in June 2009, the secretary of the U.S. Department of Health & Human Services announced a goal for hospitals to reduce CLABSIs by 75% in three years.[6] Since October 2009, a federally funded voluntary program has been helping hospitals in every state achieve this goal.

References

1. Pronovost P., Vehr E.: *Safe Patients, Smart Hospitals: How One Doctor's Checklist Can Help Us Change Health Care from the Inside Out.* New York City: Hudson Street Press, 2010.

2. Pronovost P.J., et al.: Improving patient safety in intensive care units in Michigan. *J Crit Care* 23:207–221, Jun. 2008.

3. O'Grady N.P., et al.: Guidelines for the prevention of intravascular catheter-related infections. Centers for Disease Control and Prevention. *MMWR Recomm Rep* 51(RR-10):1–29, Aug. 9, 2002.

4. Kilo C.M.: A framework for collaborative improvement: Lessons from the Institute for Healthcare Improvement's Breakthrough Series. *Qual Manag Health Care* 6:1–13, Sep. 1998.

5. Watson S., et al.: Preventing central line–associated bloodstream infections and improving safety culture: A statewide experience. *Jt Comm J Qual Patient Saf* 35:593–597, Dec. 2009.

6. Agency for Healthcare Research and Quality: *Eliminating CLABSI: A National Patient Safety Imperative.* http://www.ahrq.gov/qual/onthecusprpt/onthecusp4.htm (accessed Sep. 23, 2011).

The primary feature of the Spread Strategy 2 in this case study was the use of a specific QI method—the Breakthrough Series collaborative approach.[30] Yet in this collaborative—as in most collaboratives—the results achieved by project teams in different organizations across a long period of time differed greatly.[31] Many questions remain about the cost-effectiveness of collaboratives and the sustainability of the changes, as Mittman[31] and others have pointed out. It is not clear whether one approach, such

as a collaborative, would be as effective for spreading such changes as a patient-centered medical home model[32] or computerized provider order entry,[33] for example.

Spread, Learning Networks, and Campaigns

For McCannon and Perla,[34] QI collaboratives and campaigns can be understood as examples of "learning networks"—the "instrumental mechanisms in sustainable, large-scale improvement," such as the Institute for Healthcare Improvement's 5 Million Lives Campaign,[35] which has involved hospitals and other health care organizations not only in the United States but throughout the world. Learning networks "succeed by connecting everyone who is seeking to improve—individuals, facilities, states, regions, and countries—in communities of directed learning that focus on the painstaking work of changing behavior on a large scale (as opposed to merely raising broad awareness of better practice)."[34(p. 286)] Canada Safer Healthcare Now!,[36] Denmark's Danish Safer Hospital Programme,[37] and the United Kingdom National Health Service's Patient Safety! Campaign[38] represent other examples of learning networks.[34]

Yuan et al. define improvement campaigns as an "organized, multifaceted approach to quality improvement" that involves "open enrollment; a specified target and a firm deadline; feasible interventions for which efficacy is documented in the peer-reviewed literature and reflected in standards set by relevant specialty societies and government agencies; structured activities and tools to advance improvement, exchange ideas, and share experiences of participating organizations; open access to campaign materials; voluntary participation; and a mass of organizations enrolled."[39(p. 3)]

Sidebar 7-4. Scale-up in International Health

Scale-up in international health can be directed at achieving a widespread use of the following:

- *Practices,* primarily ways to carry out a work task, as in a sequence of steps to be followed for immunizing a young child
- *Products,* such as a portable solar-power refrigerator for storing vaccines or low-cost HIV/AIDS testing kits
- *A combination of practices,* such as a number of interventions that improve care for expectant mothers
- *Ways of organizing a service,* such as creating a coordinated team of practitioners for tuberculosis prevention and treatment
- *Interventions of other types,* such as a new way of paying providers (for example, co-payment or community-based insurance systems)

Traditionally, scale-up in international health has involved the following:

- *Identifying a practice or model* that is effective (an "exemplar") for a particular health need or problem
- *Documenting the practice's or model's features* that appear to be essential to the results (the change "content"—the "what"), and communicating them simply in a way that others can understand (for example, a "packaged description" of the practice or model, often as part of a simple pack of teaching materials)
- *Documenting features of the situational context* that may be important for making it possible to carry out the practice or model and to make it more likely that it will be effective and sustained as a routine part of the service (for example, number of staff and required skills, financial resources, availability of computers)
- *A method or strategy* (the change "implementation method"—the "how") for enabling others to understand, to adapt, and to put a similar practice or model into operation (for example, "barefoot facilitators" or "honey bees," who visit, teach, and support service units to use the new approach)
- *Monitoring the speed and extent* to which others implement the practice or model and evaluating the intermediate results and health outcomes

Spread of Improved Methods and Service Models in Low- and Medium-Income Countries

In addition to the literature on implementation from high-income countries with well-developed health systems, resources, and infrastructures to support implementation of improvements, there is also an extensive literature about spread in low-income countries that is relevant to leaders of all health care organizations, no matter where they are located.[40,41] The specific uses of scale-up, as defined in Sidebar 7-1, is addressed in Sidebar 7-4 (above).

In international health scale-up, the practice or model found to be effective was often instituted as a pilot or a service that had received special support to develop "the new way" or was in some way not typical of the exiting services. In this case, scale-up entails taking what was developed in this special situation and putting it into practice in other settings, which may vary considerably in staffing or other features. This usually requires a scale-up support system for some period of time, or at least until the new approach is recognized as the new "normal" way.

Typically, traditional systems and structures are not designed to support the new practice or model, so scale-up needs to adjust them, usually by training, to accommodate the new practice or model. Similarly, existing systems and structures need to be adapted to sustain the practice or model. Sometimes, additional staff or financial resources are required on a permanent basis to sustain the improvement. If the improvement is likely to save money in the long term, an investment financing mechanism may be required (for more details, see Simmons et al.[42] and Peters et al[43]).

Summary

Whereas some improvements might be best carried out by a top-down directed and prescribed implementation, with detailed accountability or inspection for control, other improvements might be better as principle-led, with a participatory planned adaptive approach and expert-led regular reviews and midcourse corrections. Other improvements may be best viewed as "facilitated evolution," in which radical changes are likely, requiring regular reviews and local correction and leadership. In the latter, the spread approach is more about creating the incentives and enabling conditions for organizations or units to improve, with the focus on facilitating adoption and adaptation rather than on driving prescribed change and goals or "targets."

Some spread programs have been successful as a result of local researchers' action- and collaborative-research approach, such as the U.S. Department of Veterans Affairs Quality Enhancement Research Initiative.[44] In this approach, the researchers provide independent documentation and data about progress and consequences to those making the change and, in an analytic capacity, diagnose causes of lack of progress and possible ways forward, which are then used as hypotheses for testing. Similar collaborative, action, participatory, or "embedded" approaches to research in health care improvement might provide new knowledge and more effective change than traditional independent researcher approaches.

LEADING MORE EFFECTIVE IMPROVEMENT BY DRAWING ON OTHERS' EXPERIENCE AND THE EVIDENCE

The sample of implementation experience and research, as covered in this chapter, can be summarized in (1) an "equation" that specifies the contributing factors for success, and (2) steps for successful implementation.

Understanding the Critical Factors for Success

The following equation can be used to help estimate the likely success of an improvement and what needs to be done to increase the chances of its success:

$$\text{Initial idea or proven change} + \text{Implementation actions} + \text{Critical conditions} = \text{Results of implementation strategy}$$

Leaders can use this equation to remind people in their organization that, although their efforts are important, they represent only one of three influences on the success or failure of an improvement intervention. The results of the implementation strategy (improved outcomes) depend on the following:

- The strength of the *evidence* of effectiveness of the improvement, or the likely effectiveness of the *initial idea*
- The *implementation actions*—that is, what a leader, an implementation team, and others do to carry out changes. Leaders and their organizations must determine the "how" to implement, which sometimes involves adapting the content of the intervention (the "what" that they implement). This calls for local knowledge and influence and the ability to use systematic methods to make the adaptation.
- The *critical conditions*—the factors, such as financial and regulatory requirements—in the local organizational, regional, and national environment. Leaders working at the clinical level tend to have little control over these factors, which nonetheless can significantly help or hinder implementation. However, leaders can influence these factors by "managing upward," such as by providing evidence of how financing systems reward poor quality.

Steps for Successful Implementation

Pre-Implementation

- *Form a project team and steering group with the right mix of positions or skills.* This can be done at the start or later, when the intervention is chosen. The project team membership can be modified to suit the tasks at different times. Form a project steering group that includes key opinion leaders to provide advice but also to gather ideas and to persuade others of the value of the change.
- *Identify the most important gaps to address between current and best performance.* Different methods can be used, using different data and processes to involve providers and possibly patients. This step includes prioritizing which areas to work on, identifying

measurable outcomes, and setting targets.

- *Search for effective solutions.* It is often more effective and less resource-intensive to use a proven solution, and the existence of such a solution should influence the choice of which performance gap to work on (as in the above step).
- *Make an assessment of readiness for change.* Carrying out a "readiness for change" assessment can help identify which issues will need to be addressed before or during implementation and can help improve the implementation plan.[18]
- *Plan implementation.* This step should involve those persons who will need to change their own work practices or the work processes that they oversee to implement the improvement. It needs to include a schedule of regular reviews of implementation progress, with modification of the plan to take account of ongoing progress.

Pilot Testing and Refining

- Pilot testing and refining is needed for proven and unproven ideas. Proven ideas may need to be adapted locally, so testing is necessary to find out whether the local version is effective or has "lost its active ingredient" as a result of local modification. Also, many changes are easier to "sell" and to make if they are presented as temporary experiments; then, when you have evidence that the changes work in the local environment, it is easier to make the change permanent. Evidence from "elsewhere" is often not credible for skeptical local personnel.
- *"Package" a description of change principles or prescriptions.* If the intervention is successful and a decision is made to extend it to a wider group of patients or providers, then descriptions that allow the intervention to be reproduced are necessary, together with

guidance about which aspects of the intervention can and cannot be modified.

Spreading with a Strategy, Structure, and Systems

- Few interventions diffuse without an intentional spread strategy. The strategy should include a framework for the structure for spread, as well as different substrategies.
- Responsibilities for spread may need to be allocated to additional staff if they cannot be handled by current staff.

The checklist in Sidebar 7-5 (pages 172–174) can be used to help plan a strategy.

FINAL REFLECTIONS

Providers are more likely to change if they are involved in choosing the change and planning how to implement it.

My own experience in implementing QI interventions suggests that a leader should consider how to enable uptake of the changes that have been proven to result in improvement. The term *enabled uptake,* rather than implementation, is intended to emphasize the choices that providers have about whether to and how they might change what they do and how they should organize their practices accordingly. It suggests the need for "user-pull"—a desire to take up the change, which reduces the push implied by implementation. This involves helping local providers adapt the improvement to their own settings when they usually have little or no experience in doing so. It also highlights the continuing need for new knowledge about how adaptation is best carried out.

Sidebar 7-5. A Checklist for Spreading Quality Improvement

The purpose of the checklist is to help leaders assess the current situation, decide priorities for action, and select an action or intervention to increase the chances of successful implementation or spread.

Scoring key (scores 0–4): 4, already done; 3, partly done; 2, started; 1, not started; 0, not needed.

To add details, create a table and note for each item who is responsible, for what exactly, and by when.

1. Understanding "Participant-Users" and Designing "Pull" Strategies
"Users" "use" the proposed change to benefit patients and adapt it to fit their situations.

- We have clarified which individuals will need to change, and which behaviors, and how many in which clinics. Score _____
- Information has been gathered about their likely initial reactions to the proposed change (formally or informally gathered information). Score _____
- Information has been gathered about which aspects of the change they will be most attracted to (which fits with how they like to think of themselves, money, and time saved or gained). Score _____

(continued on page 173)

Sidebar 7-5. A Checklist for Spreading Quality Improvement (continued)

- Information has been gathered to identify significant differences in response and interest between different individuals or units. Score _____
- Different communication and selling strategies have been developed for different user segments. Score _____
- Each unit has a checklist to help assess its "readiness" for this change and the conditions it needs for successful implementation. Score _____

2. Infrastructure for Spread
- A group and/or individuals have been made accountable and understand their responsibility for planning and coordinating spread activities at each organizational level and facility. Score _____
- The group and/or individuals are clear as to whom they are accountable and when and what they should report. Score _____
- The group and/or individuals have the needed knowledge and skills for implementation and spread or access to the expertise. Score _____
- Individuals know their responsibility for gathering data to measure spread and for making reports (for example, quarterly) and have the expertise and resources. Score _____
- Key meetings to review progress and replan actions have been scheduled up to one year ahead. Score_____
- Individuals who are needed for these meetings have agreed to participate and have the required decision-making authority so unnecessary delays in referring upward for decisions can be avoided. Score _____ **3. Plan for Spread**
- The plan is agreed in terms of who does what and when, with indicators that can be used to follow progress of spread. Score _____
- How and when this plan is to be updated has been agreed. Score _____
- The plan includes local demonstration sites and their roles as "hubs" for sharing experiences with local units. Score _____

4. Defining the Change
A clear specification has been made widely available of the change to be spread, covering the following:
- The change—that is, the difference in process or provider behavior—to be achieved. Score _____
- The method or actions to bring about this change. Score _____
- The specification makes clear which aspects of the change must be exactly replicated and which aspects could or should be modified. Score _____

(continued on page 174)

Sidebar 7-5. A Checklist for Spreading Quality Improvement (continued)

5. Motivating and Communicating the Change
- Respected, credible opinion leaders have been selected and influenced to support the change and to advocate for it. Score _____
- A clinical champion in each unit has agreed to spend time advocating for and leading change in the unit. Score_____
- Other reasons or evidence for making the change apart from the clinical evidence are understood by user-participants in the change. Score_____
- User-participants can explain "what is in it for me personally and professionally," and a document itemizes the benefits. Score _____
- Administrators or managers have been selected, influenced, and supported to advocate for and to take part in the change. Score _____

6. Measuring Spread
- At least three key indicators of spread progress have been identified and are feasible to implement. Score _____
- At least one of the indicators will give enough early warning of problems to allow quick action to speed spread. Score _____
- The persons collecting and reporting the indicator data are clear about their responsibilities and know why other people need the data, and the persons receiving the data are clear about what to do with the data. Score _____

7. Securing Other Resources for Spread
- Provision has been made for units to have electronic clinical decision support tools or substitute methods at the point of care for identifying patients in their populations who, for example, are not yet receiving statins and angiotensin-converting enzyme inhibitors. Score _____
- Other resources needed have been identified, and creative plans for securing them or alternatives have been developed. Score _____
- A procedure is in place for replanning and prioritizing to match resources to what needs to be done. Score _____

8. Working Toward a Favorable Context for Spread
- The factors and reasons supporting the change in the wider organizational, regulatory, and health reform context have been identified. Score_____
- The barriers to the change have been identified. Score_____
- A strategy has been developed to reduce the influence of barriers that could potentially be modified. Score_____
- Each unit implementing the change has a tool and can use it for identifying local barriers to and resources for change. Score _____

References

1. Institute of Medicine: *Crossing the Quality Chasm: A New Health System for the 21st Century.* Washington, DC: National Academy Press, 2001.

2. Øvretveit J.: *Does Improving Quality Save Money? A Review of Evidence of Which Improvements to Quality Reduce Costs to Health Service Providers.* London: The Health Foundation, 2009. http://www.health.org.uk/publications/does-improving-quality-save-money/ (accessed Sep. 23, 2011).

3. Øvretveit J.: *Does Clinical Coordination Improve Quality and Save Money? A Review of the Evidence .* The Health Foundation, 2011. http://www.health.org.uk/publications/does-clinical-coordination-improve-quality-and-save-money (accessed Sep. 23, 2011).

4. U.S. Agency for Healthcare Research and Quality (AHRQ): *Making Health Care Safer: A Critical Analysis of Patient Safety Practices.* Jul. 2001. AHRQ publication no. 01-E057. AHRQ, Rockville, MD. http://archive.ahrq.gov/clinic/tp/ptsaftp.htm (accessed Sep. 23, 2011).

5. Greenhalgh T., et al.: Diffusion of innovations in service organizations: A systematic review and recommendations. *Milbank Q* 82(4):581–629, 2004.

6. Schilling L.: Sustaining improvement: What does it take? In Schilling L. (ed.): *Implementing and Sustaining Improvement in Health Care.* Oak Brook, IL: Joint Commission Resources, 2009, pp. 219–225.

7. The Joint Commission: *Looking for The Joint Commission Standards?* http://www.jointcommission.org/standards_information/standards.aspx (accessed Sep. 23, 2011).

8. Joint Commission International (JCI): *Joint Commission International Accreditation Standards for Hospitals,* 4th ed. Oak Brook, IL: Joint Commission Resources, 2010.

9. The Joint Commission: *Performance Measurement.* http://www.jointcommission.org/performance_measurement.aspx (accessed Sep. 23, 2011).

10. Joint Commission International: *Joint Commission International Library of Measures.* http://www.jointcommissioninternational.org/JCInsight/Joint-Commission-International-Library-of-Measures/ (accessed Sep. 23, 2011).

11. The Joint Commission: *Facts About the National Patient Safety Goals.* Jul. 13, 2011. http://www.jointcommission.org/facts_about_the_national_patient_safety_goals/ (accessed Sep. 23, 2011).

12. Inamdar N., Kaplan R.S., Bower M.: Applying the balanced scorecard in healthcare provider organizations. *J Healthc Manag* 47:179–195, May–Jun. 2002.

13. National Committee for Quality Assurance: *What Is HEDIS?* http://www.ncqa.org/tabid/187/default.aspx (accessed Sep. 23, 2011).

14. Pardini-Kiely K., et al.: Improving and sustaining core measure performance through effective accountability of clinical microsystems in an academic medical center. *Jt Comm J Qual Patient Saf* 36:387–398, Sep. 2010.

15. Maupin J.M., Roth D.J., Krapes J.M.: Use of the Modified Early Warning Score decreases code blue events. *Jt Comm J Qual Patient Saf* 35:598–603, Dec. 2009.

16. Neily J., et al: One-year follow-up after a collaborative breakthrough series on reducing falls and fall-related injuries. *Jt Comm J Qual Patient Saf* 31:275–285, May 2005.

17. National Institute of Clinical Studies: *Identifying Barriers to Evidence Uptake.* Feb. 2006. http://www.nhmrc.gov.au/_files_nhmrc/file/nics/material_resources/Identifying%20Barriers%20to%20Evidence%20Uptake.pdf (accessed Sep. 23, 2011).

18. Weiner B.J., Amick H., Lee S.Y.: Conceptualization and measurement of organizational readiness for change: A review of the literature in health services research and other fields. *Med Care Res Rev* 65:379–436, Aug. 2008.

19. Joint Commission Center for Transforming Healthcare: *2011 Hand Hygiene Project Storyboard.* http://www.centerfortransforminghealthcare.org/UserFiles/file/hand_hygiene_storyboard.pdf (accessed Sep. 23, 2011).

20. Berman S.: An interview with Mark Chassin. *Jt Comm J Qual Patient Saf* 36:475–479, Oct. 2010.

21. Antithrombotic Trialists' Collaboration: Collaborative meta-analysis of randomised trials of antiplatelet therapy for prevention of death, myocardial infarction, and stroke in high risk patients. *BMJ* 324(7439): 71–86, Jan. 12, 2002. Erratum in: *BMJ* 324(7330): 141, Jan. 19, 2002.

22. Forgatch M.S., Patterson G.R., DeGarmo D.S.: Evaluating fidelity: Predictive validity for a measure of competent adherence to the Oregon model of parent management training. *Behav Ther* 36(1):3–13, 2005.

23. Resnick S.G., Neale M.S., Rosenheck R.A.: Impact of public support payments, intensive psychiatric community care, and program fidelity on employment outcomes for people with severe mental illness. *J Nerv Ment Dis* 191:139–144, Mar. 2003.

24. Noel P.E.: The impact of therapeutic case management on participation in adolescent substance abuse treatment. *Am J Drug Alcohol Abuse* 32(3):311–327, 2006.

25. Thomas R.E., Baker P., Lorenzetti D.: Family-based programmes for preventing smoking by children and adolescents. *Cochrane Database Syst Rev* CD004493, Jan. 24, 2007.

26. Flottorp S., Oxman A.D.: Identifying barriers and tailoring interventions to improve the management of urinary tract infections and sore throat: A pragmatic study using qualitative methods. *BMC Health Serv Res* 3:3, Feb. 4, 2003.

27. Baker R., et al.: Tailored interventions to overcome identified barriers to change: Effects on professional practice and health care outcomes. *Cochrane Database Syst Rev* CD005470, Mar. 17, 2010.

28. Langley G.K., et al.: *The Improvement Guide: A Practical Approach to Enhancing Organizational Performance.* San Francisco: Jossey-Bass, 1996.

29. Vedel I., et al.: Healthcare professionals and managers' participation in developing an intervention: A pre-intervention study in the elderly care context. *Implement Sci* 4, Apr. 2009. http://www.implementationscience.com/content/4/1/21 (accessed Sep. 23, 2001).

30. Kilo C.M.: A framework for collaborative improvement: Lessons from the Institute for Healthcare Improvement's Breakthrough Series. *Qual Manag Health Care* 6:1–13, Sep. 1998.

31. Mittmann B.S.: Creating the evidence base for quality improvement collaboratives. *Ann Intern Med* 140:897–901, Jun. 11, 2004.

32. Rittenhouse D.R., Shortell S.M.: The patient-centered medical home: Will it stand the test of health reform? *JAMA* 301:2038–2040, May 20, 2009.

33. Shekelle P.G., Morton S.C., Keeler E.B.: *Costs and Benefits of Health Information Technology,* Evidence Report/Technology Assessment No. 132. AHRQ publication no. 06-E006. U.S. Agency for Healthcare Research and Quality, Apr. 2006. http://www.ahrq.gov/downloads/pub/evidence/pdf/hitsyscosts/hitsys.pdf (accessed Sep. 23, 2011).

34. McCannon C.J., Perla R.J.: Learning networks for sustainable, large-scale improvement. *Jt Comm J Qual Patient Saf* 35:286–291, May 2009.

35. McCannon C.J., Schall M.W., Perla R.J.: *Planning for Scale: A Guide for Designing Large-Scale Improvement Initiatives.* IHI Innovation Series white paper. Cambridge, MA: Institute for Healthcare Improvement, 2008.

36. Canadian Patient Safety Institute: *Safer Healthcare Now!* http://www.saferhealthcarenow.ca/EN/Pages/default.aspx (accessed Sep. 23, 2011).

37. Sikker Patient: *About the Danish Safer Hospital Programme.* http://www.sikkerpatient.dk/about-sikker-patient/the-danish-safer-hospital-programme.aspx (accessed Sep. 23, 2011).

38. National Health Service: *About Patient Safety First.* http://www.patientsafetyfirst.nhs.uk/Content.aspx?path=/About-the-campaign/ (accessed Sep. 23, 2011).

39. Yuan C.T., et al.: *Blueprint for the Dissemination of Evidence-Based Practices in Health Care.* Commonwealth Fund, May 2010. http://www.commonwealthfund.org/~/media/Files/Publications/Issue%20Brief/2010/May/1399_Bradley_blueprint_dissemination_evidencebased_practices_ib.pdf (accessed Sep. 23, 2011).

40. Øvretveit J., et al.: Review of strategies to strengthen health services. In Peters D.H., et al. (eds.): *Improving Health Service Delivery in Developing Countries: From Evidence to Action.* Washington, DC: International Bank for Reconstruction and Development/World Bank, 2009, pp. 35–67.

41. Øvretveit J.: Widespread focused improvement: Lessons from international health for spreading specific improvements to health services in high-income countries. *Int J Qual Health Care* 23:239–246, Jun. 2011.

42. Simmons R., Fajans P., Ghiron L. (eds.): *Scaling Up Health Service Delivery: From Pilot Innovations to Policies and Programmes.* World Health Organization, 2006. http://whqlibdoc.who.int/publications/2007/9789241563512_eng.pdf (accessed Sep. 23, 2011).

43. Peters D.H., et al. (eds.): *Improving Health Service Delivery in Developing Countries: From Evidence to Action.* Washington, DC: International Bank for Reconstruction and Development/World Bank, 2009.

44. U.S. Department of Veterans Affairs: *Quality Enhancement Research Initiative.* http://www.queri.research.va.gov/ (accessed Sep. 23, 2011).

Index